A

A

With expert r ... se to romance, adventure, good health, or career opportunities while gaining valuable insight into yourself and others. Offering a daily outlook for 18 full months, this fascinating guide shows you:

- The important dates in your life
- What to expect from an astrological reading
- How the stars can help you stay healthy and fit

  And more!

Let this sound advice guide you through a year of heavenly possibilities—for today and for every day of 2010!

SYDNEY OMARR'S® DAY-BY-DAY ASTROLOGICAL GUIDE FOR

ARIES—March 21–April 19
TAURUS—April 20–May 20
GEMINI—May 21–June 20
CANCER—June 21–July 22
LEO—July 23–August 22
VIRGO—August 23–September 22
LIBRA—September 23–October 22
SCORPIO—October 23–November 21
SAGITTARIUS—November 22–December 21
CAPRICORN—December 22–January 19
AQUARIUS—January 20–February 18
PISCES—February 19–March 20

IN 2010

SYDNEY OMARR'S®

DAY-BY-DAY ASTROLOGICAL GUIDE FOR

SCORPIO

OCTOBER 23–NOVEMBER 21

2010

by Trish MacGregor
with Carol Tonsing

A SIGNET BOOK

SIGNET
Published by New American Library, a division of
Penguin Group (USA) Inc., 375 Hudson Street,
New York, New York 10014, USA
Penguin Group (Canada), 90 Eglinton Avenue East, Suite 700, Toronto,
Ontario M4P 2Y3, Canada (a division of Pearson Penguin Canada Inc.)
Penguin Books Ltd., 80 Strand, London WC2R 0RL, England
Penguin Ireland, 25 St. Stephen's Green, Dublin 2,
Ireland (a division of Penguin Books Ltd.)
Penguin Group (Australia), 250 Camberwell Road, Camberwell, Victoria 3124,
Australia (a division of Pearson Australia Group Pty. Ltd.)
Penguin Books India Pvt. Ltd., 11 Community Centre, Panchsheel Park,
New Delhi - 110 017, India
Penguin Group (NZ), 67 Apollo Drive, Rosedale, North Shore 0645
New Zealand (a division of Pearson New Zealand Ltd.)
Penguin Books (South Africa) (Pty.) Ltd., 24 Sturdee Avenue,
Rosebank, Johannesburg 2196, South Africa

Penguin Books Ltd., Registered Offices:
80 Strand, London WC2R 0RL, England

First Printing, June 2009
10 9 8 7 6 5 4 3 2 1

First published by Signet, an imprint of New American Library,
a division of Penguin Group (USA) Inc.

Printed in the United States of America

PUBLISHER'S NOTE
While the author has made every effort to provide accurate telephone numbers and Internet addresses at the time of publication, neither the publisher nor the author assumes any responsibility for errors, or for changes that occur after publication. Further, publisher does not have any control over and does not assume any responsibility for author or third-party Web sites or their content.

CONTENTS

Introduction: Seize the Moment 1
1. The Top Trends of 2010: Transition Times 3
2. How to Find Your Best Times This Year 9
3. Introduction to Astrology 22
4. The Moon: Your Inner Light 33
5. The Planets: The Power of Ten 39
6. Where It All Happens: Your Rising Sign 95
7. The Keys to Reading Your Horoscope: The Glyphs 104
8. Join the Astrology Community 116
9. The Best Astrology Software: Take Your Knowledge to the Next Level 124
10. Ask the Expert: A Personal Reading Could Help 130
11. Loving Every Sign in the Zodiac 136
12. Financial Tips from the Stars 145
13. Children of 2010 152
14. Give the Perfect Gift to Every Sign 163
15. Your Pet-Scope for 2010: How to Choose Your Best Friend for Life 170
16. Your Scorpio Personality and Potential: The Roles You Play in Life 177

17. Scorpio Fashion and Decor Tips: Elevate Your Mood with Scorpio Style! 183
18. The Scorpio Way to Stay Healthy and Age Well 188
19. Add Scorpio Star Power to Your Career: What It Takes to Succeed in 2010 191
20. Learn from Scorpio Celebrities 194
21. Your Scorpio Relationships with Every Other Sign: The Green Lights and Red Flags 198
22. The Big Picture for Scorpio in 2010 207
23. Eighteen Months of Day-by-Day Predictions: July 2009 to December 2010 213

INTRODUCTION

Seize the Moment

"Timing is everything" is a saying worth repeating this year. Astrology is the art of interpreting moments in time, and astrology fans from the rich and famous to the readers of daily horoscope columns realize that some moments are more favorable for certain actions than others. Knowing that they can plan their actions in tune with the rhythm of the cosmic cycles gives them confidence that they are making wise choices. This could be a challenging year for many, so let this guide help you seize the moment and turn those challenges into opportunities by using the tools astrology provides.

In our toolbox for 2010, you'll find secrets of astrological timing—how to find the most auspicious dates this year. For those who are new to astrology or would like to know more about it, we offer easy techniques to start using astrology in your daily life. You'll learn all about your sun sign and how to interpret the mysterious symbols on a horoscope chart. You can use the convenient tables in this book to look up other planets in your horoscope, each of which sheds light on a different facet of your personality.

Many people turn to astrology to help them find love or figure out what went wrong with a relationship. At your service is the world's oldest dating and mating coach, ready to help you decide whether that new passion has potential or might burn out fast. We'll go through the pros and cons of all the possible sun-sign combinations, with celebrities to illustrate the romantic chemistry.

Contemplating a career change? Our sun-sign chapters can help you build your confidence and focus your job search in the most fulfilling direction by highlighting your natural talents and abilities.

Many readers have explored astrology on the Internet, where there are a mind-boggling variety of sites. Our suggestions are well worth your surfing time. We show you where to get free horoscopes, connect with other astrology fans, find the right astrology software for your ability, and even find an accredited college that specializes in astrological studies.

Whether it's money matters, fashion tips, or ideas for vacation getaways, we'll provide ways to use astrology in your life every day. Before giving yourself or your home a makeover, be sure to consult your sun sign, for the colors and styles that will complement your personality.

To make the most of each day, there are eighteen months of on-target daily horoscopes. So here's hoping this year's guide will help you use your star power wisely to make 2010 a happy, successful year!

CHAPTER 1

The Top Trends of 2010: Transition Times

Astrologers judge the trends of a year by following the slow-moving planets, from Jupiter through Pluto. A change in sign indicates a new cycle, with new emphasis. The farthest planets (Uranus, Neptune, and Pluto) which stay in a sign for at least seven years, cause a very significant change in the atmosphere when they change signs. Shifts in Jupiter, which changes every year, and Saturn, every two years, are more obvious in current events and daily lives. Jupiter generally brings a fortunate, expansive emphasis to its new sign, while Saturn's two-year cycle is a reality check, bringing tests of maturity, discipline, and responsibility. This year, Jupiter in Pisces and Saturn in Libra are in auspicious signs for most of the year, which should act as a balance to more volatile elements in the comos.

Little Pluto—The Mighty Mite

Though astronomers have demoted tiny Pluto from being a full-fledged planet to a dwarf planet, astrologers have been tracking its influence since Pluto was discovered in 1930 and have witnessed that this minuscule celestial body has a powerful effect on both a personal and global level. So Pluto, which moved into the sign of Capricorn in 2008, will still be called a "planet" by astrologers and will be given just as much importance as before.

Until 2024, Pluto will exert its influence in this practical, building, healing earth sign. Capricorn relates to structures, institutions, order, mountains and mountain countries, mineral rights, issues involving the elderly and growing older—all of which will be emphasized in the coming years. It is the sign of established order, corporations, big business—all of which will be accented. Possibly, it will fall to business structures to create a new sense of order in the world.

You should now feel the rumblings of change in the Capricorn area of your horoscope and in the world at large. The last time Pluto was in Capricorn was the years up to and during the Revolutionary War; therefore this should be an important time in the U.S. political scene, as well as a reflection of the aging and maturing of American society in general. Both the rise and the fall of the Ottoman Empire happened under Pluto in Capricorn.

The Pisces Factor

This year, Jupiter moves from experimental, humanitarian Aquarius to creative, imaginative Pisces. Jupiter is the coruler of Pisces, along with Neptune, so this is a particularly auspicious place for the planet of luck and expansion to be. During the year that Jupiter remains in a sign, the fields associated with that sign are the ones that currently arouse excitement and enthusiasm, usually providing excellent opportunities.

Jupiter in Pisces expands the influence of Neptune in Aquarius; there should be many artistic and scientific breakthroughs. International politics also comes under this influence, as Neptune in Aquarius raises issues of global boundaries and political structures not being as solid as they seem. This could continue to produce rebellion and chaos in the environment. However, with the generally benevolent force of Jupiter backing up the creative side of Neptune, it is possible that highly original and effective solutions to global problems will be found, which could transcend the current social and cultural barriers.

Another place we notice the Jupiter influence is in fashion, which should veer into a Pisces fantasy mood, with more theatrical, dramatic styles and a special emphasis on footwear. Look for exciting beachwear and seaside resorts that appeal to our desire to escape reality.

Those born under Pisces should have many opportunities during the year. However, the key is to keep your feet on the ground. The flip side of Jupiter is that there are no limits. You can expand off the planet under a Jupiter transit, which is why the planet is often called the "Gateway to Heaven." If something is going to burst (such as an artery) or overextend or go over the top in some way, it could happen under a supposedly lucky Jupiter transit, so be aware.

Those born under Virgo may find their best opportunities working with partners this year, as Jupiter will be transiting their seventh house of relationships.

During the summer months, Jupiter dips into Aries, which should give us a preview of happenings next year. In this headstrong fire sign, Jupiter promotes pioneering ventures, start-ups, all that is new and exciting. It can also promote impatience with more conservative forces, especially in early summer, which looks like the most volatile time this year. Jupiter returns to Pisces in September for the rest of the year.

Saturn in Libra

Saturn, the planet of limitation, testing, and restriction, will be moving through Libra, the sign of its exhaltation and one of its most auspicious signs, this year. In Libra, Saturn can steady the scales of justice and promote balanced, responsible judgment. There should be much deliberation over duty, honor, and fairness, which will be ongoing for the next two years, balancing the more impulsive energy of other planets. Far-reaching new legislation and diplomatic moves are possible, perhaps resolving difficult international standoffs. As this placement works well with the humanitarian Aquarius influence of Neptune, there should be new hope of resolving conflicts. Previously, Saturn was in Libra during the early 1920s, the early 1950s, and again in the early 1980s.

Continuing Trends

Uranus and Neptune continue to do a kind of astrological dance called a "mutual reception." This is a supportive relationship where Uranus is in Pisces, the sign ruled by Neptune, while Neptune is in Aquarius, the sign ruled by Uranus. When this dance is over in 2011, it is likely that we will be living under very different political and social circumstances.

Uranus in Pisces and Aries

Uranus, known as the Great Awakener, tends to cause both upheaval and innovation in the sign it transits. This year, it is accompanied by Jupiter, as it is preparing to leave Pisces and dip its toe into Aries from June to mid-August. However, the Pisces influence will predominate, since Jupiter will be in Pisces most of the year.

During previous episodes of Uranus in Pisces, great religions and spiritual movements have come into being, most recently Mormonism and Christian Fundamentalism. In its most positive mode, Pisces promotes imagination and creativity, the art of illusion in theater and film, and the inspiration of great artists.

A water sign, Pisces is naturally associated with all things liquid—such as oceans, oil, and alcohol—and with those creatures that live in the water—fish, the fishing industry, fish habitats, and fish farming. Currently there is a great debate going on about overfishing, contamination of fish, and fish farming. The underdogs, the enslaved, and the disenfranchised should also benefit from Uranus in Pisces. Since Uranus is a disruptive influence that aims to challenge the status quo, the forces of nature that manifest now will most likely be in the Pisces area—the oceans, seas, and rivers. We have so far seen unprecedented rainy seasons, floods, mud slides, and disastrous hurricanes. Note that 2005's devastating Hurricane Katrina hit an area known for both the oil and fishing industries.

Pisces is associated with the prenatal phase of life, which is related to regenerative medicine. The controversy over embryonic stem cell research will continue to be debated, but recent developments may make the arguments moot. Petroleum issues, both in the oil-producing countries and offshore oil drilling, will come to a head. Uranus in Pisces suggests that development of new hydroelectric sources may provide the power we need to continue our current power-thirsty lifestyle.

As in previous eras, there should continue to be a flourishing of the arts. We are seeing many new artistic forms developing now, such as computer-created actors and special effects. The sky's the limit on this influence.

Those who have problems with Uranus are those who resist change, so the key is to embrace the future.

As Uranus prepares to enter Aries, an active fire sign, we should have a preview of coming influences over the summer.

Neptune in Aquarius

Neptune is a planet of imagination and creativity, but also of deception and illusion. Neptune is associated with hospitals, which have been the subject of much controversy. On the positive side, hospitals are acquiring cutting-edge technology. The atmosphere of many hospitals is already changing from the intimidating and sterile environment of the past to that of a health-promoting spa. Alternative therapies, such as massage, diet counseling, and aromatherapy, are becoming commonplace, which expresses this Neptune trend. New procedures in plastic surgery, also a Neptune glamour field, and antiaging therapies are giving the illusion of youth.

However, issues involving the expense and quality of health care, medication, and the evolving relationship between doctors, drug companies, and HMOs reflect a darker side of this trend.

Neptune is finishing up its stay in Aquarius and will begin its transit of Pisces, which it rules, in 2011. So this should be a time of transition into a much more Neptunian era, when Pisces-related issues will be of paramount importance.

Lunar Eclipses Are Movers and Shakers

Eclipses could shake up the financial markets and rock your world in 2010. The eclipses in late June and July are the ones to watch as they coincide with a close contact of Jupiter and Uranus in Aries. This is a potentially volatile time, so it would be wise to be prepared. As several recent studies have shown the stock market to be linked to the lunar cycle, track investments more carefully during this time.

New Celestial Bodies

Our solar system is getting crowded, as astronomers continue to discover new objects circling the sun. In addition to the familiar planets, there are dwarf planets, comets, cometoids, asteroids, and strange icy bodies in the Kuiper Belt beyond Neptune. A dwarf planet christened Eris, discovered in 2005, is now being observed and analyzed by astrologers. Eris was named after a goddess of discord and strife. In mythology, she was a troublemaker who made men think their opinions were right and others wrong. What an appropriate name for a planet discovered during a time of discord in the Middle East and elsewhere! Eris has a companion moon named Dysnomia for her daughter, described as a demon spirit of lawlessness. With mythological associations like these, we wonder what the effect of this mother-daughter duo will be. Once Eris's orbit is established, astrologers will track the impact of this planet on our horoscopes. Eris takes about 560 years to orbit the sun, which means its emphasis in a given astrological sign will affect several generations.

CHAPTER 2

How to Find Your Best Times This Year

It's no secret that some of the most powerful and famous people, from Julius Caesar to Queen Elizabeth I, from financier J. P. Morgan to Ronald Reagan, have consulted astrologers before they made their moves. If astrology helps the rich and famous stay on course through life's ups and downs, why not put it to work for you? Anyone can follow the planetary movements, and once you know how to interpret them, you won't need an expert to grasp the overall trends and make use of them.

For instance, when mischievous Mercury creates havoc with communications, it's time to back up your vital computer files, read between the lines of contracts, and be very patient with coworkers. When Venus passes through your sign, you're more alluring, so it's time to try out a new outfit or hairstyle, and then ask someone you'd like to know better to dinner. Venus timing can also help you charm clients with a stunning sales pitch or make an offer they won't refuse.

In this chapter you will find the tricks of astrological time management. You can find your red-letter days as well as which times to avoid. You will also learn how to make the magic of the moon work for you. Use the information in this chapter and the planet tables in this book and also the moon sign listings in your daily forecasts.

Here are the happenings to note on your agenda:

- Dates of your sun sign (high-energy period)
- The month previous to your sun sign (low-energy time)

- Dates of planets in your sign this year
- Full and new moons (Pay special attention when these fall in your sun sign!)
- Eclipses
- Moon in your sun sign every month, as well as moon in the opposite sign (listed in daily forecast)
- Mercury retrogrades
- Other retrograde periods

Your Most Proactive Time

Every birthday starts off a new cycle of solar energy for you. You should feel a new surge of vitality as the powerful sun enters your sign. This is the time when predominant energies are most favorable to you. So go for it! Start new projects, and make your big moves (especially when the new moon is in your sign, doubling your charisma). You'll get the recognition you deserve now, when everyone is attuned to your sun sign. Look in the tables in this book to see if other planets will also be passing through your sun sign at this time. Venus (love, beauty), Mars (energy, drive), and Mercury (communication, mental sharpness) reinforce the sun and give an extra boost to your life in the areas they affect. Venus will rev up your social and love life, making you seem especially attractive. Mars amplifies your energy and drive. Mercury fuels your brainpower and helps you communicate. Jupiter signals an especially lucky period of expansion.

There are two downtimes related to the sun. During the month before your birthday period, when you are winding up your annual cycle, you could be feeling especially vulnerable and depleted. So at that time get extra rest, watch your diet, and take it easy. Don't overstress yourself. Use this time to gear up for a big push when the sun enters your sign.

Another downtime is when the sun is in the sign opposite your sun sign (six months from your birthday). This is a reactive time, when the prevailing energies are very different from yours. You may feel at odds with the world. You'll have to work harder for recognition because people are not on your wavelength. However, this could be a good time to work on a team, in cooperation with others, or behind the scenes.

Be a Moon Watcher

The moon is a powerful tool to divine the mood of the moment. You can work with the moon in two ways. Plan by the sign the moon is in; plan by the phase of the moon. The sign will tell you the kind of activities that suit the moon's mood. The phase will tell you the best time to start or finish a certain activity.

Working with the phases of the moon is as easy as looking up at the night sky. During the new moon, when both the sun and moon are in the same sign, begin new ventures—especially activities that are favored by that sign. Then you'll utilize the powerful energies pulling you in the same direction. You'll be focused outward, toward action, and in a doing mode. Postpone breaking off, terminating, deliberating, or reflecting—activities that require introspection and passive work. These are better suited to a later moon phase.

Get your project under way during the first quarter. Then go public at the full moon, a time of high intensity, when feelings come out into the open. This is your time to shine—to express yourself. Be aware, however, that because pressures are being released, other people will also be letting off steam. Since confrontations are possible, take advantage of this time either to air grievances or to avoid arguments.

About three days after the full moon comes the disseminating phase, a time when the energy of the cycle begins to wind down. From the last quarter of the moon to the next new moon, it's a time to cut off unproductive relationships, do serious thinking, and focus on inward-directed activities.

You'll feel some new and full moons more strongly than others, especially when they fall in your sun sign. That full moon happens at your low-energy time of year, and is likely to be an especially stressful time in a relationship, when any hidden problems or unexpressed emotions could surface.

Full and New Moons in 2010

All dates are calculated for eastern standard time and eastern daylight time.

New Moon—January 15 in Capricorn (solar eclipse)
Full Moon—January 30 in Leo

New Moon—February 13 in Aquarius
Full Moon—February 28 in Virgo

New Moon—March 15 in Pisces
Full Moon—March 29 in Libra

New Moon—April 14 in Aries
Full Moon—April 28 in Scorpio

New Moon—May 13 in Taurus
Full Moon—May 27 in Sagittarius

New Moon—June 12 in Gemini
Full Moon—June 26 in Capricorn (lunar eclipse)

New Moon—July 11 in Cancer (solar eclipse)
Full Moon—July 25 in Aquarius

New Moon—August 9 in Leo
Full Moon—August 24 in Pisces

New Moon—September 8 in Virgo
Full Moon—September 23 in Aries

New Moon—October 7 in Libra
Full Moon—October 22 in Aries

New Moon—November 5 in Scorpio
Full Moon—November 21 in Taurus

New Moon—December 5 in Sagittarius
Full Moon—December 21 in Gemini (lunar eclipse)

Timing by the Moon's Sign

To forecast the daily emotional "weather," to determine your monthly high and low days, or to synchronize your activities with the cycles of the moon, take note of the moon's sign under your daily forecast at the end of the book. Here are some of the activities favored and the moods you are likely to encounter under each moon sign.

Moon in Aries: Get Moving

The new moon in Aries is an ideal time to start new projects. Everyone is pushy, raring to go, rather impatient, and short-tempered. Leave details and follow-up for later. Competitive sports or martial arts are great ways to let off steam. Quiet types could use some assertiveness, but it's a great day for dynamos. Be careful not to step on too many toes.

Moon in Taurus: Lay the Foundations for Success

Do solid, methodical tasks like follow-through or backup work. Make investments, buy real estate, do appraisals, or do some hard bargaining. Attend to your property. Get out in the country or spend some time in your garden. Enjoy creature comforts, music, a good dinner, or sensual lovemaking. Forget starting a diet—this is a day when you'll feel self-indulgent.

Moon in Gemini: Communicate

Talk means action today. Telephone, write letters, and fax! Make new contacts; stay in touch with steady customers. You can juggle lots of tasks today. It's a great time for mental activity of any kind. Don't try to pin people down—they too are feeling restless. Keep it light. Flirtations and socializing are good. Watch gossip—and don't give away secrets.

Moon in Cancer: Pay Attention to Loved Ones

This is a moody, sensitive, emotional time. People respond to personal attention and mothering. Stay at home, have a family dinner, or call your mother. Nostalgia, memories, and psychic powers are heightened. You'll want to hang on to people and things (don't clean out your closets now). You could have shrewd insights into what others really need and want. Pay attention to dreams, intuition, and gut reactions.

Moon in Leo: Be Confident

Everybody is in a much more confident, warm, generous mood. It's a good day to ask for a raise, show what you can do, or dress like a star. People will respond to flattery and enjoy a bit of drama and theater. You may be extravagant, treat yourself royally, and show off a bit—but don't break the bank! Be careful not to promise more than you can deliver.

Moon in Virgo: Be Practical

Do practical, down-to-earth chores. Review your budget, make repairs, or be an efficiency expert. Not a day to ask for a raise. Tend to personal care and maintenance. Have a health checkup, go on a diet, or buy vitamins or health food. Make your home spotless. Take care of details and piled-up chores. Reorganize your work and life so they run more smoothly and efficiently. Save money. Be prepared for others to be in critical, fault-finding moods.

Moon in Libra: Be Diplomatic

Attend to legal matters. Negotiate contracts. Arbitrate. Do things with your favorite partner. Socialize. Be romantic. Buy a special gift or a beautiful object. Decorate yourself or your surroundings. Buy new clothes. Throw a party. Have an elegant, romantic evening. Smooth over any ruffled feathers. Avoid confrontations. Stick to civilized discussions.

Moon in Scorpio: Solve Problems

This is a day to do things with passion. You'll have excellent concentration and focus. Try not to get too intense emotionally. Avoid sharp exchanges with loved ones. Others may tend to go to extremes, get jealous, or overreact. Great for troubleshooting, problem solving, research, scientific work—and making love. Pay attention to those psychic vibes.

Moon in Sagittarius: Sell and Motivate

A great time for travel, philosophical discussions, or setting long-range career goals. Work out, do sports, or buy athletic equipment. Others will be feeling upbeat, exuberant, and adventurous. Taking risks is favored. You may feel like gambling, betting on the horses, visiting a local casino, or buying a lottery ticket. Teaching, writing, and spiritual activities also get the green light. Relax outdoors. Take care of animals.

Moon in Capricorn: Get Organized

You can accomplish a lot now, so get on the ball! Attend to business. Issues concerning your basic responsibilities, duties, family, and elderly parents could crop up. You'll be expected to deliver on promises. Weed out the deadwood from your life. Get a dental checkup. Not a good day for gambling or taking risks.

Moon in Aquarius: Join the Group

A great day for doing things with groups—clubs, meetings, outings, politics, or parties. Campaign for your candidate. Work for a worthy cause. Deal with larger issues that affect humanity—the environment and metaphysical questions. Buy a computer or electronic gadget. Watch TV. Wear something outrageous. Try something you've never done before. Present an original idea. Don't stick to a rigid schedule; go with the flow. Take a class in meditation, mind control, or yoga.

Moon in Pisces: Be Creative

This can be a very creative day, so let your imagination work overtime. Film, theater, music, and ballet could inspire you. Spend some time resting and reflecting, reading, or writing poetry. Daydreams can also be profitable. Help those less fortunate. Lend a listening ear to someone who may be feeling blue. Don't overindulge in self-pity or escapism. People are especially vulnerable to substance abuse. Turn your thoughts to romance and someone special.

Eclipses Clear the Air

Eclipses can bring on milestones in your life, if they aspect a key point in your horoscope. In general, they shake up the status quo, bringing hidden areas out into the open. During this time, problems you've been avoiding or have brushed aside can surface to demand your attention. A good coping strategy is to accept whatever comes up as a challenge that could make a positive difference in your life. And don't forget the power of your sense of humor. If you can laugh at something, you'll never be afraid of it.

When the natural rhythms of the sun and moon are disturbed, it's best to postpone important activities. Be sure to mark eclipse days on your calendar, especially if the eclipse falls in your birth sign. This year, those born under Capricorn, Cancer, and Gemini should take special note of the feelings that arise. If your moon is in one of these signs, you may be especially affected. With lunar eclipses, some possibilities could be a break from attachments, or the healing of an illness or substance abuse that was triggered by the subconscious. The temporary event could be a healing time, when you gain perspective. During solar eclipses, when you might be in a highly subjective state, pay attention to the hidden subconscious patterns that surface, the emotional truth that is revealed at this time.

The effect of the eclipse can reverberate for some time, often months after the event. But it is especially important to stay cool and make no major moves during the period known as the shadow of the eclipse, which begins about a week before and lasts until at least three days after the eclipse. After three days, the daily rhythms should return to normal, and you can proceed with business as usual.

This Year's Eclipse Dates

January 15: Solar Eclipse in Capricorn
June 26: Lunar Eclipse in Capricorn
July 11: Solar Eclipse in Cancer
December 21: Lunar Eclipse in Gemini

Retrogrades: When the Planets Seem to Backstep

All the planets, except for the sun and moon, have times when they appear to move backward—or retrograde—as it seems from our point of view on Earth. At these times, planets do not work as they normally do. So it's best to "take a break" from that planet's energies in our life and to do some work on an inner level.

Mercury Retrograde: The Key Is in "Re"

Mercury goes into retrograde most often, and its effects can be especially irritating. When it reaches a short distance ahead of the sun several times a year, it seems to move backward from our point of view. Astrologers often compare retrograde motion to the optical illusion that occurs when we ride on a train that passes another train traveling at a different speed—the second train appears to be moving in reverse.

What this means to you is that the Mercury-ruled areas of your life—analytical thought processes, communications, scheduling—are subject to all kinds of confusion. Be prepared. Communications equipment can break down. Schedules may be changed on short notice. People are late for appointments or don't show up at all. Traffic is terrible. Major purchases malfunction, don't work out, or get delivered in the wrong color. Letters don't arrive or are delivered to the wrong address. Employees will make errors that have to be corrected later. Contracts don't work out or must be renegotiated.

Since most of us can't put our lives on "hold" during Mercury retrogrades, we should learn to tame the trickster and make it work for us. The key is in the prefix re-. This is the time to go back over things in your life, reflect on what you've done during the previous months. Now you can get deeper insights, and spot errors you've missed. So take time to review and re-evaluate what has happened. Rest and reward yourself—it's a good time to take a vacation, especially if you revisit a favorite place. Reorganize your work and finish up projects that are backed up. Clean out your desk and closets. Throw away what you can't recycle. If you must sign contracts or agreements, do so with a contingency clause that lets you reevaluate the terms later.

Postpone major purchases or commitments for the time being. Don't get married (unless you're remarrying the same person). Try not to rely on other people keeping appointments, contracts, or agreements to the letter; have several alternatives. Double-check and read between the lines. Don't buy anything connected with communications or transportation (if you must, be sure to cover yourself).

Mercury retrograding through your sun sign will intensify its effect on your life.

If Mercury was retrograde when you were born, you may be one of the lucky people who don't suffer the frustrations of this period. If so, your mind probably works in a very intuitive, insightful way.

The sign in which Mercury is retrograding can give you an idea of what's in store—as well as the sun signs that will be especially challenged.

Mercury Retrogrades in 2010

Mercury has four retrograde periods this year, since it will be retrograde as the year begins. During the retrograde periods, it will be especially important to watch all activities which involve mental processes and communication.

December 26, 2009, to January 15 in Capricorn
April 17 to May 11 in Taurus
August 20 to September 12 in Virgo
December 10 to December 30 from Capricorn to Sagittarius

Venus Retrograde: Relationships Are Affected

Retrograding Venus can cause your relationships to take a backward step, or you may feel that a key relationship is on hold. Singles may be especially lonely, yet find it difficult to connect with someone special. If you wish to make amends in an already troubled relationship, make peaceful overtures at this time. You may feel more extravagant or overindulge in shopping or sweet treats. Shopping till you drop and buying what you cannot afford are bad at this time. It's *not* a good time to redecorate—you'll hate the color of the walls later. Postpone getting a new hairstyle. It only lasts for a relatively short time this year; however, Scorpio and Libra should take special note.

Venus Retrogrades in 2010

Venus retrogrades from October 8 to November 18, from Scorpio to Libra.

Use the Power of Mars

Mars shows how and when to get where you want to go. Timing your moves with Mars on your side can give you a big push. On the other hand, pushing Mars the wrong way can guarantee that you'll run into frustrations around every corner. Your best times to forge ahead are during the weeks when Mars is traveling through your sun sign or your Mars sign (look these up in the planet tables in this book). Also consider times when Mars is in a compatible sign (fire signs with air signs, or earth signs with water signs). You'll be sure to have planetary power on your side.

Mars began a lengthy retrograde in extravagant Leo on December 20, 2009. Your patience may have been tested more than usual during last year's festivities. The Mars retrograde in Leo will last until March 10, during which time there are sure to be repercussions on the international level.

Mars Retrogrades in 2010

Mars turns retrograde in Leo on December 20, 2009, until March 10, 2010.

When Other Planets Retrograde

The slower-moving planets stay retrograde for many months at a time (Jupiter, Saturn, Neptune, Uranus, and Pluto).

When Saturn is retrograde, it's an uphill battle with self-discipline. You may not be in the mood for work. You may feel more like hanging out at the beach than getting things done.

Neptune retrograde promotes a dreamy escapism from reality, when you may feel you're in a fog (Pisces will feel this, especially).

Uranus retrograde may mean setbacks in areas where there have been sudden changes, when you may be forced to regroup or reevaluate the situation.

Pluto retrograde is a time to work on establishing proportion and balance in areas where there have been recent dramatic transformations.

When the planets move forward again, there's a shift in the atmosphere. Activities connected with each planet start moving ahead; plans that were stalled get rolling. Make a special note of those days on your calendar and proceed accordingly.

Other Retrogrades in 2010

The five slower-moving planets all go retrograde in 2010.

Jupiter retrogrades from July 23 in Aries to November 18 in Pisces.

Saturn retrogrades from January 13 in Libra to May 30 in Virgo.

Uranus retrogrades from July 5 in Aries to December 5 in Pisces.

Neptune retrogrades from May 31 to November 7 in Aquarius.

Pluto retrogrades from April 6 to September 13 in Capricorn.

CHAPTER 3

Introduction to Astrology

Astrology is a powerful tool that can help you discover and access your personal potential, understand others and interpret events in your life and the world at large. You don't have to be an expert in astrology to put it to work for you. It's easy to pick up enough basic knowledge to go beyond the realm of your sun sign into the deeper areas of this fascinating subject, which combines science, art, spirituality, and psychology. Perhaps from here you'll upgrade your knowledge with computer software that calculates charts for everyone you know in a nanosecond or join an astrology group in your city.

In this chapter, we'll introduce you to the basics of astrology. You'll be able to define a sign and figure out why astrologers say what they do about each sign. As you look at your astrological chart, you'll have a good idea of what's going on in each portion of the horoscope. Let's get started.

Know the Difference Between Signs and Constellations

Most readers know their signs, but many often confuse them with constellations. *Signs* are actually a type of celestial real estate, located on the *zodiac*, an imaginary 360-degree belt circling the earth. This belt is divided into twelve equal 30-degree portions, which are the *signs*. There's a lot of confusion about the difference between the *signs* and the *constellations* of the zodiac, patterns of stars which originally marked the twelve divisions, like signposts. Though a *sign* is named after the *constellation* that once marked the same area, the constellations are no longer in the same place relative to the earth that they were many centuries ago. Over hundreds of years, the earth's orbit has shifted, so that from our point of view here on earth, the constellations seem to have moved. However, the signs remain in place. (Most Western astrology uses the twelve-equal-part division of the zodiac, though there are some other methods of astrology that still use the constellations instead of the signs.)

Most people think of themselves in terms of their sun sign. A *sun sign* refers to the sign the sun is orbiting through at a given moment (from our point of view here on earth). For instance, if someone says, "I'm an Aries," the sun was passing through Aries when that person was born. However, there are nine other planets (plus asteroids, fixed stars, and sensitive points) that also form our total astrological personality, and some or many of these will be located in other signs. No one is completely "Aries," with all their astrological components in one sign! (Please note that, in astrology, the sun and moon are usually referred to as "planets," though of course they're not. Though there is some controversy over Pluto, it is still called a "planet" by astrologers.)

As we mentioned before, the sun signs are *places* on the zodiac. They do not *do* anything (the planets are the doers). However, they are associated with many things, depending on their location on the zodiac.

How Do We Define a Sign's Characteristics?

The definitions of the signs evolved systematically from four interrelated components: a sign's element, its quality, its polarity or sex, and its order in the progression of the zodiac. All these factors work together to tell us what the sign is like.

The system is magically mathematical: the number 12—as in the twelve signs of the zodiac—is divisible by 4, by 3, and by

2. There are four elements, three qualities, and two polarities, which follow one another in sequence around the zodiac.

The four elements (earth, air, fire, and water) are the building blocks of astrology. The use of an element to describe a sign probably dates from man's first attempts to categorize what he saw. Ancient sages believed that all things were composed of combinations of these basic elements—earth, air, fire, and water. This included the human character, which was fiery/choleric, earthy/melancholy, airy/sanguine, or watery/phlegmatic. The elements also correspond to our emotional (water), physical (earth), mental (air), and spiritual (fire) natures. The energies of each of the elements were then observed to relate to the time of year when the sun was passing through a certain segment of the zodiac.

Those born with the sun in fire signs—Aries, Leo, Sagittarius—embody the characteristics of that element. Optimism, warmth, hot tempers, enthusiasm, and "spirit" are typical of these signs. Taurus, Virgo, and Capricorn are "earthy"—more grounded, physical, materialistic, organized, and deliberate than fire sign people. Air sign people—Gemini, Libra, and Aquarius—are mentally oriented communicators. Water signs—Cancer, Scorpio, and Pisces—are emotional, sensitive, and creative.

Think of what each element does to the others: water puts out fire or evaporates under heat. Air fans the flames or blows them out. Earth smothers fire, drifts and erodes with too much wind, and becomes mud or fertile soil with water. Those are often perfect analogies for the relationships between people of different sun-sign elements. This astrochemistry was one of the first ways man described his relationships. Fortunately, no one is entirely "air" or "water." We all have a bit, or a lot, of each element in our horoscopes. It is this unique mix that defines each astrological personality.

Within each element, there are three qualities that describe types of behavior associated with the sign. Those of cardinal signs are activists, go-getters. These four signs—Aries, Cancer, Libra, and Capricorn—begin each season. Fixed signs, which happen in the middle of the season, are associated with builders and stabilizers. You'll find that Taurus, Leo, Scorpio, and Aquarius are usually gifted with concentration, stamina, and focus. Mutable signs—Gemini, Virgo, Sagittarius, and Pisces—fall at the end of each season and thus are considered catalysts for change. People born under mutable signs are flexible and adaptable.

The polarity of a sign is either its positive or negative "charge." It can be masculine, active, positive, and yang, like air or fire signs, or it can be feminine, reactive, negative, and yin, like the water and earth signs. The polarities alternate, moving energy around the zodiac like the poles of a battery.

Finally, we consider the sign's place in the order of the zodiac. This is vital to the balance of all the forces and the transmission of energy moving through the signs. You may have noticed that your sign is quite different from your neighboring sign on either side. Yet each seems to grow out of its predecessor like links in a chain and transmits a synthesis of energy gathered along the "chain" to the following sign, beginning with the fire-powered positive charge of Aries.

How the Signs Add Up

SIGN	ELEMENT	QUALITY	POLARITY	PLACE
Aries	fire	cardinal	masculine	first
Taurus	earth	fixed	feminine	second
Gemini	air	mutable	masculine	third
Cancer	water	cardinal	feminine	fourth
Leo	fire	fixed	masculine	fifth
Virgo	earth	mutable	feminine	sixth
Libra	air	cardinal	masculine	seventh
Scorpio	water	fixed	feminine	eighth
Sagittarius	fire	mutable	masculine	ninth
Capricorn	earth	cardinal	feminine	tenth
Aquarius	air	fixed	masculine	eleventh
Pisces	water	mutable	feminine	twelfth

Each Sign Has a Special Planet

Each sign has a "ruling" planet that is most compatible with its energies. Mars adds its fiery assertive characteristics to Aries. The sensual beauty and comfort-loving side of Venus rules Taurus, whereas the idealistic side of Venus rules Libra. Quick-moving Mercury rules two mutable signs, Gemini and Virgo. Its mental agility belongs to Gemini while its analytical side is best expressed in Virgo. The changeable emotional moon is associated with Cancer, while the outgoing Leo personality is ruled by the sun. Scorpio originally shared Mars, but when Pluto was discovered in the last century, its powerful magnetic energies were deemed more suitable to the intense vibrations of the fixed water sign Scorpio. Though Pluto has, as of this writing, been downgraded, it is still considered by astrologers to be a powerful force in the horoscope. Disciplined Capricorn is ruled by Saturn, and expansive Sagittarius by Jupiter. Unpredictable Aquarius is ruled by Uranus and creative, imaginative Pisces by Neptune. In a horoscope, if a planet is placed in the sign it rules, it is sure to be especially powerful.

The Layout of a Horoscope Chart

A horoscope chart is a map of the heavens at a given moment in time. It looks like a wheel with twelve spokes. In between each of the "spokes" is a section called a *house*.

Each house deals with a different area of life and is influenced by a special sign and a planet. Astrologers look at the houses to tell in what area of life an event is happening or about to happen.

The house is governed by the sign passing over the spoke (or cusp of the house) at that particular moment. Though the first house is naturally associated with Aries and Mars, it would also have an additional Capricorn influence if that sign was passing over the house cusp at the time the chart was cast. The sequence of the houses starts with the first house located at the left center spoke (or the number 9 position, if you were reading a clock). The houses are then read *counterclockwise* around the chart, with the fourth house at the bottom of the chart, the tenth house at the top or twelve o'clock position.

Where do the planets belong? Around the horoscope, planets are placed within the houses according to their location at the time of the chart. That is why it is so important to have an accurate time; with no specific time, the planets have no specific location in the houses and one cannot determine which area of life they will apply to. Since the signs move across the houses as the earth turns, planets in a house will naturally intensify the importance of that house. The house that contains the sun is naturally one of the most prominent.

The First House: Self

The sign passing over the first house at the time of your birth is known as your ascendant, or rising sign. The first house is the house of "firsts"—the first impression you make, how you initiate matters, the image you choose to project. This is where you advertise yourself, where you project your personality. Planets that fall here will intensify the way you come across to others. It is the home of Aries and the planet Mars.

The Second House: The Material You

This house is where you experience the material world, what you value. Here are your attitudes about money, possessions, and finances, as well as your earning and spending capacity. On a deeper level, this house reveals your sense of self-worth, the inner values that draw wealth in various forms. It is the natural home of Taurus and the planet Venus.

The Third House: Your Thinking Process

This house describes how you communicate with others, how you reach out to others nearby and interact with the immediate environment. It shows how your thinking process works and the way you express your thoughts. Are you articulate or tongue-tied? Can you think on your feet? This house also shows your first relationships, your experiences with brothers and sisters, as well as how you deal with people close to you, such as your neighbors or pals. It's where you take short trips, write letters, or use the telephone. It shows how your mind works in terms of left-brain logical and analytical functions. It is the home of Gemini and the planet Mercury.

The Fourth House: Your Home Life

The fourth house shows the foundation of life, the psychological underpinnings. Located at the bottom of the chart, this house shows how you are nurtured and made to feel secure—your roots! It shows your early home environment and the circumstances at the end of your life (your final "home"), as well as the place you call home now. Astrologers look here for information about the parental nurturers in your life. It is the home of Cancer and the moon.

The Fifth House: Your Self-Expression

The Leo house is where the creative potential develops. Here you express yourself and procreate, in the sense that children are outgrowths of your creative ability. But this house most represents your inner childlike self, who delights in play. If your inner security has been established by the time you reach this house, you are now free to have fun, romance, and love affairs and to give of yourself. This is also the place astrologers look for playful love affairs, flirtations, and brief romantic encounters (rather than long-term commitments). It is the home of Leo and the sun.

The Sixth House: Care and Maintenance

The sixth house has been called the "care and maintenance" department. This house shows how you take care of your body and organize yourself to perform efficiently in the world. Here is where you get things done, where you look after others and fulfill service duties, such as taking care of pets. Here is what you do to survive on a day-to-day basis. The sixth house demands order in your life; otherwise there would be chaos. The house is your "job" (as opposed to your career, which is the domain of the tenth house), your diet, and your health and fitness regimens. It is the home of Virgo and the planet Mercury.

The Seventh House: Your Relationships

This house shows your attitude toward your partners and those with whom you enter commitments, contracts, or agreements. Here is the way you relate to others, as well as your close, intimate, one-on-one relationships (including open enemies—those you "face off" with). Open hostilities, lawsuits, divorces, and marriages happen here. If the first house represents the "I," the seventh or opposite house is the "not I"—the complementary partner you attract by the way you come across. If you are having trouble with partnerships, consider what you are attracting by the energies of your first and seventh house. It is the home of Libra and the planet Venus.

The Eighth House: Your Power House

The eighth house refers to how you merge with something or someone, and how you handle power and control. This is one of the most mysterious and powerful houses, where your energy transforms itself from "I" to "we." As you give up power and control by uniting with something or someone, two kinds of energies merge and become something greater, leading to a regeneration of the self on a higher level. Here are your attitudes toward sex, shared resources, and taxes (what you share with the government). Because this house involves what belongs to others, you face issues of control and power struggles, or undergo a deep psychological transformation as you bond with another. Here you transcend yourself through dreams, drugs, and occult or psychic experiences that reflect the collective unconscious. It is the home of Scorpio and the planet Pluto.

The Ninth House: Your Worldview

The ninth house shows your search for wisdom and higher knowledge: your belief system. As the third house represents the "lower mind," its opposite on the wheel, the ninth house, is the "higher mind," the abstract, intuitive, spiritual mind that asks "big" questions, like "Why we are here?" After the third house has explored what was close at hand, the ninth stretches out to broaden you mentally with higher education and travel. Here you stretch spiritually with religious activity. Since you are concerned with how everything is related, you tend to push boundaries and take risks. Here is where you express your ideas in a book or thesis, where you pontificate, philosophize, or preach. It is the home of Sagittarius and the planet Jupiter.

The Tenth House: Your Public Life

The tenth house is associated with your public life and high-profile activities. Located directly overhead at the "high noon" position on the horoscope wheel, this is the most "visible" house in the chart, the one where the world sees you. It deals with your career (but not your routine "job") and your reputation. Here is where you go public, take on responsibilities (as opposed to the fourth house, where you stay home). This will affect the career you choose and your "public relations." This house is also associated with your father figure or the main authority figure in your life. It is the home of Capricorn and the planet Saturn.

The Eleventh House: Your Social Concerns

The eleventh house is where you extend yourself to a group, a goal, or a belief system. This house is where you define what you really want: the kinds of friends you have, your political affiliations, and the kind of groups you identify with as an equal. Here is where you become concerned with "what other people think" or where you rebel against social conventions. It's where you become a socially conscious humanitarian or a partying social butterfly. It's where you look to others to stimulate you and discover your kinship to the rest of humanity. The sign on this house can help you understand what you gain and lose from friendships. It is the home of Aquarius and the planet Uranus.

The Twelfth House: Where You Become Selfless

Old-fashioned astrologers used to put a rather negative spin on this house, calling it the "house of self-undoing." When we "undo ourselves," we surrender control, boundaries, limits, and rules. The twelfth house is where the boundaries between yourself and others become blurred and you become selfless. But instead of being self-undoing, the twelfth house can be a place of great creativity and talent. It is the place where you can tap into the collective unconscious, where your imagination is limitless.

In your trip around the zodiac, you've gone from the "I" of self-assertion in the first house to the final house, which symbolizes the dissolution that happens before rebirth. The twelfth house is where accumulated experiences are processed in the unconscious. Spiritually oriented astrologers look to this house for evidence of past lives and karma. Places where we go for solitude or to do spiritual or reparatory work belong here, such as retreats, religious institutions, or hospitals. Here is also where we withdraw from society voluntarily or involuntarily, and where we are put in prison because of antisocial activity. Selfless giving through charitable acts is part of this house, as is helpless receiving or dependence on charity.

In your daily life, the twelfth house reveals your deepest intimacies, your best-kept secrets, especially those you hide from yourself and repress deep in the unconscious. It is where we surrender a sense of a separate self to a deep feeling of wholeness, such as selfless service in religion or any activity that involves merging with the greater whole. Many sports stars have important planets in the twelfth house, which enable them to play in the zone, finding an inner, almost mystical, strength that transcends their limits. The twelfth house is the home of Pisces and the planet Neptune.

Which Are the Most Powerful Houses?

Houses are stronger or weaker depending on how many planets are inhabiting them. If there are many planets in a given house, it follows that the activities of that house will be especially important in your life. If the planet that rules the house is also located there, this too adds power to the house. The most powerful houses are the first, fourth, seventh, and tenth. These are the houses on "the angles" of a horoscope.

CHAPTER 4

The Moon: Your Inner Light

In some astrology-conscious lands, the moon is given as much importance in a horoscope as the sun. Astrologers often refer to these two bodies as the "lights," an appropriate description, since the sun and moon are not planets, but a star and a satellite. But it is also true that these two bodies shed the most "light" on a horoscope reading.

As the sun shines *out* in a horoscope, revealing the personality, the moon shines *in*. The sign the moon was transiting at the time of your birth reveals much about the inner you, secrets like what you really care about, what makes you feel comfortable and secure. It represents the receptive, reflective, female, nurturing self. It also reflects the one who nurtured you, the mother or mother figure in your chart. In a man's chart, the moon position describes his receptive, emotional, yin side, as well as the woman in his life who will have the deepest effect, usually his mother. (Venus reveals the kind of woman who will attract him physically.)

The moon is more at home in some signs than in others. It rules maternal Cancer and is exalted in Taurus—both comforting, home-loving signs where the natural emotional energies of the moon are easily and productively expressed. But when the moon is in the opposite signs—Capricorn and Scorpio—it leaves the comfortable nest and deals with emotional issues of power and achievement in the outside world. If you were born with the moon in one of these signs, you may find your emotional role in life more challenging.

To determine your moon sign, it is worthwhile to have an accurate horoscope cast, either by an astrologer, a computer program, or one of the online astrology sites that offer free charts. Since detailed moon tables are too extensive for this book, check through the following listing to find the moon sign that feels most familiar.

Moon in Aries

This placement makes you both independent and ardent. You are an idealist, and you tend to fall in and out of love easily. You love a challenge but could cool once your quarry is captured. Your emotional reactions are fast and fiery, quickly expressed and quickly forgotten. You may not think before expressing your feelings. It's not easy to hide how you feel. Channeling all your emotional energy could be one of your big challenges.

Celebrity example: Angelina Jolie

Moon in Taurus

You are a sentimental soul who is very fond of the good life and gravitates toward solid, secure relationships. You like displays of affection and creature comforts—all the tangible trappings of a cozy, safe, calm atmosphere. You are sensual and steady emotionally, but very stubborn, possessive, and determined. You can't be pushed and tend to dislike changes. You should make an effort to broaden your horizons and to take a risk sometimes. You may become very attached to your home turf, your garden, and your possessions. You may also be a collector of objects that are meaningful to you.

Celebrity example: Prince Charles

Moon in Gemini

You crave mental stimulation and variety in life, which you usually get via a varied social life, the excitement of flirtation, or multiple professional involvements. You may marry more than once and have a rather chaotic emotional life due to your difficulty with commitment and settling down, as well as your need to be constantly on the go. (Be sure to find a partner who is as outgoing as you are.) You will have to learn at some point to focus your energies because you tend to be somewhat fragmented—to do two things at once, to have two homes, or even to have two lovers. If you can find a creative way to express your many-faceted nature, you'll be ahead of the game.

Celebrity example: Jim Carrey

Moon in Cancer

This is the most powerful lunar position, which is sure to make a deep imprint on your character. Your needs are very much associated with your reaction to the needs of others. You are very sensitive, caring, and self-protective, though some of you may mask this with a hard shell, like the moon-sensitive crab. This placement also gives an excellent memory, keen intuition, and an uncanny ability to perceive the needs of others. All of the lunar phases will affect you, especially full moons and eclipses, so you would do well to mark them on your calendar. Because you're happiest at home, you may work at home or turn your office into a second home, where you can nurture and comfort people. (You may tend to mother the world.) With natural psychic, intuitive ability, you might be drawn to occult work in some way. Or you may get professionally involved with providing food and shelter to others.

Celebrity example: Tom Cruise

Moon in Leo

This warm, passionate moon takes everything to heart. You are attracted to all that is noble, generous, and aristocratic in life (and you may be a bit of a snob). You have an innate ability to take command emotionally, but you do need strong support, loyalty, and loud applause from those you love. You are possessive of your loved ones and your turf and will roar if anyone threatens to take over your territory.

Celebrity example: Paul McCartney

Moon in Virgo

You are rather cool until you decide if others measure up. But once someone or something meets your high standards, you hold up your end of the arrangement perfectly. You may, in fact, drive yourself too hard to attain some notion of perfection. Try to be a bit easier on yourself and others. Don't always act the censor! You love to be the teacher; you are drawn to situations where you can change others for the better, but sometimes you must learn to accept others for what they are—enjoy what you have!

Celebrity example: John F. Kennedy

Moon in Libra

Like other air-sign moons, you think before you feel. Therefore, you may not immediately recognize the emotional needs of others. However, you are relationship-oriented and may find it difficult to be alone or to do things alone. After you have learned emotional balance by leaning on yourself first, you can have excellent partnerships. It is best for you to avoid extremes, which set your scales swinging and can make your love life precarious. You thrive in a rather conservative, traditional, romantic relationship, where you receive attention and flattery—but not possessiveness—from your partner. You'll be your most charming in an elegant, harmonious atmosphere.

Celebrity example: Leonardo DiCaprio

Moon in Scorpio

This is a moon that enjoys and responds to intense, passionate feelings. You may go to extremes and have a very dramatic emotional life, full of ardor, suspicion, jealousy, and obsession. It would be much healthier to channel your need for power and control into meaningful work. This is a good position for anyone in the fields of medicine, police work, research, the occult, psychoanalysis, or intuitive work, because life-and-death situations don't faze you. However, you do take personal disappointments very hard.

Celebrity example: Elizabeth Taylor

Moon in Sagittarius

You take life's ups and downs with good humor and the proverbial grain of salt. You'll love 'em and leave 'em or take off on a great adventure at a moment's notice. "Born free" could be your slogan. Attracted by the exotic, you have mental and physical wanderlust. You may be too much in search of new mental and spiritual stimulation to ever settle down.

Celebrity example: Donald Trump

Moon in Capricorn

Are you ever accused of being too cool and calculating? You have an earthy side, but you take prestige and position very seriously. Your strong drive to succeed extends to your romantic life, where you will be devoted to improving your lifestyle and rising to the top. A structured situation where you can advance methodically makes you feel wonderfully secure. You may be attracted to someone older or very much younger or from a different social world. It may be difficult to look at the lighter side of emotional relationships. Though this moon is placed in the sign to your detriment, the good news is that you tend to be very dutiful and responsible to those you care for.

Celebrity example: Brad Pitt

Moon in Aquarius

You are a people collector with many friends of all backgrounds. You are happiest surrounded by people, and you may feel uneasy when left alone. Though you usually stay friends with lovers, intense emotions and demanding one-on-one relationships turn you off. You don't like anything to be too rigid or scheduled. Though tolerant and understanding, you can be emotionally unpredictable; you may opt for an unconventional love life. With plenty of space, you will be able to sustain relationships with liberal, freedom-loving types.

Celebrity example: Princess Diana

Moon in Pisces

You are very responsive and empathetic to others, especially if they have problems or are the underdog. (Be on guard against attracting too many people with sob stories.) You'll be happiest if you can express your creative imagination in the arts or in the spiritual or healing professions. Because you may tend to escape in fantasies or overreact to the moods of others, you need an emotional anchor to help you keep a firm foothold in reality. Steer clear of too much escapism (especially in alcohol) or reclusiveness. Places near water soothe your moods. Working in a field that gives you emotional variety will also help you be productive.

Celebrity example: Elvis Presley

CHAPTER 5

The Planets: The Power of Ten

If you know a person's sun sign, you can learn some very useful generic information, but when you know the placement of all ten planets (eight planets plus the sun and moon), you've got a much more accurate profile of the person's character. Then the subject of the horoscope becomes a unique individual, as well as a member of a certain sun sign. You'll discover what makes him angry (Mars), pleased (Venus), or fearful (Saturn).

The planets are the doers of the horoscope, each representing a basic force in life. The sign and house where the planet is located indicate how and where its force will operate. For a moment, think of the horoscope as real estate. Prime property is close to the rising sign or at the top of the chart. If two or more planets are grouped together in one sign, they usually operate like a team, playing off each other, rather than expressing their energy singularly. But a loner, a planet that stands far away from the others, is usually outstanding and often calls the shots.

The sign of a planet also has a powerful influence. In some signs, the planet's energies are very much at home and can easily express themselves. In others, the planet has to work harder and is slightly out of sorts. The sign that most corresponds to the planet's energies is said to be ruled by that planet and obviously is the best place for that planet to be. The next best place is a sign where it is exalted, or especially harmonious. On the other hand, there are places in the horoscope where a planet has to stretch itself to play its role, such as the sign opposite a planet's rulership, which embodies the opposite area of life, and the sign opposite its exaltation. However, a planet that must work harder can also be more complete, because it must grow to meet the challenges of living in a more difficult sign. Like world leaders who've had to struggle for greatness, this planet may actually develop strength and character.

Here's a list of the best places for each planet to be. Note that, as new planets were discovered in the last century, they replaced the traditional rulers of signs which best complemented their energies.

ARIES—Mars
TAURUS—Venus, in its most sensual form
GEMINI—Mercury, in its communicative role
CANCER—the moon
LEO—the sun
VIRGO—also Mercury, this time in its more critical capacity
LIBRA—also Venus, in its more aesthetic, judgmental form
SCORPIO—Pluto, co-ruled by Mars
SAGITTARIUS—Jupiter
CAPRICORN—Saturn
AQUARIUS—Uranus, replacing Saturn, its original ruler
PISCES—Neptune, replacing Jupiter, its original ruler

Those who have many planets in exalted signs are lucky indeed, for here is where the planet can accomplish the most and be its most influential and creative.

SUN—exalted in Aries, where its energy creates action
MOON—exalted in Taurus, where instincts and reactions operate on a highly creative level
MERCURY—exalted in Aquarius, where it can reach analytical heights
VENUS—exalted in Pisces, a sign whose sensitivity encourages love and creativity
MARS—exalted in Capricorn, a sign that puts energy to work productively
JUPITER—exalted in Cancer, where it encourages nurturing and growth
SATURN—at home in Libra, where it steadies the scales of justice and promotes balanced, responsible judgment

URANUS—powerful in Scorpio, where it promotes transformation

NEPTUNE—especially favored in Cancer, where it gains the security to transcend to a higher state

PLUTO—exalted in Pisces, where it dissolves the old cycle, to make way for transition to the new

The Personal Planets: Mercury, Venus, and Mars

These planets work in your immediate personal life.

Mercury affects how you communicate and how your mental processes work. Are you a quick study who grasps information rapidly, or do you learn more slowly and thoroughly? How is your concentration? Can you express yourself easily? Are you a good writer? All these questions can be answered by your Mercury placement.

Venus shows what you react to. What turns you on? What appeals to you aesthetically? Are you charming to others? Are you attractive to look at? Your taste, your refinement, your sense of balance and proportion are all Venus-ruled.

Mars is your outgoing energy, your drive and ambition. Do you reach out for new adventures? Are you assertive? Are you motivated? Self-confident? Hot-tempered? How you channel your energy and drive is revealed by your Mars placement.

Mercury Shows How Your Mind Works

Since Mercury never travels far from the sun, read Mercury in your sun sign, and then the signs preceding and following it. Then decide which reflects the way you think.

Mercury in Aries

Your mind is very active and assertive. It approaches a plan aggressively. You never hesitate to say what you think, never shy away from a battle. In fact, you may relish a verbal confrontation. Tact is not your strong point, so you may have to learn not to trip over your tongue.

Mercury in Taurus

This is a much more cautious Mercury. Though you may be a slow learner, you have good concentration and mental stamina. You want to make your ideas really happen. You'll attack a problem methodically and consider every angle thoroughly, never jumping to conclusions. You'll stick with a subject until you master it.

Mercury in Gemini

You are a wonderful communicator with great facility for expressing yourself both verbally and in writing. You love gathering all kinds of information. You probably finish other people's sentences and express yourself with eloquent hand gestures. You can talk to anybody anytime and probably have phone and E-mail bills to prove it. You read anything from sci-fi to Shakespeare and might need an extra room just for your book collection. Though you learn fast, you may lack focus and discipline. Watch a tendency to jump from subject to subject.

Mercury in Cancer

You rely on intuition more than logic. Your mental processes are usually colored by your emotions, so you may seem shy or hesitant to voice your opinions. However, this placement gives you the advantage of great imagination and empathy in the way you communicate with others.

Mercury in Leo

You are enthusiastic and very dramatic in the way you express yourself. You like to hold the attention of groups and could be a great public speaker. Your mind thinks big, so you'd prefer to deal with the overall picture rather than with the details.

Mercury in Virgo

This is one of the best places for Mercury. It should give you critical ability, attention to details, and thorough analysis. Your mind focuses on the practical side of things. This type of thinking is very well suited to being a teacher or editor.

Mercury in Libra

You're either a born diplomat who smoothes over ruffled feathers or a talented debater. Many lawyers have this placement. However, since you're forever weighing the pros and cons of a situation, you may vacillate when making decisions.

Mercury in Scorpio

This is an investigative mind that stops at nothing to get the answers. You may have a sarcastic, stinging wit, a gift for the cutting remark. There's always a grain of truth to your verbal sallies, thanks to your penetrating insight.

Mercury in Sagittarius

You are a super salesman with a tendency to expound. Though you are very broad-minded, you can be dogmatic when it comes to telling others what's good for them. You won't hesitate to tell the truth as you see it, so watch a tendency toward tactlessness. On the plus side, you have a great sense of humor. This position of Mercury is often considered by astrologers to be at a disadvantage because Sagittarius opposes Gemini, the sign Mercury rules, and squares off with Virgo, another Mercury-ruled sign. What often happens is that Mercury in Sagittarius oversteps its bounds and loses sight of the facts in a situation. Do a reality check before making promises that you may not be able to deliver.

Mercury in Capricorn

This placement endows good mental discipline. You have a love of learning and a very orderly approach to your subjects. You will patiently plod through the facts and figures until you have mastered the tasks. You grasp structured situations easily, but may be short on creativity.

Mercury in Aquarius

An independent, original thinker, you'll have more cutting-edge ideas than the average person. You'll be quick to check out any unusual opportunities. Your opinions are so well-researched and grounded that once your mind is made up, it is difficult to change.

Mercury in Pisces

You have the psychic intuitive mind of a natural poet. Learn to make use of your creative imagination. You may think in terms of helping others, but check a tendency to be vague and forgetful of details.

Venus Is the Popularity Planet

Venus tells how you relate to others and to your environment. It shows where you receive pleasure and what you love to do. Find your Venus placement on the chart in this book by looking for the year of your birth in the left-hand column. Then follow the line of that year across the page until you reach the time period of your birthday. The sign heading that column will be your Venus. If you were born on a day when Venus was changing signs, check the signs preceding or following that day to determine if that feels more like your Venus nature.

Venus in Aries

You can't stand to be bored, confined, or ordered around. But a good challenge, maybe even a rousing row, turns you on. Confess—don't you pick a fight now and then just to get someone stirred up? You're attracted by the chase, not the catch, which could cause some problems in your love life, if the object of your affection becomes too attainable. You like to wear red and can spot a trend before anyone else.

Venus in Taurus

All your senses work in high gear. You love to be surrounded by glorious tastes, smells, textures, sounds, and visuals—austerity is not for you. Neither is being rushed. You like time to enjoy your pleasures. Soothing surroundings with plenty of creature comforts are your cup of tea. You like to feel secure in your nest, with no sudden jolts or surprises. You like familiar objects—in fact, you may hate to let anything or anyone go.

Venus in Gemini

You are a lively, sparkling personality who thrives in a situation that affords a constant variety and a frequent change of scenery. A varied social life is important to you, with plenty of mental stimulation and a chance to engage in some light flirtation. Commitment may be difficult, because playing the field is so much fun.

Venus in Cancer

An atmosphere where you feel protected, coddled, and mothered is best for you. You love to be surrounded by children in a cozy, homelike situation. You are attracted to those who are tender and nurturing, who make you feel secure and well provided for. You may be quite secretive about your emotional life or attracted to clandestine relationships.

Venus in Leo

First-class attention in large doses turns you on, and so does the glitter of real gold and the flash of mirrors. You like to feel like a star at all times, surrounded by your admiring audience. The side effect is that you may be attracted to flatterers and tinsel, while the real gold requires some digging.

Venus in Virgo

Everything neatly in its place? On the surface, you are attracted to an atmosphere where everything is in perfect order, but underneath are some basic, earthy urges. You are attracted to those who appeal to your need to teach, be of service, or play out a Pygmalion fantasy. You are at your best when you are busy doing something useful.

Venus in Libra

Elegance and harmony are your key words. You can't abide an atmosphere of contention. Your taste tends toward the classic, with light harmonies of color—nothing clashing, trendy, or outrageous. You love doing things with a partner and should be careful to pick one who is decisive, but patient enough to let you weigh the pros and cons. And steer clear of argumentative types.

Venus in Scorpio

Mysteries intrigue you—in fact, anything that is too open and aboveboard is a bit of a bore. You surely have a stack of whodunits by the bed, along with an erotic magazine or two. You like to solve puzzles. You may also be fascinated with the occult, crime, or scientific research. Intense, all-or-nothing situations add spice to your life, and you love to ferret out the secrets of others. But you could get burned by your flair for living dangerously. The color black, spicy food, dark wood furniture, and heady perfume put you in the right mood.

Venus in Sagittarius

If you are not actually a world traveler, your surroundings are sure to reflect your love of faraway places. You like a casual outdoor atmosphere and a dog or two to pet. There should be plenty of room for athletic equipment and suitcases. You're attracted to kindred souls who love to travel and who share your freedom-loving philosophy of life. Athletics and spiritual or New Age pursuits could be other interests.

Venus in Capricorn

No fly-by-night relationships for you! You want substance in life, and you are attracted to whatever will help you get where you are going. Status objects turn you on. And so do those who have a serious, responsible, businesslike approach, or who remind you of a beloved parent. It is characteristic of this placement to be attracted to someone of a different generation. Antiques, traditional clothing, and dignified behavior are becoming to you.

Venus in Aquarius

This Venus wants to make friends, to be "cool." You like to be in a group, particularly one pushing a worthy cause. You feel quite at home surrounded by people, and could even court fame, yet all the while, you tend to remain detached from intense commitment. Original ideas and unpredictable people fascinate you. You prefer spontaneity and delightful surprises, rather than a well-planned schedule of events.

Venus in Pisces

This Venus loves to give of yourself, and you find plenty of takers. Stray animals and people appeal to your heart and your pocketbook, but be careful to look at their motives realistically once in a while. You are extremely vulnerable to sob stories of all kinds. Fantasy, the arts (especially film, dance, and theater), and psychic or spiritual activities also speak to you.

Mars: The Action Hero

Mars is the mover and shaker in your life. It shows how you pursue your goals, whether you have energy to burn or proceed in a slow, steady pace. It will also show how you get angry. Do you explode, or do a slow burn, or hold everything inside and then get revenge later?

To find your Mars, turn to the chart on pages 82–94. Then find your birth year in the left-hand column and find the line headed by the month of your birth. There you will find an abbreviation of your Mars sign. If the description of your Mars sign doesn't ring true, read the description of the signs preceding and following it. You might have been born on a day when Mars was changing signs, in which case your Mars might fall into the adjacent sign.

Mars in Aries

In the sign it rules, Mars shows its brilliant fiery nature. You have an explosive temper and can be quite impatient. On the other hand, you have tremendous courage, energy, and drive. You'll let nothing stand in your way as you race to be first! Obstacles are met head-on and broken through by force. However, problems that require patience and persistence to solve can have you exploding in rage. You're a great starter, but not necessarily around for the finish.

Mars in Taurus

Slow, steady, concentrated energy gives you the power to last until the finish line. You've great stamina, and you never give up. Your tactic is to wear away obstacles with your persistence. Often you come out a winner because you've had the patience to hang in there. When angered, you do a slow burn.

Mars in Gemini

You can't sit still for long. This Mars craves variety. You often have two or more things going on at once—it's all an amusing game to you. Your life can get very complicated, but that only adds spice and stimulation. What drives you into a nervous, hyper state? Boredom, sameness, routine, and confinement. You can do wonderful things with your hands, and you have a way with words.

Mars in Cancer

You rarely attack head-on. Instead, you'll keep things to yourself, make plans in secret, and always cover your actions. This might be interpreted by some as manipulative, but you are only being self-protective. You get furious when anyone knows too much about you. But you do like to know all about others. Your mothering and feeding instincts can be put to good use, if you work in the food, hotel, or child-care-related businesses. You may have to overcome your fragile sense of security, which prompts you not to take risks and to get physically upset when criticized. Don't take things so personally!

Mars in Leo

You have a very dominant personality that takes center stage—modesty is not one of your traits, nor is taking a back seat. You prefer giving the orders and have been known to make a dramatic scene if they are not obeyed. Properly used, this Mars confers leadership ability, endurance, and courage.

Mars in Virgo

You are the fault-finder of the zodiac, who notices every detail. Mistakes of any kind make you very nervous. You may worry, even if everything is going smoothly. You may not express your anger directly, but you sure can nag. You have definite likes and dislikes, and you are sure you can do the job better than anyone else. You are certainly more industrious and detail-oriented than other signs. Your Mars energy is often most positively expressed in some kind of teaching role.

Mars in Libra

This Mars will have a passion for beauty, justice, and art. Generally, you will avoid confrontations at all costs. You prefer to spend your energy finding diplomatic solutions or weighing pros and cons. Your other techniques are passive aggression or exercising your well-known charm to get people to do what you want.

Mars in Scorpio

This is a powerful placement, so intense that it demands careful channeling into worthwhile activities. Otherwise, you could become obsessed with your sexuality or might use your need for power and control to manipulate others. You are strong-willed, shrewd, and very private about your affairs, and you'll usually have a secret agenda behind your actions. Your great stamina, focus, and discipline would be excellent assets for careers in the military or medical fields, especially research or surgery. When angry, you don't get mad—you get even!

Mars in Sagittarius

This expansive Mars often propels people into sales, travel, athletics or philosophy. Your energies function well when you are on the move. You have a hot temper and are inclined to say what you think before you consider the consequences. You shoot for high goals—and talk endlessly about them—but you may be weak on groundwork. This Mars needs a solid foundation. Watch a tendency to take unnecessary risks.

Mars in Capricorn

This is an ambitious Mars with an excellent sense of timing. You have an eye for those who can be of use to you, and you may dismiss people ruthlessly when you're angry. But you drive yourself hard and deliver full value. This is a good placement for an executive. You'll aim for status and a high material position in life, and keep climbing despite the odds. A great Mars to have!

Mars in Aquarius

This is the most rebellious Mars. You seem to have a drive to assert yourself against the status quo. You may enjoy provoking people, shocking them out of traditional views. Or this placement could express itself in an offbeat sex life. Somehow you often find yourself in unconventional situations. You enjoy being a leader of an active group, which pursues forward-looking studies, politics, or goals.

Mars in Pisces

This Mars is a good actor who knows just how to appeal to the sympathies of others. You create and project wonderful fantasies or use your sensitive antennae to crusade for those less fortunate. You get what you want through creating a veil of illusion and glamour. This is a good Mars for someone in the creative and imaginative fields—a dancer, a performer, a photographer, or an actor. Many famous film stars have this placement. Watch a tendency to manipulate by making others feel sorry for you.

Jupiter Is the Optimist

This big, bright, swirling mass of gases is associated with abundance, prosperity, and the kind of windfall you get without too much hard work. You're optimistic under Jupiter's influence, when anything seems possible. You'll travel, expand your mind with higher education, and publish to share your knowledge widely. On the other hand, Jupiter's influence is neither discriminating nor disciplined. It represents the principle of growth without judgment. Therefore, if not kept in check, it could result in extravagance, weight gain, laziness, and carelessness.

Be sure to look up your Jupiter in the tables in this book. When the current position of Jupiter is favorable, you may get that lucky break. This is a great time to try new things, take risks, travel, or get more education. Opportunities seem to open up easily, so take advantage of them.

Once a year, Jupiter changes signs. That means you are due for an expansive time every twelve years, when Jupiter travels through your sun sign. You'll also have periods every four years when Jupiter is in the same element as your sun sign.

Jupiter in Aries

You are the soul of enthusiasm and optimism. Your luckiest times are when you are getting started on an exciting project or selling an ideal that you really believe in. You may have to watch a tendency to be arrogant with those who do not share your enthusiasm. You follow your impulses, often ignoring budget or other commonsense limitations. To produce real, solid benefits, you'll need patience and the will to follow through wherever this Jupiter falls in your horoscope.

Jupiter in Taurus

You'll spend money on beautiful material things, especially those that come from nature—items made of rare woods, natural fabrics, or precious gems, for instance. You can't have too much comfort or too many sensual pleasures. Watch a tendency to overindulge in good food, or to overpamper yourself with nothing but the best. Spartan living is not for you! You may be especially lucky in matters of real estate.

Jupiter in Gemini

You are the great talker of the zodiac, and you may be a great writer too. But restlessness could be your weak point. You jump around and talk too much; you could be a jack-of-all-trades. Keeping a secret is especially difficult, so you'll also have to watch a tendency to spill the beans. Since you love to be at the center of a beehive of activity, you'll have a vibrant social life. Your best opportunities will come through your talent for language: speaking, writing, communicating, and selling.

Jupiter in Cancer

You are luckiest in situations where you can find emotional closeness or deal with basic security needs, such as food, nurturing, or shelter. You may be a great collector, and you may simply love to accumulate things—you are the one who stashes things away for a rainy day. You probably have a very good memory and love children—in fact, you may have many children to care for. The food, hotel, child-care, and shipping businesses hold good opportunities for you.

Jupiter in Leo

You are a natural showman who loves to live in a larger-than-life way. Yours is a personality full of color that always finds its way into the limelight. You can't have too much attention. Showbiz is a natural place for you, and so is any area where you can play to a crowd. Exercising your flair for drama, your natural playfulness, and your romantic nature brings you good fortune. But watch a tendency to be overextravagant or to monopolize center stage.

Jupiter in Virgo

You actually love those minute details others find boring. To you, they make all the difference between the perfect and the ordinary. You are the fine craftsman who spots every flaw. You expand your awareness by finding the most efficient methods and by being of service to others. Many will be drawn to medical or teaching fields. You'll also have luck in publishing, crafts, nutrition, and service professions. Watch out for a tendency to overwork.

Jupiter in Libra

This is an other-directed Jupiter that develops best with a partner, for the stimulation of others helps you grow. You are also most comfortable in harmonious, beautiful situations, and you work well with artistic people. You have a great sense of fair play and an ability to evaluate the pros and cons of a situation. You usually prefer to play the role of diplomat rather than that of adversary.

Jupiter in Scorpio

You love the feeling of power and control, of taking things to their limit. You can't resist a mystery, and your shrewd, penetrating mind sees right through to the heart of most situations and people. You have luck in work that provides for solutions to matters of life and death. You may be drawn to undercover work, behind-the-scenes intrigue, psychotherapy, the occult, and sex-related ventures. Your challenge will be to develop a sense of moderation and tolerance for other beliefs. You may have luck in handling other people's money—insurance, taxes, and inheritance can bring you a windfall.

Jupiter in Sagittarius

Independent, outgoing, and idealistic, you'll shoot for the stars. This Jupiter compels you to travel far and wide, both physically and mentally, via higher education. You may have luck while traveling in an exotic place. You also have luck with outdoor ventures, exercise, and animals, particularly horses. Since you tend to be very open about your opinions, watch a tendency to be tactless and to exaggerate. Instead, use your wonderful sense of humor to make your point.

Jupiter in Capricorn

Jupiter is much more restrained in Capricorn, the sign of rules and authority. Here, Jupiter can make you overwork and heighten any ambition or sense of duty you may have. You'll expand in areas that advance your position, putting you higher up the social or corporate ladder. You are lucky working within the establishment in a very structured situation, where you can show off your ability to organize and reap rewards for your hard work.

Jupiter in Aquarius

This is another freedom-loving Jupiter, with great tolerance and originality. You are at your best when you are working for a humanitarian cause and in the company of many supporters. This is a good Jupiter for a political career. You'll relate to all kinds of people on all social levels. You have an abundance of original ideas, but you are best off away from routine and any situation that imposes rigid rules. You need mental stimulation!

Jupiter in Pisces

You are a giver whose feelings and pocketbook are easily touched by others, so choose your companions with care. You could be the original sucker for a hard-luck story. Better find a worthy hospital or charity to appreciate your selfless support. You have a great creative imagination and may attract good fortune in fields related to oil, perfume, pharmaceuticals, petroleum, dance, footwear, and alcohol. But beware not to overindulge in alcohol—focus on a creative outlet instead.

Saturn Puts on the Brakes

Jupiter speeds you up with lucky breaks, and then along comes Saturn to slow you down with the disciplinary brakes. It is the planet that can help you achieve lasting goals. Saturn has unfairly been called a malefic planet, one of the bad guys of the zodiac. On the contrary, Saturn is one of our best friends—the kind who tells you what you need to hear, even if it's not good news. Under a Saturn transit, we grow up, take responsibility for our lives, and emerge from whatever test this planet has in store as far wiser, more capable, and mature human beings. After all, it is when we are under pressure that we grow stronger.

When Saturn hits a critical point in your horoscope, you can count on an experience that will make you slow up, pull back, and reexamine your life. It is a call to eliminate what is not working and to shape up. By the end of its twenty-eight-year trip around the zodiac, Saturn will have tested you in all areas of your life. The major tests happen in seven-year cycles, when Saturn passes over the angles of your chart—your rising sign, the top of your chart or midheaven, your descendant, and the nadir or bottom of your chart. This is when the real life-changing experiences happen. But you are also in for a testing period whenever Saturn passes a planet in your chart or stresses that planet from a distance. Therefore, it is useful to check your planetary positions with the timetable of Saturn to prepare in advance, or at least to brace yourself.

When Saturn returns to its location at the time of your birth, at approximately age twenty-eight, you'll have your first Saturn return. At this time, a person usually takes stock or settles down to find his mission in life and assumes full adult duties and responsibilities.

Another way Saturn helps us is to reveal the karmic lessons from previous lives and give us the chance to overcome them. So look at Saturn's challenges as much-needed opportunities for self-improvement. Under a Jupiter influence, you'll have more fun, but Saturn gives you solid, long-lasting results.

Look up your natal Saturn in the tables in this book for clues on where you need work.

Saturn in Aries

Saturn here puts the brakes on Aries's natural drive and enthusiasm. There is often an angry side to this placement. You don't let anyone push you around and you know what's best for yourself. Following orders is not your strong point, nor is diplomacy. You tend to be quick to go on the offensive in relationships, attacking first, before anyone attacks you. Because no one quite lives up to your standards, you often wind up doing everything yourself. You'll have to learn to cooperate and tone down any self-centeredness. Pat Buchanan has this Saturn.

Saturn in Taurus

A big issue is getting control of the cash flow. There will be lean periods that can be frightening, but you have the patience and endurance to stick them out and the methodical drive to prosper in the end. Learn to take a philosophical attitude like Ben Franklin, who also had this placement, and who said, "A penny saved is a penny earned."

Saturn in Gemini

You are a serious student of life, who may have difficulty communicating or sharing your knowledge. You may be shy, speak slowly, or have fears about communicating, like Eleanor Roosevelt. You dwell in the realms of science, theory, or abstract analysis, even when you are dealing with the emotions, like Sigmund Freud, who also had this placement.

Saturn in Cancer

Your tests come with establishing a secure emotional base. In doing so, you may have to deal with some very basic fears centering on your early home environment. Most of your Saturn tests will have emotional roots in those early-childhood experiences. You may have difficulty remaining objective in terms of what you try to achieve, so it will be especially important for you to deal with negative feelings such as guilt, paranoia, jealousy, resentment, and suspicion. Galileo and Michelangelo also navigated these murky waters.

Saturn in Leo

This is an authoritarian Saturn—a strict, demanding parent who may deny the pleasure principle in your zeal to see that rules are followed. Though you may feel guilty about taking the spotlight, you are very ambitious and loyal. You have to watch a tendency toward rigidity, also toward overwork and holding back affection. Joseph Kennedy and Billy Graham share this placement.

Saturn in Virgo

This is a cautious, exacting Saturn, intensely hard on yourself. Most of all, you give yourself the roughest time with your constant worries about every little detail, often making yourself sick. You may have difficulties setting priorities and getting the job done. Your tests will come in learning tolerance and understanding of others. Charles de Gaulle, Mae West, and Nathaniel Hawthorne had this meticulous Saturn.

Saturn in Libra

Saturn is exalted here, which makes this planet an ally. You may choose very serious, older partners in life, perhaps stemming from a fear of dependency. You need to learn to stand solidly on your own before you commit to another. Since you are extremely cautious, you deliberate every involvement—with good reason. It is best that you find an occupation that makes good use of your sense of duty and honor. Steer clear of fly-by-night situations. Both Khrushchev and Mao Tse-tung had this placement.

Saturn in Scorpio

You have great staying power. This Saturn tests you in situations involving the control of others. You may feel drawn to some kind of intrigue or undercover work, like J. Edgar Hoover. Or there may be an air of mystery surrounding your life and death, like Marilyn Monroe and Robert Kennedy, who both had this placement. There are lessons to be learned from your sexual involvements. Often sex is used for manipulation or is somehow out of the ordinary. The Roman emperor Caligula and the transsexual Christine Jorgensen are extreme cases.

Saturn in Sagittarius

Your challenges and lessons will come from tests of your spiritual and philosophical values, as happened to Martin Luther King Jr. and Gandhi. You are high-minded and sincere with this reflective, moral placement. Uncompromising in your ethical standards, you could become a benevolent despot.

Saturn in Capricorn

With the help of Saturn at maximum strength, your judgment will improve with age. And, like Spencer Tracy's screen image, you'll be the gray-haired hero with a strong sense of responsibility. You advance in life slowly but steadily, always with a strong hand at the helm and an eye for the advantageous situation. Like Pat Robertson, you're likely to stand for conservative values. Negatively, you may be a loner, prone to periods of melancholy.

Saturn in Aquarius

Your tests come from relationships with groups. Do you care too much about what others think? Do you feel like an outsider, like Greta Garbo? You may fear being different from others and therefore slight your own unique, forward-looking gifts. Or like Lord Byron and Howard Hughes, you may take the opposite tack and rebel in the extreme. You can apply discipline to accomplish great humanitarian goals, as Albert Schweitzer did.

Saturn in Pisces

Your fear of the unknown and the irrational may lead you to the safety and protection of an institution. You may go on the run like Jesse James to avoid looking too deeply inside. Or you might go in the opposite, more positive direction and develop a disciplined psychoanalytic approach, which puts you more in control of your feelings. Some of you will take refuge in work with hospitals, charities, or religious institutions. Queen Victoria, who had this placement, symbolized an era when institutions of all kinds were sustained. Discipline applied to artistic work, especially poetry and dance, or spiritual work, such as yoga or meditation, might be helpful.

How Uranus, Neptune, and Pluto Influence Your Generation

These three planets remain in signs such a long time that a whole generation bears the imprint of the sign. Mass movements, great sweeping changes, fads that characterize a generation, and even the issues of the conflicts and wars of the time are influenced by these outer three planets. When one of these distant planets changes signs, there is a definite shift in the atmosphere, the feeling of the end of an era.

Since these planets are so far away from the sun—too distant to be seen by the naked eye—they pick up signals from the universe at large. These planetary receivers literally link the sun with distant energies, and then perform a similar function in your horoscope by linking your central character with intuitive, spiritual, transformative forces from the cosmos. Each planet has a special domain and will reflect this in the area of your chart where it falls.

Uranus Is the Surprise Ingredient

Uranus is the surprise ingredient that sets you and your generation apart. There is nothing ordinary about this quirky green planet that seems to be traveling on its side, surrounded by a swarm of moons. Is it any wonder that astrologers assigned it to Aquarius, the most eccentric and gregarious sign? Uranus seems to wend its way around the sun, marching to its own tune.

Significantly, Uranus follows Saturn, the planet of limitations and structures. Often we get caught up in the structures we have created to give ourselves a sense of security. However, if we lose contact with our spiritual roots in the process, Uranus is likely to jolt us out of our comfortable rut and wake us up.

Uranus energy is electrical, happening in sudden flashes. It is not influenced by karma or past events, nor does it regard tradition, sex, or sentiment. Uranus's key words are surprise and awakening. Suddenly, there's that flash of inspiration, that bright idea, or that totally new approach that revolutionizes whatever scheme you were undertaking. A Uranus event takes you by surprise, for better or for worse. The Uranus place in your life is where you awaken and become your own person, leaving the structures of Saturn behind. And it is probably the most unconventional place in your chart.

Look up the sign of Uranus at the time of your birth and see where you follow your own tune.

Uranus in Aries

Birth Dates:

March 31, 1927–November 4, 1927
January 13, 1928–June 6, 1934
October 10, 1934–March 28, 1935

Your generation is original, creative, and pioneering. It developed the computer, the airplane, and the cyclotron. You let nothing hold you back from exploring the unknown, and you have a powerful mixture of fire and electricity behind you. Women of your generation were among the first to be liberated. You were the unforgettable style setters. You have a surprise in store for everyone. As with Yoko Ono, Grace Kelly, and Jacqueline Onassis, your life may be jolted by sudden and violent changes.

Uranus in Taurus

Birth Dates:

June 6, 1934–October 10, 1934
March 28, 1935–August 7, 1941
October 5, 1941–May 15, 1942

The great territorial shakeups of World War II began during your generation. You're independent; you're probably self-employed or you would like to be. You have original ideas about making money, and you brace yourself for sudden changes of fortune. This Uranus can cause shake-ups, particularly in finances, but it can also make you a born entrepreneur, like Martha Stewart.

Uranus in Gemini

Birth Dates:

August 7, 1941–October 5, 1941
May 15, 1942–August 30, 1948
November 12, 1948–June 10, 1949

You were the first children to be influenced by television, and in your adult years, your generation stocks up on answering machines, cell phones, computers, and fax machines—any new way you can communicate. You have an inquiring mind, but your interests may be rather short-lived. This Uranus can be easily fragmented if there is no structure and focus.

Uranus in Cancer

Birth Dates:

August 30–November 12, 1948
June 10, 1949–August 24, 1955
January 28, 1956–June 10, 1956

This generation came at a time when divorce was becoming commonplace, so your home image is unconventional. You may have an unusual relationship with your parents, or come from a broken home or an unconventional one. You'll have unorthodox ideas about parenting, intimacy, food, and shelter. You may also be interested in dreams, psychic phenomena, and memory work.

Uranus in Leo

Birth Dates:

August 24, 1955–January 28, 1956
June 10, 1956–November 1, 1961
January 10, 1962–August 10, 1962

This generation understood how to use electronic media. Many of your group are now leaders in the high-tech industries, and you also understand how to use the new media to promote yourself. Like Isadora Duncan, you may have a very eccentric kind of charisma and a life that is sparked by unusual love affairs. Your children may have traits that are out of the ordinary. Where this planet falls in your chart, you'll have a love of freedom, be a bit of an egomaniac, and show the full force of your personality in a unique way, like tennis great Martina Navratilova.

Uranus in Virgo

Birth Dates:

November 1, 1961–January 10, 1962
August 10, 1962–September 28, 1968
May 20, 1969–June 24, 1969

You'll have highly individual work methods, and many will be finding newer, more practical ways to use computers. Like Einstein, who had this placement, you'll break the rules brilliantly. Your generation came at a time of student rebellions, the civil rights movement, and the general acceptance of health foods. Chances are, you're concerned about pollution and cleaning up the environment. You may also be involved with nontraditional healing methods.

Uranus in Libra

Birth Dates:

September 28, 1968–May 20, 1969
June 24, 1969–November 21, 1974
May 1, 1975–September 8, 1975

Your generation will be always changing partners. Born during the era of women's liberation, you may have come from a broken home and may have no clear image of what a marriage entails. There will be many sudden splits and experiments before you settle down. Your generation will be much involved in legal and political reforms and in changing artistic and fashion looks.

Uranus in Scorpio

Birth Dates:

November 21, 1974–May 1, 1975
September 8, 1975–February 17, 1981
March 20, 1981–November 16, 1981

Interest in transformation, meditation, and life after death signaled the beginning of New Age consciousness. Your generation recognizes no boundaries, no limits, and no external controls. You'll have new attitudes toward death and dying, psychic phenomena, and the occult. Like Mae West and Casanova, you'll shock 'em sexually.

Uranus in Sagittarius

Birth Dates:
February 17, 1981–March 20, 1981
November 16, 1981–February 15, 1988
May 27, 1988–December 2, 1988

Could this generation be the first to travel in outer space? The new generation with this placement included Charles Lindbergh and a time when the first zeppelins and the Wright Brothers were conquering the skies. Uranus here forecasts great discoveries, mind expansion, and long-distance travel. Like Galileo and Martin Luther, those born in these years will generate new theories about the cosmos and man's relation to it.

Uranus in Capricorn

Birth Dates:
December 20, 1904–January 30, 1912
September 4, 1912–November 12, 1912
February 15, 1988–May 27, 1988
December 2, 1988–April 1, 1995
June 9, 1995–January 12, 1996

This generation, now reaching adulthood, will challenge traditions. In these years, we got organized with the help of technology put to practical use. The Internet was born after the great economic boom of the 1990s. Great leaders who were movers and shakers of history, like Julius Caesar and Henry VIII, were born under this placement.

Uranus in Aquarius

Birth Dates:
January 30, 1912–September 4, 1912
November 12, 1912–April 1, 1919

August 16, 1919–January 22, 1920
April 1, 1995–June 9, 1995
January 12, 1996–March 10, 2003
September 15, 2003–December 30, 2003

Uranus in Aquarius is the strongest placement for this planet. Recently, we've had the opportunity to witness the full force of its power of innovation, as well as its sudden wake-up calls and insistence on humanitarian values. This was a time of high-tech development, when home computers became as ubiquitous as television. It was a time of globalization, surprise attacks (9/11), and underdeveloped countries demanding attention. The last generation with this placement produced great innovative minds, such as Leonard Bernstein and Orson Welles. The next will become another radical breakthrough generation, much concerned with global issues that involve all humanity.

Uranus in Pisces

Birth Dates:

April 1, 1919–August 16, 1919
January 22, 1920–March 31, 1927
November 4, 1927–January 12, 1928
March 10, 2003–September 15, 2003
December 30, 2003–May 28, 2010

Uranus is now in Pisces, ushering in a new generation. In the past century, Uranus in Pisces focused attention on the rise of electronic entertainment—radio and the cinema—and the secretiveness of Prohibition. This produced a generation of idealists exemplified by Judy Garland's theme, "Somewhere over the Rainbow." Uranus in Pisces also hints at stealth activities, at hospital and prison reform, at high-tech drugs and medical experiments, at shake-ups in the petroleum industry and new locations for Pisces-ruled off-shore drilling. Issues regarding the water and oil supply, water-related storm damage (Hurricane Katrina), sudden hurricanes, droughts, and floods demand our attention.

Neptune Is the Magic Solvent

Neptune is often maligned as the planet of illusions that dissolves reality, enabling you to escape the material world. Under Neptune's influence, you see what you want to see. But Neptune also encourages you to create. It embodies glamour, subtlety, mystery, and mysticism, and governs anything that takes you beyond the mundane world, including out-of-body experiences.

Neptune breaks through and transcends your ordinary perceptions to take you to another level, where you experience either confusion or ecstasy. Its force can pull you off course only if you allow this to happen. Those who use Neptune wisely can translate their daydreams into poetry, theater, design, or inspired moves in the business world, avoiding the tricky con artist side of this planet.

Find your Neptune listed below:

Neptune in Cancer

Birth Dates:

July 19, 1901–December 25, 1901
May 21, 1902–September 23, 1914
December 14, 1914–July 19, 1915
March 19, 1916–May 2, 1916

Dreams of the homeland, idealistic patriotism, and glamorization of the nurturing assets of women characterized this time. You who were born here have unusual psychic ability and deep insights into basic needs of others.

Neptune in Leo

Birth Dates:

September 23, 1914–December 14, 1914
July 19, 1915–March 19, 1916
May 2, 1916–September 21, 1928
February 19, 1929–July 24, 1929

Neptune in Leo brought us the glamour and high living of the 1920s and the big spenders of that time. Neptune temptations of gambling, seduction, theater, and lavish entertaining distracted from the realities of the age. Those born in that generation also made great advances in the arts.

Neptune in Virgo

Birth Dates:

September 21, 1928–February 19, 1929
July 24, 1929–October 3, 1942
April 17, 1943–August 2, 1943

Neptune in Virgo encompassed the 1930s, the Great Depression, and the beginning of World War II, when a new order was born. This was a time of facing what didn't work. Many were unemployed and found solace at the movies, watching the great Virgo star Greta Garbo or the escapist dance films of Busby Berkeley. New public services were born. Those with Neptune in Virgo later spread the gospel of health and fitness. This generation's devotion to spending hours at the office inspired the word *workaholic*.

Neptune in Libra

Birth Dates:

October 3, 1942–April 17, 1943
August 2, 1943–December 24, 1955
March 12, 1956–October 19, 1956
June 15, 1957–August 6, 1957

This was the time of World War II, and the immediate postwar period, when the world regained balance and returned to relative stability. Neptune in Libra was the romantic generation who would later be concerned with relating. As this generation matured, there was a new trend toward marriage and commitment. Racial and sexual equality became important issues, as they redesigned traditional roles to suit modern times.

Neptune in Scorpio

Birth Dates:

December 24, 1955–March 12, 1956
October 19, 1956–June 15, 1957
August 6, 1957–January 4, 1970

May 3, 1970–November 6, 1970

Neptune in Scorpio brought in a generation that would become interested in transformative power. Born in an era that glamorized sex, drugs, rock and roll, and Eastern religion, they matured in a more sobering time of AIDS, cocaine abuse, and New Age spirituality. As they evolve, they will become active in healing the planet from the results of the abuse of power.

Neptune in Sagittarius

Birth Dates:

January 4, 1970–May 3, 1970
November 6, 1970–January 19, 1984
June 23, 1984–November 21, 1984

Neptune in Sagittarius was the time when space travel became a reality. The Neptune influence glamorized new approaches to mysticism, religion, and mind expansion. This generation will take a new approach to spiritual life, with emphasis on visions, mysticism, and clairvoyance.

Neptune in Capricorn

Birth Dates:

January 19, 1984–June 23, 1984
November 21, 1984–January 29, 1998

Neptune in Capricorn brought a time when delusions about material power were glamorized in the mideighties and nineties. There was a boom in the stock market, and the Internet era spawned young tycoons who later lost all their wealth. It was also a time when the psychic and occult worlds spawned a new category of business enterprise, and sold services on television.

Neptune in Aquarius

Birth Dates:

January 29, 1998–April 4, 2011

This should continue to be a time of breakthroughs. Here the creative influence of Neptune reaches a universal audience. This is a time of dissolving barriers and globalization—when we truly become one world. During this transit of high-tech Aquarius, new kinds of entertainment media reach across cultural differences. However, the transit of Neptune has also raised boundary issues between cultures, especially in Middle Eastern countries with Neptune-ruled oil fields. As Neptune raises issues of social and political structures not being as solid as they seem, this could continue to produce rebellion and chaos in the environment. However, by using imagination (Neptune) in partnership with a global view (Aquarius), we could reach creative solutions.

Those born with this placement should be true citizens of the world, with a remarkable creative ability to transcend social and cultural barriers.

Pluto Can Transform You

Though Pluto is a tiny, mysterious body in space, its influence is great. When Pluto zaps a strategic point in your horoscope, your life changes dramatically.

Little Pluto is the power behind the scenes; it affects you at deep levels of consciousness, causing events to come to the surface that will transform you and your generation. Nothing escapes, or is sacred, with this probing planet. Its purpose is to wipe out the past so something new can happen.

The Pluto place in your horoscope is where you have invisible power (Mars governs the visible power), where you can transform, heal, and affect the unconscious needs of the masses. Pluto tells lots about how your generation projects power and what makes it seem cool to others. And when Pluto changes signs, there is a whole new concept of what's cool. Pluto's strange elliptical orbit occasionally runs inside the orbit of neighboring Neptune. Because of its eccentric path, the length of time Pluto stays in any given sign can vary from thirteen to thirty-two years. It covered only seven signs in the last century.

Pluto in Gemini

Late 1800s–May 26, 1914

This was a time of mass suggestion and breakthroughs in communications, when many brilliant writers, such as Ernest Hemingway and F. Scott Fitzgerald, were born. Henry Miller, D. H. Lawrence, and James Joyce scandalized society by using explicit sexual images and language in their literature. "Muck-raking" journalists exposed corruption. Pluto-ruled Scorpio president Theodore Roosevelt said, "Speak softly, but carry a big stick." This generation had an intense need to communicate and made major breakthroughs in knowledge. A compulsive restlessness and a thirst for a variety of experiences characterize many of this generation.

Pluto in Cancer

Birth Dates:

May 26, 1914–June 14, 1939

Dictators and mass media arose to wield emotional power over the masses. Women's rights were a popular issue. Deep sentimental feelings, acquisitiveness, and possessiveness characterized these times and people. Most of the great stars of the Hollywood era who embodied the American image were born during this period: Grace Kelly, Esther Williams, Frank Sinatra, and Lana Turner, to name a few.

Pluto in Leo

Birth Dates:

June 14, 1939–August 19, 1957

The performing arts played on the emotions of the masses. Mick Jagger, John Lennon, and rock and roll were born at this time. So were baby boomers like Bill and Hillary Clinton. Those born here tend to be self-centered, powerful, and boisterous. This generation does its own thing, for better or for worse. They are quick to embrace self-transformation in the form of antiaging and plastic surgery techniques, to stay forever young and stay relevant in society.

Pluto in Virgo

Birth Dates:

August 19, 1957–October 5, 1971
April 17, 1972–July 30, 1972

This is the yuppie generation that sparked a mass movement toward fitness, health, and career. It is a much more sober, serious, and driven generation than the fun-loving Pluto in Leo. During this time, machines were invented to process detail work efficiently. Inventions took a practical turn with answering machines, fax machines, car phones, and home-office equipment—all making the workplace far more efficient.

Pluto in Libra

Birth Dates:

October 5, 1971–April 17, 1972
July 30, 1972–November 5, 1983
May 18, 1984–August 27, 1984

A mellower generation, people born at this time are concerned with partnerships, working together, and finding diplomatic solutions to problems. Marriage is important to this generation, and they will define it by combining traditional values with equal partnership. This was a time of women's liberation, gay rights, the ERA, and legal battles over abortion—all of which transformed our ideas about relationships.

Pluto in Scorpio

Birth Dates:

November 5, 1983–May 18, 1984
August 27, 1984–January 17, 1995

Pluto was in its ruling sign for a comparatively short period of time. However, this was a time of record achievements, destructive sexually transmitted diseases, nuclear power controversies, and explosive political issues. Pluto destroys in order to create new understanding—the phoenix rising from the ashes—which should be some consolation for those of you who felt Pluto's force before 1995. Sexual shockers were par for the course during these intense years, when black clothing, transvestites, body piercing, tattoos, and sexually explicit advertising pushed the boundaries of good taste.

Pluto in Sagittarius

Birth Dates:

January 17, 1995–April 20, 1995

November 10, 1995–January 27, 2008

June 13, 2008–November 26, 2008

During the most recent Pluto transit, we were pushed to expand our horizons and find deeper spiritual meaning in life.

Pluto's opposition with Saturn in 2001 brought an enormous conflict between traditional societies and the forces of change. It signaled a time when religious convictions exerted power in our political life as well.

Since Sagittarius is associated with travel, Pluto, the planet of extremes, made space travel a reality for wealthy adventurers, who paid for the privilege of travel on space shuttles. Globalization transformed business and traditional societies as outsourcing became the norm.

New dimensions in electronic publishing, concern with animal rights and the environment, and an increasing emphasis on extreme forms of religion were other signs of Pluto in Sagittarius. Charismatic religious leaders asserted themselves and questions of the boundaries between church and state arose. There were also sexual scandals associated with the church, which transformed the religious power structure.

Pluto in Capricorn

Birth Dates:

January 25, 2008–June 13, 2008

November 26, 2008–January 20, 2024

As Pluto in Jupiter-ruled Sagittarius signaled a time of expansion and globalization, Pluto's entry into Saturn-ruled Capricorn in 2008 signaled a time of adjustment, of facing reality and limitations, then finding pragmatic solutions. It will be a time when a new structure is imposed, when we become concerned with what actually works.

As Capricorn is associated with corporations and also with

responsibility and duty, look for dramatic changes in business practices, hopefully with more attention paid to ethical and social responsibility as well as the bottom line. Big business will have enormous power during this transit, perhaps handling what governments have been unable to accomplish. There will be an emphasis on trimming down, perhaps a new belt-tightening regime. And, since Capricorn is the sign of Father Time, there will be a new emphasis on the aging of the population. The generation born now is sure to be a more practical and realistic one than that of their older Pluto in Sagittarius siblings.

VENUS SIGNS 1901–2010

	Aries	Taurus	Gemini	Cancer	Leo	Virgo
1901	3/29–4/22	4/22–5/17	5/17–6/10	6/10–7/5	7/5–7/29	7/29–8/23
1902	5/7–6/3	6/3–6/30	6/30–7/25	7/25–8/19	8/19–9/13	9/13–10/7
1903	2/28–3/24	3/24–4/18	4/18–5/13	5/13–6/9	6/9–7/7	7/7–8/17
						9/6–11/8
1904	3/13–5/7	5/7–6/1	6/1–6/25	6/25–7/19	7/19–8/13	8/13–9/6
1905	2/3–3/6	3/6–4/9	7/8–8/6	8/6–9/1	9/1–9/27	9/27–10/21
	4/9–5/28	5/28–7/8				
1906	3/1–4/7	4/7–5/2	5/2–5/26	5/26–6/20	6/20–7/16	7/16–8/11
1907	4/27–5/22	5/22–6/16	6/16–7/11	7/11–8/4	8/4–8/29	8/29–9/22
1908	2/14–3/10	3/10–4/5	4/5–5/5	5/5–9/8	9/8–10/8	10/8–11/3
1909	3/29–4/22	4/22–5/16	5/16–6/10	6/10–7/4	7/4–7/29	7/29–8/23
1910	5/7–6/3	6/4–6/29	6/30–7/24	7/25–8/18	8/19–9/12	9/13–10/6
1911	2/28–3/23	3/24–4/17	4/18–5/12	5/13–6/8	6/9–7/7	7/8–11/18
1912	4/13–5/6	5/7–5/31	6/1–6/24	6/24–7/18	7/19–8/12	8/13–9/5
1913	2/3–3/6	3/7–5/1	7/8–8/5	8/6–8/31	9/1–9/26	9/27–10/20
	5/2–5/30	5/31–7/7				
1914	3/14–4/6	4/7–5/1	5/2–5/25	5/26–6/19	6/20–7/15	7/16–8/10
1915	4/27–5/21	5/22–6/15	6/16–7/10	7/11–8/3	8/4–8/28	8/29–9/21
1916	2/14–3/9	3/10–4/5	4/6–5/5	5/6–9/8	9/9–10/7	10/8–11/2
1917	3/29–4/21	4/22–5/15	5/16–6/9	6/10–7/3	7/4–7/28	7/29–8/21
1918	5/7–6/2	6/3–6/28	6/29–7/24	7/25–8/18	8/19–9/11	9/12–10/5
1919	2/27–3/22	3/23–4/16	4/17–5/12	5/13–6/7	6/8–7/7	7/8–11/8
1920	4/12–5/6	5/7–5/30	5/31–6/23	6/24–7/18	7/19–8/11	8/12–9/4
1921	2/3–3/6	3/7–4/25	7/8–8/5	8/6–8/31	9/1–9/25	9/26–10/20
	4/26–6/1	6/2–7/7				
1922	3/13–4/6	4/7–4/30	5/1–5/25	5/26–6/19	6/20–7/14	7/15–8/9
1923	4/27–5/21	5/22–6/14	6/15–7/9	7/10–8/3	8/4–8/27	8/28–9/20
1924	2/13–3/8	3/9–4/4	4/5–5/5	5/6–9/8	9/9–10/7	10/8–11/12
1925	3/28–4/20	4/21–5/15	5/16–6/8	6/9–7/3	7/4–7/27	7/28–8/21
1926	5/7–6/2	6/3–6/28	6/29–7/23	7/24–8/17	8/18–9/11	9/12–10/5
1927	2/27–3/22	3/23–4/16	4/17–5/11	5/12–6/7	6/8–7/7	7/8–11/9

Libra	Scorpio	Sagittarius	Capricorn	Aquarius	Pisces
8/23–9/17	9/17–10/12	10/12–1/16	1/16–2/9	2/9–3/5	3/5–3/29
			11/7–12/5	12/5–1/11	
10/7–10/31	10/31–11/24	11/24–12/18	12/18–1/11	2/6–4/4	1/11–2/6
					4/4–5/7
8/17–9/6	12/9–1/5			1/11–2/4	2/4–2/28
11/8–12/9					
9/6–9/30	9/30–10/25	1/5–1/30	1/30–2/24	2/24–3/19	3/19–4/13
		10/25–11/18	11/18–12/13	12/13–1/7	
10/21–11/14	11/14–12/8	12/8–1/1/06			1/7–2/3
8/11–9/7	9/7–10/9	10/9–12/15	1/1–1/25	1/25–2/18	2/18–3/14
	12/15–12/25	12/25–2/6			
9/22–10/16	10/16–11/9	11/9–12/3	2/6–3/6	3/6–4/2	4/2–4/27
			12/3–12/27	12/27–1/20	
11/3–11/28	11/28–12/22	12/22–1/15			1/20–2/4
8/23–9/17	9/17–10/12	10/12–11/17	1/15–2/9	2/9–3/5	3/5–3/29
			11/17–12/5	12/5–1/15	
10/7–10/30	10/31–11/23	11/24–12/17	12/18–12/31	1/1–1/15	1/16–1/28
				1/29–4/4	4/5–5/6
11/19–12/8	12/9–12/31		1/1–1/10	1/11–2/2	2/3–2/27
9/6–9/30	1/1–1/4	1/5–1/29	1/30–2/23	2/24–3/18	3/19–4/12
	10/1–10/24	10/25–11/17	11/18–12/12	12/13–12/31	
10/21–11/13	11/14–12/7	12/8–12/31		1/1–1/6	1/7–2/2
8/11–9/6	9/7–10/9	10/10–12/5	1/1–1/24	1/25–2/17	2/18–3/13
	12/6–12/30	12/31			
9/22–10/15	10/16–11/8	1/1–2/6	2/7–3/6	3/7–4/1	4/2–4/26
		11/9–12/2	12/3–12/26	12/27–12/31	
11/3–11/27	11/28–12/21	12/22–12/31		1/1–1/19	1/20–2/13
8/22–9/16	9/17–10/11	1/1–1/14	1/15–2/7	2/8–3/4	3/5–3/28
		10/12–11/6	11/7–12/5	12/6–12/31	
10/6–10/29	10/30–11/22	11/23–12/16	12/17–12/31	1/1–4/5	4/6–5/6
11/9–12/8	12/9–12/31		1/1–1/9	1/10–2/2	2/3–2/26
9/5–9/30	1/1–1/3	1/4–1/28	1/29–2/22	2/23–3/18	3/19–4/11
	9/31–10/23	10/24–11/17	11/18–12/11	12/12–12/31	
10/21–11/13	11/14–12/7	12/8–12/31		1/1–1/6	1/7–2/2
8/10–9/6	9/7–10/10	10/11–11/28	1/1–1/24	1/25–2/16	2/17–3/12
	11/29–12/31				
9/21–10/14	1/1	1/2–2/6	2/7–3/5	3/6–3/31	4/1–4/26
	10/15–11/7	11/8–12/1	12/2–12/25	12/26–12/31	
11/13–11/26	11/27–12/21	12/22–12/31		1/1–1/19	1/20–2/12
8/22–9/15	9/16–10/11	1/1–1/14	1/15–2/7	2/8–3/3	3/4–3/27
		10/12–11/6	11/7–12/5	12/6–12/31	
10/6–10/29	10/30–11/22	11/23–12/16	12/17–12/31	1/1–4/5	4/6–5/6
11/10–12/8	12/9–12/31	1/1–1/7	1/8	1/9–2/1	2/2–2/26

VENUS SIGNS 1901–2010

	Aries	Taurus	Gemini	Cancer	Leo	Virgo
1928	4/12–5/5	5/6–5/29	5/30–6/23	6/24–7/17	7/18–8/11	8/12–9/4
1929	2/3–3/7	3/8–4/19	7/8–8/4	8/5–8/30	8/31–9/25	9/26–10/19
	4/20–6/2	6/3–7/7				
1930	3/13–4/5	4/6–4/30	5/1–5/24	5/25–6/18	6/19–7/14	7/15–8/9
1931	4/26–5/20	5/21–6/13	6/14–7/8	7/9–8/2	8/3–8/26	8/27–9/19
1932	2/12–3/8	3/9–4/3	4/4–5/5	5/6–7/12	9/9–10/6	10/7–11/1
			7/13–7/27	7/28–9/8		
1933	3/27–4/19	4/20–5/28	5/29–6/8	6/9–7/2	7/3–7/26	7/27–8/20
1934	5/6–6/1	6/2–6/27	6/28–7/22	7/23–8/16	8/17–9/10	9/11–10/4
1935	2/26–3/21	3/22–4/15	4/16–5/10	5/11–6/6	6/7–7/6	7/7–11/8
1936	4/11–5/4	5/5–5/28	5/29–6/22	6/23–7/16	7/17–8/10	8/11–9/4
1937	2/2–3/8	3/9–4/13	7/7–8/3	8/4–8/29	8/30–9/24	9/25–10/18
	4/14–6/3	6/4–7/6				
1938	3/12–4/4	4/5–4/28	4/29–5/23	5/24–6/18	6/19–7/13	7/14–8/8
1939	4/25–5/19	5/20–6/13	6/14–7/8	7/9–8/1	8/2–8/25	8/26–9/19
1940	2/12–3/7	3/8–4/3	4/4–5/5	5/6–7/4	9/9–10/5	10/6–10/31
			7/5–7/31	8/1–9/8		
1941	3/27–4/19	4/20–5/13	5/14–6/6	6/7–7/1	7/2–7/26	7/27–8/20
1942	5/6–6/1	6/2–6/26	6/27–7/22	7/23–8/16	8/17–9/9	9/10–10/3
1943	2/25–3/20	3/21–4/14	4/15–5/10	5/11–6/6	6/7–7/6	7/7–11/8
1944	4/10–5/3	5/4–5/28	5/29–6/21	6/22–7/16	7/17–8/9	8/10–9/2
1945	2/2–3/10	3/11–4/6	7/7–8/3	8/4–8/29	8/30–9/23	9/24–10/18
	4/7–6/3	6/4–7/6				
1946	3/11–4/4	4/5–4/28	4/29–5/23	5/24–6/17	6/18–7/12	7/13–8/8
1947	4/25–5/19	5/20–6/12	6/13–7/7	7/8–8/1	8/2–8/25	8/26–9/18
1948	2/11–3/7	3/8–4/3	4/4–5/6	5/7–6/28	9/8–10/5	10/6–10/31
			6/29–8/2	8/3–9/7		
1949	3/26–4/19	4/20–5/13	5/14–6/6	6/7–6/30	7/1–7/25	7/26–8/19
1950	5/5–5/31	6/1–6/26	6/27–7/21	7/22–8/15	8/16–9/9	9/10–10/3
1951	2/25–3/21	3/22–4/15	4/16–5/10	5/11–6/6	6/7–7/7	7/8–11/9
1952	4/10–5/4	5/5–5/28	5/29–6/21	6/22–7/16	7/17–8/9	8/10–9/3
1953	2/2–3/3	3/4–3/31	7/8–8/3	8/4–8/29	8/30–9/24	9/25–10/18
	4/1–6/5	6/6–7/7				

Libra	Scorpio	Sagittarius	Capricorn	Aquarius	Pisces
9/5–9/28	1/1–1/3	1/4–1/28	1/29–2/22	2/23–3/17	3/18–4/11
	9/29–10/23	10/24–11/16	11/17–12/11	12/12–12/31	
10/20–11/12	11/13–12/6	12/7–12/30	12/31	1/1–1/5	1/6–2/2
8/10–9/6	9/7–10/11	10/12–11/21	1/1–1/23	1/24–2/16	2/17–3/12
	11/22–12/31				
9/20–10/13	1/1–1/3	1/4–2/6	2/7–3/4	3/5–3/31	4/1–4/25
	10/14–11/6	11/7–11/30	12/1–12/24	12/25–12/31	
11/2–11/25	11/26–12/20	12/21–12/31		1/1–1/18	1/19–2/11
8/21–9/14	9/15–10/10	1/1–1/13	1/14–2/6	2/7–3/2	3/3–3/26
		10/11–11/5	11/6–12/4	12/5–12/31	
10/5–10/28	10/29–11/21	11/22–12/15	12/16–12/31	1/1–4/5	4/6–5/5
11/9–12/7	12/8–12/31		1/1–1/7	1/8–1/31	2/1–2/25
9/5–9/27	1/1–1/2	1/3–1/27	1/28–2/21	2/22–3/16	3/17–4/10
	9/28–10/22	10/23–11/15	11/16–12/10	12/11–12/31	
10/19–11/11	11/12–12/5	12/6–12/29	12/30–12/31	1/1–1/5	1/6–2/1
8/9–9/6	9/7–10/13	10/14–11/14	1/1–1/22	1/23–2/15	2/16–3/11
	11/15–12/31				
9/20–10/13	1/1–1/3	1/4–2/5	2/6–3/4	3/5–3/30	3/31–4/24
	10/14–11/6	11/7–11/30	12/1–12/24	12/25–12/31	
11/1–11/25	11/26–12/19	12/20–12/31		1/1–1/18	1/19–2/11
8/21–9/14	9/15–10/9	1/1–1/12	1/13–2/5	2/6–3/1	3/2–3/26
		10/10–11/5	11/6–12/4	12/5–12/31	
10/4–10/27	10/28–11/20	11/21–12/14	12/15–12/31	1/1–4/5	4/6–5/5
11/9–12/7	12/8–12/31		1/1–1/7	1/8–1/31	2/1–2/24
9/3–9/27	1/1–1/2	1/3–1/27	1/28–2/20	2/21–3/16	3/17–4/9
	9/28–10/21	10/22–11/15	11/16–12/10	12/11–12/31	
10/19–11/11	11/12–12/5	12/6–12/29	12/30–12/31	1/1–1/4	1/5–2/1
8/9–9/6	9/7–10/15	10/16–11/7	1/1–1/21	1/22–2/14	2/15–3/10
	11/8–12/31				
9/19–10/12	1/1–1/4	1/5–2/5	2/6–3/4	3/5–3/29	3/30–4/24
	10/13–11/5	11/6–11/29	11/30–12/23	12/24–12/31	
11/1–11/25	11/26–12/19	12/20–12/31		1/1–1/17	1/18–2/10
8/20–9/14	9/15–10/9	1/1–1/12	1/13–2/5	2/6–3/1	3/2–3/25
		10/10–11/5	11/6–12/5	12/6–12/31	
10/4–10/27	10/28–11/20	11/21–12/13	12/14–12/31	1/1–4/5	4/6–5/4
11/10–12/7	12/8–12/31		1/1–1/7	1/8–1/31	2/1–2/24
9/4–9/27	1/1–1/2	1/3–1/27	1/28–2/20	2/21–3/16	3/17–4/9
	9/28–10/21	10/22–11/15	11/16–12/10	12/11–12/31	
10/19–11/11	11/12–12/5	12/6–12/29	12/30–12/31	1/1–1/5	1/6–2/1

VENUS SIGNS 1901–2010

	Aries	Taurus	Gemini	Cancer	Leo	Virgo
1954	3/12–4/4	4/5–4/28	4/29–5/23	5/24–6/17	6/18–7/13	7/14–8/8
1955	4/25–5/19	5/20–6/13	6/14–7/7	7/8–8/1	8/2–8/25	8/26–9/18
1956	2/12–3/7	3/8–4/4	4/5–5/7	5/8–6/23	9/9–10/5	10/6–10/31
			6/24–8/4	8/5–9/8		
1957	3/26–4/19	4/20–5/13	5/14–6/6	6/7–7/1	7/2–7/26	7/27–8/19
1958	5/6–5/31	6/1–6/26	6/27–7/22	7/23–8/15	8/16–9/9	9/10–10/3
1959	2/25–3/20	3/21–4/14	4/15–5/10	5/11–6/6	6/7–7/8	7/9–9/20
					9/21–9/24	9/25–11/9
1960	4/10–5/3	5/4–5/28	5/29–6/21	6/22–7/15	7/16–8/9	8/10–9/2
1961	2/3–6/5	6/6–7/7	7/8–8/3	8/4–8/29	8/30–9/23	9/24–10/17
1962	3/11–4/3	4/4–4/28	4/29–5/22	5/23–6/17	6/18–7/12	7/13–8/8
1963	4/24–5/18	5/19–6/12	6/13–7/7	7/8–7/31	8/1–8/25	8/26–9/18
1964	2/11–3/7	3/8–4/4	4/5–5/9	5/10–6/17	9/9–10/5	10/6–10/31
			6/18–8/5	8/6–9/8		
1965	3/26–4/18	4/19–5/12	5/13–6/6	6/7–6/30	7/1–7/25	7/26–8/19
1966	5/6–5/31	6/1–6/26	6/27–7/21	7/22–8/15	8/16–9/8	9/9–10/2
1967	2/24–3/20	3/21–4/14	4/15–5/10	5/11–6/6	6/7–7/8	7/9–9/9
					9/10–10/1	10/2–11/9
1968	4/9–5/3	5/4–5/27	5/28–6/20	6/21–7/15	7/16–8/8	8/9–9/2
1969	2/3–6/6	6/7–7/6	7/7–8/3	8/4–8/28	8/29–9/22	9/23–10/17
1970	3/11–4/3	4/4–4/27	4/28–5/22	5/23–6/16	6/17–7/12	7/13–8/8
1971	4/24–5/18	5/19–6/12	6/13–7/6	7/7–7/31	8/1–8/24	8/25–9/17
1972	2/11–3/7	3/8–4/3	4/4–5/10	5/11–6/11		
			6/12–8/6	8/7–9/8	9/9–10/5	10/6–10/30
1973	3/25–4/18	4/18–5/12	5/13–6/5	6/6–6/29	7/1–7/25	7/26–8/19
1974	5/5–5/31	6/1–6/25	6/26–7/21	7/22–8/14	8/15–9/8	9/9–10/2
1975	2/24–3/20	3/21–4/13	4/14–5/9	5/10–6/6	6/7–7/9	7/10–9/2
					9/3–10/4	10/5–11/9
1976	4/8–5/2	5/2–5/27	5/27–6/20	6/20–7/14	7/14–8/8	8/8–9/1
1977	2/2–6/6	6/6–7/6	7/6–8/2	8/2–8/28	8/28–9/22	9/22–10/17
1978	3/9–4/2	4/2–4/27	4/27–5/22	5/22–6/16	6/16–7/12	7/12–8/6
1979	4/23–5/18	5/18–6/11	6/11–7/6	7/6–7/30	7/30–8/24	8/24–9/17
1980	2/9–3/6	3/6–4/3	4/3–5/12	5/12–6/5	9/7–10/4	10/4–10/30
			6/5–8/6	8/6–9/7		
1981	3/24–4/17	4/17–5/11	5/11–6/5	6/5–6/29	6/29–7/24	7/24–8/18

Libra	Scorpio	Sagittarius	Capricorn	Aquarius	Pisces
8/9–9/6	9/7–10/22	10/23–10/27	1/1–1/22	1/23–2/15	2/16–3/11
	10/28–12/31				
9/19–10/13	1/1–1/6	1/7–2/5	2/6–3/4	3/5–3/30	3/31–4/24
	10/14–11/5	11/6–11/30	12/1–12/24	12/25–12/31	
11/1–11/25	11/26–12/19	12/20–12/31		1/1–1/17	1/18–2/11
8/20–9/14	9/15–10/9	1/1–1/12	1/13–2/5	2/6–3/1	3/2–3/25
		10/10–11/5	11/6–12/6	12/7–12/31	
10/4–10/27	10/28–11/20	11/21–12/14	12/15–12/31	1/1–4/6	4/7–5/5
11/10–12/7	12/8–12/31		1/1–1/7	1/8–1/31	2/1–2/24
9/3–9/26	1/1–1/2	1/3–1/27	1/28–2/20	2/21–3/15	3/16–4/9
	9/27–10/21	10/22–11/15	11/16–12/10	12/11–12/31	
10/18–11/11	11/12–12/4	12/5–12/28	12/29–12/31	1/1–1/5	1/6–2/2
8/9–9/6	9/7–12/31		1/1–1/21	1/22–2/14	2/15–3/10
9/19–10/12	1/1–1/6	1/7–2/5	2/6–3/4	3/5–3/29	3/30–4/23
	10/13–11/5	11/6–11/29	11/30–12/23	12/24–12/31	
11/1–11/24	11/25–12/19	12/20–12/31		1/1–1/16	1/17–2/10
8/20–9/13	9/14–10/9	1/1–1/12	1/13–2/5	2/6–3/1	3/2–3/25
		10/10–11/5	11/6–12/7	12/8–12/31	
10/3–10/26	10/27–11/19	11/20–12/13	2/7–2/25	1/1–2/6	4/7–5/5
			12/14–12/31	2/26–4/6	
11/10–12/7	12/8–12/31		1/1–1/6	1/7–1/30	1/31–2/23
9/3–9/26	1/1	1/2–1/26	1/27–2/20	2/21–3/15	3/16–4/8
	9/27–10/21	10/22–11/14	11/15–12/9	12/10–12/31	
10/18–11/10	11/11–12/4	12/5–12/28	12/29–12/31	1/1–1/4	1/5–2/2
8/9–9/7	9/8–12/31		1/1–1/21	1/22–2/14	2/15–3/10
9/18–10/11	1/1–1/7	1/8–2/5	2/6–3/4	3/5–3/29	3/30–4/23
	10/12–11/5	11/6–11/29	11/30–12/23	12/24–12/31	
10/31–11/24	11/25–12/18	12/19–12/31		1/1–1/16	1/17–2/10
8/20–9/13	9/14–10/8	1/1–1/12	1/13–2/4	2/5–2/28	3/1–3/24
		10/9–11/5	11/6–12/7	12/8–12/31	
10/3–10/26	10/27–11/19	11/20–12/13	12/14–12/31	3/1–4/6	4/7–5/4
			1/30–2/28	1/1–1/29	
11/10–12/7	12/8–12/31		1/1–1/6	1/7–1/30	1/31–2/23
9/1–9/26	9/26–10/20	1/1–1/26	1/26–2/19	2/19–3/15	3/15–4/8
10/17–11/10	11/10–12/4	12/4–12/27	12/27–1/20/78		1/4–2/2
8/6–9/7	9/7–1/7			1/20–2/13	2/13–3/9
9/17–10/11	10/11–11/4	1/7–2/5	2/5–3/3	3/3–3/29	3/29–4/23
		11/4–11/28	11/28–12/22	12/22–1/16/80	
10/30–11/24	11/24–12/18	12/18–1/11/81			1/16–2/9
8/18–9/12	9/12–10/9	10/9–11/5	1/11–2/4	2/4–2/28	2/28–3/24
			11/5–12/8	12/8–1/23/82	

VENUS SIGNS 1901–2010

	Aries	Taurus	Gemini	Cancer	Leo	Virgo
1982	5/4–5/30	5/30–6/25	6/25–7/20	7/20–8/14	8/14–9/7	9/7–10/2
1983	2/22–3/19	3/19–4/13	4/13–5/9	5/9–6/6	6/6–7/10	7/10–8/27
					8/27–10/5	10/5–11/9
1984	4/7–5/2	5/2–5/26	5/26–6/20	6/20–7/14	7/14–8/7	8/7–9/1
1985	2/2–6/6	6/7–7/6	7/6–8/2	8/2–8/28	8/28–9/22	9/22–10/16
1986	3/9–4/2	4/2–4/26	4/26–5/21	5/21–6/15	6/15–7/11	7/11–8/7
1987	4/22–5/17	5/17–6/11	6/11–7/5	7/5–7/30	7/30–8/23	8/23–9/16
1988	2/9–3/6	3/6–4/3	4/3–5/17	5/17–5/27	9/7–10/4	10/4–10/29
			5/27–8/6	8/28–9/22	9/22–10/16	
1989	3/23–4/16	4/16–5/11	5/11–6/4	6/4–6/29	6/29–7/24	7/24–8/18
1990	5/4–5/30	5/30–6/25	6/25–7/20	7/20–8/13	8/13–9/7	9/7–10/1
1991	2/22–3/18	3/18–4/13	4/13–5/9	5/9–6/6	6/6–7/11	7/11–8/21
					8/21–10/6	10/6–11/9
1992	4/7–5/1	5/1–5/26	5/26–6/19	6/19–7/13	7/13–8/7	8/7–8/31
1993	2/2–6/6	6/6–7/6	7/6–8/1	8/1–8/27	8/27–9/21	9/21–10/16
1994	3/8–4/1	4/1–4/26	4/26–5/21	5/21–6/15	6/15–7/11	7/11–8/7
1995	4/22–5/16	5/16–6/10	6/10–7/5	7/5–7/29	7/29–8/23	8/23–9/16
1996	2/9–3/6	3/6–4/3	4/3–8/7	8/7–9/7	9/7–10/4	10/4–10/29
1997	3/23–4/16	4/16–5/10	5/10–6/4	6/4–6/28	6/28–7/23	7/23–8/17
1998	5/3–5/29	5/29–6/24	6/24–7/19	7/19–8/13	8/13–9/6	9/6–9/30
1999	2/21–3/18	3/18–4/12	4/12–5/8	5/8–6/5	6/5–7/12	7/12–8/15
					8/15–10/7	10/7–11/9
2000	4/6–5/1	5/1–5/25	5/25–6/13	6/13–7/13	7/13–8/6	8/6–8/31
2001	2/2–6/6	6/6–7/5	7/5–8/1	8/1–8/26	8/26–9/20	9/20–10/15
2002	3/7–4/1	4/1–4/25	4/25–5/20	5/20–6/14	6/14–7/10	7/10–8/7
2003	4/21–5/16	5/16–6/9	6/9–7/4	7/4–7/29	7/29–8/22	8/22–9/15
2004	2/8–3/5	3/5–4/3	4/3–8/7	8/7–9/6	9/6–10/3	10/3–10/28
2005	3/22–4/15	4/15–5/10	5/10–6/3	6/3–6/28	6/28–7/23	7/23–8/17
2006	5/3–5/29	5/29–6/24	6/24–7/19	7/19–8/12	8/12–9/6	9/6–9/30
2007	2/21–3/16	3/17–4/10	4/11–5/7	5/8–6/4	6/5–7/13	7/14–8/7
					8/8–10/6	10/7–11/7
2008	4/6–4/30	5/1–5/24	5/25–6/17	6/18–7/11	7/12–8/4	8/5–8/29
2009	2/2–4/11	6/6–7/5	7/5–7/31	731/–8/26	8/26–9/20	9/20–10/14
	4/24–6/6					
2010	3/7–3/31	3/31–4/25	4/25–5/20	5/20–6/14	6/14–7/10	7/10–8/7

Libra	Scorpio	Sagittarius	Capricorn	Aquarius	Pisces
10/2–10/26	10/26–11/18	11/18–12/12	1/23–3/2	3/2–4/6	4/6–5/4
			12/12–1/5/83		
11/9–12/6	12/6–1/1/84			1/5–1/29	1/29–2/22
9/1–9/25	9/25–10/20	1/1–1/25	1/25–2/19	2/19–3/14	3/14–4/7
		10/20–11/13	11/13–12/9	12/10–1/4	
10/16–11/9	11/9–12/3	12/3–12/27	12/28–1/19		1/4–2/2
8/7–9/7	9/7–1/7			1/20–2/13	2/13–3/9
9/16–10/10	10/10–11/3	1/7–2/5	2/5–3/3	3/3–3/28	3/28–4/22
		11/3–11/28	11/28–12/22	12/22–1/15	
10/29–11/23	11/23–12/17	12/17–1/10			1/15–2/9
8/18–9/12	9/12–10/8	10/8–11/5	1/10–2/3	2/3–2/27	2/27–3/23
			11/5–12/10	12/10–1/16/90	
10/1–10/25	10/25–11/18	11/18–12/12	1/16–3/3	3/3–4/6	4/6–5/4
			12/12–1/5		
11/9–12/6	12/6–12/31	12/31–1/25/92		1/5–1/29	1/29–2/22
8/31–9/25	9/25–10/19	10/19–11/13	1/25–2/18	2/18–3/13	3/13–4/7
			11/13–12/8	12/8–1/3/93	
10/16–11/9	11/9–12/2	12/2–12/26	12/26–1/19		1/3–2/2
8/7–9/7	9/7–1/7			1/19–2/12	2/12–3/8
9/16–10/10	10/10–11/13	1/7–2/4	2/4–3/2	3/2–3/28	3/28–4/22
		11/3–11/27	11/27–12/21	12/21–1/15	
10/29–11/23	11/23–12/17	12/17–1/10/97			1/15–2/9
8/17–9/12	9/12–10/8	10/8–11/5	1/10–2/3	2/3–2/27	2/27–3/23
			11/5–12/12	12/12–1/9	
9/30–10/24	10/24–11/17	11/17–12/11	1/9–3/4	3/4–4/6	4/6–5/3
11/9–12/5	12/5–12/31	12/31–1/24		1/4–1/28	1/28–2/21
8/31–9/24	9/24–10/19	10/19–11/13	1/24–2/18	2/18–3/12	3/13–4/6
			11/13–12/8	12/8	
10/15–11/8	11/8–12/2	12/2–12/26	12/26/01–	12/8/00–1/3/01	1/3–2/2
			1/18/02		
8/7–9/7	9/7–1/7/03		12/26/01–1/18	1/18–2/11	2/11–3/7
9/15–10/9	10/9–11/2	1/7–2/4	2/4–3/2	3/2–3/27	3/27–4/21
		11/2–11/26	11/26–12/21	12/21–1/14/04	
10/28–11/22	11/22–12/16	12/16–1/9/05		1/1–1/14	1/14–2/8
8/17–9/11	9/11–10/8	10/8–11/15	1/9–2/2	2/2–2/26	2/26–3/22
			11/5–12/15	12/15–1/1/06	
9/30–10/24	10/24–11/17	11/17–12/11	1/1–3/5	3/5–4/6	4/6–5/3
11/8–12/4	12/5–12/29	12/30–1/24/08		1/3–1/26	1/27–2/20
8/6–9/7	9/7–1/7			1/20–2/13	2/13–3/9
8/30–9/22	9/23–10/17	10/18–11/11	1/24–2/16	2/17–3/11	3/12–4/5
			11/12–12/6	12/7–1/2/09	
10/14–11/7	11/7–12/1	12/1–12/25	12/25–1/18/10	12/7/08–	1/3–2/2
				1/31/09	4/11–4/24
8/7–9/8	9/8–11/8			1/18/10–	2/11–3/7
11/8–11/30	11/30–1/7/11			2/11/10	

How to Use the Mars, Jupiter, and Saturn Tables

Find the year of your birth on the left side of each column. The dates when the planet entered each sign are listed on the right side of each column. (Signs are abbreviated to three letters.) Your birthday should fall on or between each date listed, and your planetary placement should correspond to the earlier sign of that period.

All planet changes are calculated for the Greenwich Mean Time zone.

MARS SIGNS 1901–2010

Year	Month	Day	Sign
1901	MAR	1	Leo
	MAY	11	Vir
	JUL	13	Lib
	AUG	31	Scp
	OCT	14	Sag
	NOV	24	Cap
1902	JAN	1	Aqu
	FEB	8	Pic
	MAR	19	Ari
	APR	27	Tau
	JUN	7	Gem
	JUL	20	Can
	SEP	4	Leo
	OCT	23	Vir
	DEC	20	Lib
1903	APR	19	Vir
	MAY	30	Lib
	AUG	6	Scp
	SEP	22	Sag
	NOV	3	Cap
	DEC	12	Aqu
1904	JAN	19	Pic
	FEB	27	Ari
	APR	6	Tau
	MAY	18	Gem
	JUN	30	Can
	AUG	15	Leo
	OCT	1	Vir
	NOV	20	Lib
1905	JAN	13	Scp
	AUG	21	Sag
	OCT	8	Cap
	NOV	18	Aqu
	DEC	27	Pic
1906	FEB	4	Ari
	MAR	17	Tau
	APR	28	Gem
	JUN	11	Can
	JUL	27	Leo
	SEP	12	Vir
	OCT	30	Lib
	DEC	17	Scp
1907	FEB	5	Sag
	APR	1	Cap
	OCT	13	Aqu
	NOV	29	Pic
1908	JAN	11	Ari
	FEB	23	Tau
	APR	7	Gem
	MAY	22	Can
	JUL	8	Leo
	AUG	24	Vir
	OCT	10	Lib
	NOV	25	Scp

1909	JAN	10	Sag
	FEB	24	Cap
	APR	9	Aqu
	MAY	25	Pic
	JUL	21	Ari
	SEP	26	Pic
	NOV	20	Ari
1910	JAN	23	Tau
	MAR	14	Gem
	MAY	1	Can
	JUN	19	Leo
	AUG	6	Vir
	SEP	22	Lib
	NOV	6	Scp
	DEC	20	Sag
1911	JAN	31	Cap
	MAR	14	Aqu
	APR	23	Pic
	JUN	2	Ari
	JUL	15	Tau
	SEP	5	Gem
	NOV	30	Tau
1912	JAN	30	Gem
	APR	5	Can
	MAY	28	Leo
	JUL	17	Vir
	SEP	2	Lib
	OCT	18	Scp
	NOV	30	Sag
1913	JAN	10	Cap
	FEB	19	Aqu
	MAR	30	Pic
	MAY	8	Ari
	JUN	17	Tau
	JUL	29	Gem
	SEP	15	Can
1914	MAY	1	Leo
	JUN	26	Vir
	AUG	14	Lib
	SEP	29	Scp
	NOV	11	Sag
	DEC	22	Cap
1915	JAN	30	Aqu
	MAR	9	Pic
	APR	16	Ari
	MAY	26	Tau
	JUL	6	Gem
	AUG	19	Can
	OCT	7	Leo
1916	MAY	28	Vir
	JUL	23	Lib
	SEP	8	Scp
	OCT	22	Sag
	DEC	1	Cap
1917	JAN	9	Aqu
	FEB	16	Pic
	MAR	26	Ari
	MAY	4	Tau
	JUN	14	Gem
	JUL	28	Can
	SEP	12	Leo
	NOV	2	Vir
1918	JAN	11	Lib
	FEB	25	Vir
	JUN	23	Lib
	AUG	17	Scp
	OCT	1	Sag
	NOV	11	Cap
	DEC	20	Aqu
1919	JAN	27	Pic
	MAR	6	Ari
	APR	15	Tau
	MAY	26	Gem
	JUL	8	Can
	AUG	23	Leo
	OCT	10	Vir
	NOV	30	Lib
1920	JAN	31	Scp
	APR	23	Lib
	JUL	10	Scp
	SEP	4	Sag
	OCT	18	Cap
	NOV	27	Aqu
1921	JAN	5	Pic
	FEB	13	Ari
	MAR	25	Tau

	MAY	6	Gem
	JUN	18	Can
	AUG	3	Leo
	SEP	19	Vir
	NOV	6	Lib
	DEC	26	Scp
1922	FEB	18	Sag
	SEP	13	Cap
	OCT	30	Aqu
	DEC	11	Pic
1923	JAN	21	Ari
	MAR	4	Tau
	APR	16	Gem
	MAY	30	Can
	JUL	16	Leo
	SEP	1	Vir
	OCT	18	Lib
	DEC	4	Scp
1924	JAN	19	Sag
	MAR	6	Cap
	APR	24	Aqu
	JUN	24	Pic
	AUG	24	Aqu
	OCT	19	Pic
	DEC	19	Ari
1925	FEB	5	Tau
	MAR	24	Gem
	MAY	9	Can
	JUN	26	Leo
	AUG	12	Vir
	SEP	28	Lib
	NOV	13	Scp
	DEC	28	Sag
1926	FEB	9	Cap
	MAR	23	Aqu
	MAY	3	Pic
	JUN	15	Ari
	AUG	1	Tau
1927	FEB	22	Gem
	APR	17	Can
	JUN	6	Leo
	JUL	25	Vir
	SEP	10	Lib
	OCT	26	Scp
	DEC	8	Sag
1928	JAN	19	Cap
	FEB	28	Aqu
	APR	7	Pic
	MAY	16	Ari
	JUN	26	Tau
	AUG	9	Gem
	OCT	3	Can
	DEC	20	Gem
1929	MAR	10	Can
	MAY	13	Leo
	JUL	4	Vir
	AUG	21	Lib
	OCT	6	Scp
	NOV	18	Sag
	DEC	29	Cap
1930	FEB	6	Aqu
	MAR	17	Pic
	APR	24	Ari
	JUN	3	Tau
	JUL	14	Gem
	AUG	28	Can
	OCT	20	Leo
1931	FEB	16	Can
	MAR	30	Leo
	JUN	10	Vir
	AUG	1	Lib
	SEP	17	Scp
	OCT	30	Sag
	DEC	10	Cap
1932	JAN	18	Aqu
	FEB	25	Pic
	APR	3	Ari
	MAY	12	Tau
	JUN	22	Gem
	AUG	4	Can
	SEP	20	Leo
	NOV	13	Vir
1933	JUL	6	Lib
	AUG	26	Scp
	OCT	9	Sag
	NOV	19	Cap

	DEC	28	Aqu
1934	FEB	4	Pic
	MAR	14	Ari
	APR	22	Tau
	JUN	2	Gem
	JUL	15	Can
	AUG	30	Leo
	OCT	18	Vir
	DEC	11	Lib
1935	JUL	29	Scp
	SEP	16	Sag
	OCT	28	Cap
	DEC	7	Aqu
1936	JAN	14	Pic
	FEB	22	Ari
	APR	1	Tau
	MAY	13	Gem
	JUN	25	Can
	AUG	10	Leo
	SEP	26	Vir
	NOV	14	Lib
1937	JAN	5	Scp
	MAR	13	Sag
	MAY	14	Scp
	AUG	8	Sag
	SEP	30	Cap
	NOV	11	Aqu
	DEC	21	Pic
1938	JAN	30	Ari
	MAR	12	Tau
	APR	23	Gem
	JUN	7	Can
	JUL	22	Leo
	SEP	7	Vir
	OCT	25	Lib
	DEC	11	Scp
1939	JAN	29	Sag
	MAR	21	Cap
	MAY	25	Aqu
	JUL	21	Cap
	SEP	24	Aqu
	NOV	19	Pic
1940	JAN	4	Ari
	FEB	17	Tau
	APR	1	Gem
	MAY	17	Can
	JUL	3	Leo
	AUG	19	Vir
	OCT	5	Lib
	NOV	20	Scp
1941	JAN	4	Sag
	FEB	17	Cap
	APR	2	Aqu
	MAY	16	Pic
	JUL	2	Ari
1942	JAN	11	Tau
	MAR	7	Gem
	APR	26	Can
	JUN	14	Leo
	AUG	1	Vir
	SEP	17	Lib
	NOV	1	Scp
	DEC	15	Sag
1943	JAN	26	Cap
	MAR	8	Aqu
	APR	17	Pic
	MAY	27	Ari
	JUL	7	Tau
	AUG	23	Gem
1944	MAR	28	Can
	MAY	22	Leo
	JUL	12	Vir
	AUG	29	Lib
	OCT	13	Scp
	NOV	25	Sag
1945	JAN	5	Cap
	FEB	14	Aqu
	MAR	25	Pic
	MAY	2	Ari
	JUN	11	Tau
	JUL	23	Gem
	SEP	7	Can
	NOV	11	Leo
	DEC	26	Can
1946	APR	22	Leo
	JUN	20	Vir

Year	Month	Day	Sign
	AUG	9	Lib
	SEP	24	Scp
	NOV	6	Sag
	DEC	17	Cap
1947	JAN	25	Aqu
	MAR	4	Pic
	APR	11	Ari
	MAY	21	Tau
	JUL	1	Gem
	AUG	13	Can
	OCT	1	Leo
	DEC	1	Vir
1948	FEB	12	Leo
	MAY	18	Vir
	JUL	17	Lib
	SEP	3	Scp
	OCT	17	Sag
	NOV	26	Cap
1949	JAN	4	Aqu
	FEB	11	Pic
	MAR	21	Ari
	APR	30	Tau
	JUN	10	Gem
	JUL	23	Can
	SEP	7	Leo
	OCT	27	Vir
	DEC	26	Lib
1950	MAR	28	Vir
	JUN	11	Lib
	AUG	10	Scp
	SEP	25	Sag
	NOV	6	Cap
	DEC	15	Aqu
1951	JAN	22	Pic
	MAR	1	Ari
	APR	10	Tau
	MAY	21	Gem
	JUL	3	Can
	AUG	18	Leo
	OCT	5	Vir
	NOV	24	Lib
1952	JAN	20	Scp
	AUG	27	Sag
	OCT	12	Cap
	NOV	21	Aqu
	DEC	30	Pic
1953	FEB	8	Ari
	MAR	20	Tau
	MAY	1	Gem
	JUN	14	Can
	JUL	29	Leo
	SEP	14	Vir
	NOV	1	Lib
	DEC	20	Scp
1954	FEB	9	Sag
	APR	12	Cap
	JUL	3	Sag
	AUG	24	Cap
	OCT	21	Aqu
	DEC	4	Pic
1955	JAN	15	Ari
	FEB	26	Tau
	APR	10	Gem
	MAY	26	Can
	JUL	11	Leo
	AUG	27	Vir
	OCT	13	Lib
	NOV	29	Scp
1956	JAN	14	Sag
	FEB	28	Cap
	APR	14	Aqu
	JUN	3	Pic
	DEC	6	Ari
1957	JAN	28	Tau
	MAR	17	Gem
	MAY	4	Can
	JUN	21	Leo
	AUG	8	Vir
	SEP	24	Lib
	NOV	8	Scp
	DEC	23	Sag
1958	FEB	3	Cap
	MAR	17	Aqu
	APR	27	Pic
	JUN	7	Ari
	JUL	21	Tau

	SEP	21	Gem
	OCT	29	Tau
1959	FEB	10	Gem
	APR	10	Can
	JUN	1	Leo
	JUL	20	Vir
	SEP	5	Lib
	OCT	21	Scp
	DEC	3	Sag
1960	JAN	14	Cap
	FEB	23	Aqu
	APR	2	Pic
	MAY	11	Ari
	JUN	20	Tau
	AUG	2	Gem
	SEP	21	Can
1961	FEB	5	Gem
	FEB	7	Can
	MAY	6	Leo
	JUN	28	Vir
	AUG	17	Lib
	OCT	1	Scp
	NOV	13	Sag
	DEC	24	Cap
1962	FEB	1	Aqu
	MAR	12	Pic
	APR	19	Ari
	MAY	28	Tau
	JUL	9	Gem
	AUG	22	Can
	OCT	11	Leo
1963	JUN	3	Vir
	JUL	27	Lib
	SEP	12	Scp
	OCT	25	Sag
	DEC	5	Cap
1964	JAN	13	Aqu
	FEB	20	Pic
	MAR	29	Ari
	MAY	7	Tau
	JUN	17	Gem
	JUL	30	Can
	SEP	15	Leo

	NOV	6	Vir
1965	JUN	29	Lib
	AUG	20	Scp
	OCT	4	Sag
	NOV	14	Cap
	DEC	23	Aqu
1966	JAN	30	Pic
	MAR	9	Ari
	APR	17	Tau
	MAY	28	Gem
	JUL	11	Can
	AUG	25	Leo
	OCT	12	Vir
	DEC	4	Lib
1967	FEB	12	Scp
	MAR	31	Lib
	JUL	19	Scp
	SEP	10	Sag
	OCT	23	Cap
	DEC	1	Aqu
1968	JAN	9	Pic
	FEB	17	Ari
	MAR	27	Tau
	MAY	8	Gem
	JUN	21	Can
	AUG	5	Leo
	SEP	21	Vir
	NOV	9	Lib
	DEC	29	Scp
1969	FEB	25	Sag
	SEP	21	Cap
	NOV	4	Aqu
	DEC	15	Pic
1970	JAN	24	Ari
	MAR	7	Tau
	APR	18	Gem
	JUN	2	Can
	JUL	18	Leo
	SEP	3	Vir
	OCT	20	Lib
	DEC	6	Scp
1971	JAN	23	Sag
	MAR	12	Cap

Year	Month	Day	Sign
	MAY	3	Aqu
	NOV	6	Pic
	DEC	26	Ari
1972	FEB	10	Tau
	MAR	27	Gem
	MAY	12	Can
	JUN	28	Leo
	AUG	15	Vir
	SEP	30	Lib
	NOV	15	Scp
	DEC	30	Sag
1973	FEB	12	Cap
	MAR	26	Aqu
	MAY	8	Pic
	JUN	20	Ari
	AUG	12	Tau
	OCT	29	Ari
	DEC	24	Tau
1974	FEB	27	Gem
	APR	20	Can
	JUN	9	Leo
	JUL	27	Vir
	SEP	12	Lib
	OCT	28	Scp
	DEC	10	Sag
1975	JAN	21	Cap
	MAR	3	Aqu
	APR	11	Pic
	MAY	21	Ari
	JUL	1	Tau
	AUG	14	Gem
	OCT	17	Can
	NOV	25	Gem
1976	MAR	18	Can
	MAY	16	Leo
	JUL	6	Vir
	AUG	24	Lib
	OCT	8	Scp
	NOV	20	Sag
1977	JAN	1	Cap
	FEB	9	Aqu
	MAR	20	Pic
	APR	27	Ari
	JUN	6	Tau
	JUL	17	Gem
	SEP	1	Can
	OCT	26	Leo
1978	JAN	26	Can
	APR	10	Leo
	JUN	14	Vir
	AUG	4	Lib
	SEP	19	Scp
	NOV	2	Sag
	DEC	12	Cap
1979	JAN	20	Aqu
	FEB	27	Pic
	APR	7	Ari
	MAY	16	Tau
	JUN	26	Gem
	AUG	8	Can
	SEP	24	Leo
	NOV	19	Vir
1980	MAR	11	Leo
	MAY	4	Vir
	JUL	10	Lib
	AUG	29	Scp
	OCT	12	Sag
	NOV	22	Cap
	DEC	30	Aqu
1981	FEB	6	Pic
	MAR	17	Ari
	APR	25	Tau
	JUN	5	Gem
	JUL	18	Can
	SEP	2	Leo
	OCT	21	Vir
	DEC	16	Lib
1982	AUG	3	Scp
	SEP	20	Sag
	OCT	31	Cap
	DEC	10	Aqu
1983	JAN	17	Pic
	FEB	25	Ari
	APR	5	Tau
	MAY	16	Gem
	JUN	29	Can

	AUG	13	Leo
	SEP	30	Vir
	NOV	18	Lib
1984	JAN	11	Scp
	AUG	17	Sag
	OCT	5	Cap
	NOV	15	Aqu
	DEC	25	Pic
1985	FEB	2	Ari
	MAR	15	Tau
	APR	26	Gem
	JUN	9	Can
	JUL	25	Leo
	SEP	10	Vir
	OCT	27	Lib
	DEC	14	Scp
1986	FEB	2	Sag
	MAR	28	Cap
	OCT	9	Aqu
	NOV	26	Pic
1987	JAN	8	Ari
	FEB	20	Tau
	APR	5	Gem
	MAY	21	Can
	JUL	6	Leo
	AUG	22	Vir
	OCT	8	Lib
	NOV	24	Scp
1988	JAN	8	Sag
	FEB	22	Cap
	APR	6	Aqu
	MAY	22	Pic
	JUL	13	Ari
	OCT	23	Pic
	NOV	1	Ari
1989	JAN	19	Tau
	MAR	11	Gem
	APR	29	Can
	JUN	16	Leo
	AUG	3	Vir
	SEP	19	Lib
	NOV	4	Scp
	DEC	18	Sag
1990	JAN	29	Cap
	MAR	11	Aqu
	APR	20	Pic
	MAY	31	Ari
	JUL	12	Tau
	AUG	31	Gem
	DEC	14	Tau
1991	JAN	21	Gem
	APR	3	Can
	MAY	26	Leo
	JUL	15	Vir
	SEP	1	Lib
	OCT	16	Scp
	NOV	29	Sag
1992	JAN	9	Cap
	FEB	18	Aqu
	MAR	28	Pic
	MAY	5	Ari
	JUN	14	Tau
	JUL	26	Gem
	SEP	12	Can
1993	APR	27	Leo
	JUN	23	Vir
	AUG	12	Lib
	SEP	27	Scp
	NOV	9	Sag
	DEC	20	Cap
1994	JAN	28	Aqu
	MAR	7	Pic
	APR	14	Ari
	MAY	23	Tau
	JUL	3	Gem
	AUG	16	Can
	OCT	4	Leo
	DEC	12	Vir
1995	JAN	22	Leo
	MAY	25	Vir
	JUL	21	Lib
	SEP	7	Scp
	OCT	20	Sag
	NOV	30	Cap
1996	JAN	8	Aqu
	FEB	15	Pic

Year	Month	Day	Sign
	MAR	24	Ari
	MAY	2	Tau
	JUN	12	Gem
	JUL	25	Can
	SEP	9	Leo
	OCT	30	Vir
1997	JAN	3	Lib
	MAR	8	Vir
	JUN	19	Lib
	AUG	14	Scp
	SEP	28	Sag
	NOV	9	Cap
	DEC	18	Aqu
1998	JAN	25	Pic
	MAR	4	Ari
	APR	13	Tau
	MAY	24	Gem
	JUL	6	Can
	AUG	20	Leo
	OCT	7	Vir
	NOV	27	Lib
1999	JAN	26	Scp
	MAY	5	Lib
	JUL	5	Scp
	SEP	2	Sag
	OCT	17	Cap
	NOV	26	Aqu
2000	JAN	4	Pic
	FEB	12	Ari
	MAR	23	Tau
	MAY	3	Gem
	JUN	16	Can
	AUG	1	Leo
	SEP	17	Vir
	NOV	4	Lib
	DEC	23	Scp
2001	FEB	14	Sag
	SEP	8	Cap
	OCT	27	Aqu
	DEC	8	Pic
2002	JAN	18	Ari
	MAR	1	Tau
	APR	13	Gem
	MAY	28	Can
	JUL	13	Leo
	AUG	29	Vir
	OCT	15	Lib
	DEC	1	Scp
2003	JAN	17	Sag
	MAR	4	Cap
	APR	21	Aqu
	JUN	17	Pic
	DEC	16	Ari
2004	FEB	3	Tau
	MAR	21	Gem
	MAY	7	Can
	JUN	23	Leo
	AUG	10	Vir
	SEP	26	Lib
	NOV	11	Sep
	DEC	25	Sag
2005	FEB	6	Cap
	MAR	20	Aqu
	MAY	1	Pic
	JUN	12	Ari
	JUL	28	Tau
2006	FEB	17	Gem
	APR	14	Can
	JUN	3	Leo
	JUL	22	Vir
	SEP	8	Lib
	OCT	23	Scp
	DEC	6	Sag
2007	JAN	16	Cap
	FEB	25	Aqu
	APR	6	Pic
	MAY	15	Ari
	JUNE	24	Tau
	AUG	7	Gem
	SEP	28	Can
	DEC	31	Gem*
2008	MAR	4	Can
	MAY	9	Leo
	JUL	1	Vir
	AUG	19	Lib
	OCT	3	Scp

	NOV	16	Sag
	DEC	27	Cap
2009	FEB	4	Aqu
	MAR	14	Pic
	APR	22	Ari
	MAY	31	Tau
	JUL	11	Gem
	AUG	25	Can
	OCT	16	Leo
2010	JUN	7	Vir
	JUL	29	Lib
	SEP	14	Scp
	OCT	28	Sag
	DEC	7	Cap

JUPITER SIGNS 1901–2010

1901	JAN	19	Cap
1902	FEB	6	Aqu
1903	FEB	20	Pic
1904	MAR	1	Ari
	AUG	8	Tau
	AUG	31	Ari
1905	MAR	7	Tau
	JUL	21	Gem
	DEC	4	Tau
1906	MAR	9	Gem
	JUL	30	Can
1907	AUG	18	Leo
1908	SEP	12	Vir
1909	OCT	11	Lib
1910	NOV	11	Scp
1911	DEC	10	Sag
1913	JAN	2	Cap
1914	JAN	21	Aqu
1915	FEB	4	Pic
1916	FEB	12	Ari
	JUN	26	Tau
	OCT	26	Ari
1917	FEB	12	Tau
	JUN	29	Gem
1918	JUL	13	Can
1919	AUG	2	Leo
1920	AUG	27	Vir
1921	SEP	25	Lib
1922	OCT	26	Scp
1923	NOV	24	Sag
1924	DEC	18	Cap
1926	JAN	6	Aqu
1927	JAN	18	Pic
	JUN	6	Ari
	SEP	11	Pic
1928	JAN	23	Ari
	JUN	4	Tau
1929	JUN	12	Gem
1930	JUN	26	Can
1931	JUL	17	Leo
1932	AUG	11	Vir
1933	SEP	10	Lib
1934	OCT	11	Scp
1935	NOV	9	Sag
1936	DEC	2	Cap
1937	DEC	20	Aqu
1938	MAY	14	Pic
	JUL	30	Aqu
	DEC	29	Pic
1939	MAY	11	Ari
	OCT	30	Pic
	DEC	20	Ari
1940	MAY	16	Tau
1941	MAY	26	Gem
1942	JUN	10	Can
1943	JUN	30	Leo
1944	JUL	26	Vir
1945	AUG	25	Lib
1946	SEP	25	Scp
1947	OCT	24	Sag
1948	NOV	15	Cap
1949	APR	12	Aqu
	JUN	27	Cap
	NOV	30	Aqu

1950	APR	15	Pic
	SEP	15	Aqu
	DEC	1	Pic
1951	APR	21	Ari
1952	APR	28	Tau
1953	MAY	9	Gem
1954	MAY	24	Can
1955	JUN	13	Leo
	NOV	17	Vir
1956	JAN	18	Leo
	JUL	7	Vir
	DEC	13	Lib
1957	FEB	19	Vir
	AUG	7	Lib
1958	JAN	13	Scp
	MAR	20	Lib
	SEP	7	Scp
1959	FEB	10	Sag
	APR	24	Scp
	OCT	5Sag	
1960	MAR	1	Cap
	JUN	10	Sag
	OCT	26	Cap
1961	MAR	15	Aqu
	AUG	12	Cap
	NOV	4	Aqu
1962	MAR	25	Pic
1963	APR	4	Ari
1964	APR	12	Tau
1965	APR	22	Gem
	SEP	21	Can
	NOV	17	Gem
1966	MAY	5	Can
	SEP	27	Leo
1967	JAN	16	Can
	MAY	23	Leo
	OCT	19	Vir
1968	FEB	27	Leo
	JUN	15	Vir
	NOV	15	Lib
1969	MAR	30	Vir
	JUL	15	Lib
	DEC	16	Scp
1970	APR	30	Lib
	AUG	15	Scp
1971	JAN	14	Sag
	JUN	5	Scp
	SEP	11	Sag
1972	FEB	6	Cap
	JUL	24	Sag
	SEP	25	Cap
1973	FEB	23	Aqu
1974	MAR	8	Pic
1975	MAR	18	Ari
1976	MAR	26	Tau
	AUG	23	Gem
	OCT	16	Tau
1977	APR	3	Gem
	AUG	20	Can
	DEC	30	Gem
1978	APR	12	Can
	SEP	5	Leo
1979	FEB	28	Can
	APR	20	Leo
	SEP	29	Vir
1980	OCT	27	Lib
1981	NOV	27	Scp
1982	DEC	26	Sag
1984	JAN	19	Cap
1985	FEB	6	Aqu
1986	FEB	20	Pic
1987	MAR	2	Ari
1988	MAR	8	Tau
	JUL	22	Gem
	NOV	30	Tau
1989	MAR	11	Gem
	JUL	30	Can
1990	AUG	18	Leo
1991	SEP	12	Vir
1992	OCT	10	Lib
1993	NOV	10	Scp
1994	DEC	9	Sag
1996	JAN	3	Cap
1997	JAN	21	Aqu
1998	FEB	4	Pic
1999	FEB	13	Ari

	JUN	28	Tau
	OCT	23	Ari
2000	FEB	14	Tau
	JUN	30	Gem
2001	JUL	14	Can
2002	AUG	1	Leo
2003	AUG	27	Vir
2004	SEP	24	Lib
2005	OCT	26	Scp
2006	NOV	24	Sag
2007	DEC	17	Cap
2009	JAN	5	Aqu
2010	JAN	18	Pis
	JUN	6	Ari
	SEP	9	Pis

SATURN SIGNS 1903–2010

1903	JAN	19	Aqu
1905	APR	13	Pic
	AUG	17	Aqu
1906	JAN	8	Pic
1908	MAR	19	Ari
1910	MAY	17	Tau
	DEC	14	Ari
1911	JAN	20	Tau
1912	JUL	7	Gem
	NOV	30	Tau
1913	MAR	26	Gem
1914	AUG	24	Can
	DEC	7	Gem
1915	MAY	11	Can
1916	OCT	17	Leo
	DEC	7	Can
1917	JUN	24	Leo
1919	AUG	12	Vir
1921	OCT	7	Lib
1923	DEC	20	Scp
1924	APR	6	Lib
	SEP	13	Scp
1926	DEC	2	Sag
1929	MAR	15	Cap
	MAY	5	Sag
	NOV	30	Cap
1932	FEB	24	Aqu
	AUG	13	Cap
	NOV	20	Aqu
1935	FEB	14	Pic
1937	APR	25	Ari
	OCT	18	Pic
1938	JAN	14	Ari
1939	JUL	6	Tau
	SEP	22	Ari
1940	MAR	20	Tau
1942	MAY	8	Gem
1944	JUN	20	Can
1946	AUG	2	Leo
1948	SEP	19	Vir
1949	APR	3	Leo
	MAY	29	Vir
1950	NOV	20	Lib
1951	MAR	7	Vir
	AUG	13	Lib
1953	OCT	22	Scp
1956	JAN	12	Sag
	MAY	14	Scp
	OCT	10	Sag
1959	JAN	5	Cap
1962	JAN	3	Aqu
1964	MAR	24	Pic
	SEP	16	Aqu
	DEC	16	Pic
1967	MAR	3	Ari
1969	APR	29	Tau
1971	JUN	18	Gem
1972	JAN	10	Tau
	FEB	21	Gem
1973	AUG	1	Can
1974	JAN	7	Gem
	APR	18	Can

1975	SEP	17	Leo
1976	JAN	14	Can
	JUN	5	Leo
1977	NOV	17	Vir
1978	JAN	5	Leo
	JUL	26	Vir
1980	SEP	21	Lib
1982	NOV	29	Scp
1983	MAY	6	Lib
	AUG	24	Scp
1985	NOV	17	Sag
1988	FEB	13	Cap
	JUN	10	Sag
	NOV	12	Cap
1991	FEB	6	Aqu
1993	MAY	21	Pic
	JUN	30	Aqu
1994	JAN	28	Pic
1996	APR	7	Ari
1998	JUN	9	Tau
	OCT	25	Ari
1999	MAR	1	Tau
2000	AUG	10	Gem
	OCT	16	Tau
2001	APR	21	Gem
2003	JUN	3	Can
2005	JUL	16	Leo
2007	SEP	2	Vir
2009	OCT	29	Lib
2010	APR	7	Vir
	JUL	21	Lib

CHAPTER 6

Where It All Happens: Your Rising Sign

To find out what's happening in a horoscope, you first have to look east. The degree of the zodiac ascending over the eastern horizon at the time you were born, which is called the rising sign or ascendant, marks the beginning of the first house, one of twelve divisions of the horoscope, each of which represents a different area of life. These "houses" contain the planets, the doers in a chart. After the rising sign, the other houses parade around the chart in sequence, with the following sign on the next house cusp. Therefore, the setup of the chart—*what* happens *where*—depends on the rising sign.

Though you can learn much about a person by the signs and interactions of the sun, moon, and planets in the horoscope, without a valid rising sign, the collection of planets has no "homes." One would have no idea which area of life could be influenced by a particular planet. For example, you might know that a person has Mars in Aries, which will describe that person's dynamic fiery energy. But if you also know that the person has a Capricorn rising sign, this Mars will fall in the fourth house of home and family, so you know where that energy will operate.

Due to the earth's rotation, the rising sign changes every two hours, which means that babies born later or earlier on the same day in the same hospital will have most planets in the same signs, but may not have the same rising sign. Therefore, their planets may fall in different houses in the chart. For instance, if Mars is in Gemini and your rising sign is Taurus,

Mars will most likely be active in the second or financial house of your chart. Someone born later in the same day when the rising sign is Virgo would have Mars positioned at the top of the chart, energizing the tenth house of career.

Most astrologers insist on knowing the exact time of a client's birth before they analyze a chart. The more accurate your birth time, the more accurately an astrologer can position the planets in your chart by determining the correct rising sign.

How Your Rising Sign Can Influence Your Sun Sign

Your rising sign has an important relationship with your sun sign. Some will complement the sun sign; others hide it under a totally different mask, as if playing an entirely different role, making it difficult to guess the person's sun sign from outer appearances. This may be the reason why you might not look or act like your sun sign's archetype. For example, a Leo with a conservative Capricorn ascendant would come across as much more serious than a Leo with a fiery Aries or Sagittarius ascendant.

Though the rising sign usually creates the first impression you make, there are exceptions. When the sun sign is reinforced by other planets in the same sign, this might overpower the impression of the rising sign. For instance, a Leo sun plus a Leo Venus and Leo Jupiter would counteract the more conservative image that would otherwise be conveyed by the person's Capricorn ascendant.

Those born early in the morning when the sun was on the horizon will be most likely to project the image of their sun sign. These people are often called a "double Aries" or a "double Virgo" because the same sun sign and ascendant reinforce each other.

Find Your Rising Sign

Look up your rising sign on the chart at the end of this chapter. Since rising signs change every two hours, it is important to know your birth time as close to the minute as possible. Even a few minutes' difference could change the rising sign and therefore the setup of your chart. If you are unsure about the exact time, but know within a few hours, check the following descriptions to see which is most like the personality you project.

Aries Rising: Alpha Energy

You are the most aggressive version of your sun sign, with boundless energy that can be used productively if it's channeled in the right direction. Watch a tendency to overreact emotionally and blow your top. You come across as openly competitive, a positive asset in business or sports. Be on guard against impatience, which could lead to head injuries. Your walk and bearing could have the telltale head-forward Aries posture. You may wear more bright colors, especially red, than others of your sign, or be a redhead. You may also have a tendency to drive your car faster.

Can you see the alpha Aries tendency in Barbra Streisand (a sun sign Taurus) and Bette Midler (a sun sign Sagittarius)?

Taurus Rising: Down-to-Earth

You're slow-moving, with a beautiful (or distinctive) speaking or singing voice. You probably surround yourself with comfort, good food, luxurious surroundings, and other sensual pleasures. You prefer welcoming others into your home to gadding about. You may have a talent for business, especially in trading, appraising, and real estate. A Taurus ascendant gives a well-padded physique that gains weight easily, like Liza Minnelli. This ascendant can also endow females with a curvaceous beauty.

Gemini Rising: A Way with Words

You're naturally sociable, with lighter, more ethereal mannerisms than others of your sign, especially if you're female. You love to communicate with people, and express your ideas easily, like former British prime minister Tony Blair. You may have a talent for writing or public speaking. You thrive on variety, a constantly changing scene, and a lively social life. However, you may relate to others at a deeper level than might be suspected. And you will be far more sympathetic and caring than you project. You will probably travel widely, changing partners and jobs several times (or juggle two at once). Physically, your nerves are quite sensitive. Occasionally, you would benefit from a calm, tranquil atmosphere away from your usual social scene.

Cancer Rising: Nurturing Instincts

You are naturally acquisitive, possessive, private, a moneymaker like Bill Gates or Michael Bloomberg. You easily pick up others' needs and feelings—a great gift in business, the arts, and personal relationships. But you must guard against overreacting or taking things too personally, especially during full-moon periods. Find creative outlets for your natural nurturing gifts, such as helping the less fortunate, particularly children. Your insights would be helpful in psychology. Your desire to feed and care for others would be useful in the restaurant, hotel, or child-care industries. You may be especially fond of wearing romantic old clothes, collecting antiques, and dining on exquisite food. Since your body may retain fluids, pay attention to your diet. To relax, escape to places near water.

Leo Rising: Diva Dazzle

You may come across as more poised than you really feel. However, you play it to the hilt, projecting a proud royal presence. A Leo ascendant gives you a natural flair for drama, like Marilyn Monroe, and you might be accused of stealing the spotlight. You'll also project a much more outgoing, optimistic, and sunny personality than others of your sign. You take care to please your public by always projecting star quality, probably tossing a luxuriant mane of hair, sporting a striking hairstyle, or dressing to impress. Females often dazzle with colorful clothing or spectacular jewelry. Since you may have a strong parental nature, you could well become a family matriarch or patriarch, like George H. W. Bush.

Virgo Rising: High Standards

Virgo rising endows you with a practical, analytical outer image. You seem neat, orderly, and more particular than others of your sign. Others in your life may feel they must live up to your high standards. Though at times you may be openly critical, this masks a well-meaning desire to have only the best for loved ones. Your sharp eye for details could be used in the financial world, or your literary skills could draw you to teaching or publishing. The healing arts, health care, and service-oriented professions attract many with a Virgo ascendant. You're likely to take good care of yourself, with great attention to health, diet, and exercise, like Madonna. You might even show some hypochondriac tendencies, like Woody Allen. Physically, you may have a very sensitive digestive system.

Libra Rising: The Charmer

Libra rising gives you a charming, social, and public persona, like John F. Kennedy and Bill Clinton. You tend to avoid confrontations in relationships, preferring to smooth the way or negotiate diplomatically rather than give in to an emotional reaction. Because you are interested in all aspects of a situation, you may be slow to reach decisions. Physically, you'll have good proportions and physical symmetry. You will move with natural grace and balance. You're likely to have pleasing, if not beautiful, facial features, with a winning smile, like Cary Grant. You'll show natural good taste and harmony in your clothes and home decor. Legal, diplomatic, or public relations professions could draw your interest.

Scorpio Rising: Air of Mystery

You project an intriguing air of mystery with this ascendant, as the Scorpio secretiveness and sense of underlying power combine with your sun sign. Like Jacqueline Kennedy Onassis, you convey that there's more to you than meets the eye. You seem like someone who is always in control and who can move comfortably in the world of power. Your physical look comes across as intense. Many of you have remarkable eyes, with a direct, penetrating gaze. But you'll never reveal your private agenda, and you tend to keep your true feelings under wraps (watch a tendency toward paranoia). You may have an interesting romantic history with secret love affairs, like Grace Kelly. Many of you heighten your air of mystery by wearing black. You're happiest near water; you should provide yourself with a seaside retreat.

Sagittarius Rising: The Explorer

You travel with this ascendant. You may also be a more outdoor, sportive type, with an athletic, casual, and outgoing air. Your moods are camouflaged with cheerful optimism or a philosophical attitude. Though you don't hesitate to speak your mind—like Ted Turner, who was called the Mouth of the South—you can also laugh at your troubles or crack a joke more easily than others of your sign. A Sagittarius ascendant can also draw you to the field of higher education or to spiritual life. You'll seem to have less attachment to things and people, and you may explore the globe. Your strong, fast legs are a physical bonus.

Capricorn Rising: Serious Business

This rising sign makes you come across as serious, goal-oriented, disciplined, and careful with cash. You are not one of the zodiac's big spenders, though you might splurge occasionally on items with good investment value. You're the conservative type in dress and environment, and you might come across as quite formal and businesslike, like Rupert Murdoch. You'll function well in a structured or corporate environment where you can climb to the top. (You are always aware of who's the boss.) In your personal life, you could be a loner or a single parent who is father and mother to your children.

Aquarius Rising: One of a Kind

You come across as less concerned about what others think and could even be a bit eccentric. Your appearance is sure to be unique and memorable. You're more at ease with groups of people than others in your sign, and you may be attracted to public life, like Jay Leno. Your appearance may be unique, either unconventional or unimportant to you. Those of you whose sun is in a water sign (Cancer, Scorpio, or Pisces) may exercise your nurturing qualities with a large group, an extended family, or a day-care or community center.

Pisces Rising: Romantic Roles

Your creative, nurturing talents are heightened and so is your ability to project emotional drama. And, like Antonio Banderas, your dreamy eyes and poetic air bring out the protective instinct in others. You could be attracted to the arts, especially theater, dance, film, and photography, or to psychology, spiritual practice, and charity work. You are happiest when you are using your creative ability to help others. Since you are vulnerable to mood swings, it is important for you to find interesting, creative work where you can express your talents and heighten your self-esteem. Accentuate the positive. Be wary of escapist tendencies, particularly involving alcohol or drugs to which you are supersensitive, like Whitney Houston.

RISING SIGNS—A.M. BIRTHS

	1 AM	2 AM	3 AM	4 AM	5 AM	6 AM	7 AM	8 AM	9 AM	10 AM	11 AM	12 NOON
Jan 1	Lib	Sc	Sc	Sc	Sag	Sag	Cap	Cap	Aq	Aq	Pis	Ar
Jan 9	Lib	Sc	Sc	Sag	Sag	Sag	Cap	Cap	Aq	Pis	Ar	Tau
Jan 17	Sc	Sc	Sc	Sag	Sag	Cap	Cap	Aq	Aq	Pis	Ar	Tau
Jan 25	Sc	Sc	Sag	Sag	Sag	Cap	Cap	Aq	Pis	Ar	Tau	Tau
Feb 2	Sc	Sc	Sag	Sag	Cap	Cap	Aq	Pis	Pis	Ar	Tau	Gem
Feb 10	Sc	Sag	Sag	Sag	Cap	Cap	Aq	Pis	Ar	Tau	Tau	Gem
Feb 18	Sc	Sag	Sag	Cap	Cap	Aq	Pis	Pis	Ar	Tau	Gem	Gem
Feb 26	Sag	Sag	Sag	Cap	Aq	Aq	Pis	Ar	Tau	Tau	Gem	Gem
Mar 6	Sag	Sag	Cap	Cap	Aq	Pis	Pis	Ar	Tau	Gem	Gem	Can
Mar 14	Sag	Cap	Cap	Aq	Aq	Pis	Ar	Tau	Tau	Gem	Gem	Can
Mar 22	Sag	Cap	Cap	Aq	Pis	Ar	Ar	Tau	Gem	Gem	Can	Can
Mar 30	Cap	Cap	Aq	Pis	Pis	Ar	Tau	Tau	Gem	Can	Can	Can
Apr 7	Cap	Cap	Aq	Pis	Ar	Ar	Tau	Gem	Gem	Can	Can	Leo
Apr 14	Cap	Aq	Aq	Pis	Ar	Tau	Tau	Gem	Gem	Can	Can	Leo
Apr 22	Cap	Aq	Pis	Ar	Ar	Tau	Gem	Gem	Gem	Can	Leo	Leo
Apr 30	Aq	Aq	Pis	Ar	Tau	Tau	Gem	Can	Can	Can	Leo	Leo
May 8	Aq	Pis	Ar	Ar	Tau	Gem	Gem	Can	Can	Leo	Leo	Leo
May 16	Aq	Pis	Ar	Tau	Gem	Gem	Can	Can	Can	Leo	Leo	Vir
May 24	Pis	Ar	Ar	Tau	Gem	Gem	Can	Can	Leo	Leo	Leo	Vir
June 1	Pis	Ar	Tau	Gem	Gem	Can	Can	Can	Leo	Leo	Vir	Vir
June 9	Ar	Ar	Tau	Gem	Gem	Can	Can	Leo	Leo	Leo	Vir	Vir
June 17	Ar	Tau	Gem	Gem	Can	Can	Can	Leo	Leo	Vir	Vir	Vir
June 25	Tau	Tau	Gem	Gem	Can	Can	Leo	Leo	Leo	Vir	Vir	Lib
July 3	Tau	Gem	Gem	Can	Can	Can	Leo	Leo	Vir	Vir	Vir	Lib
July 11	Tau	Gem	Gem	Can	Can	Leo	Leo	Leo	Vir	Vir	Lib	Lib
July 18	Gem	Gem	Can	Can	Can	Leo	Leo	Vir	Vir	Vir	Lib	Lib
July 26	Gem	Gem	Can	Can	Leo	Leo	Vir	Vir	Vir	Lib	Lib	Lib
Aug 3	Gem	Can	Can	Can	Leo	Leo	Vir	Vir	Vir	Lib	Lib	Sc
Aug 11	Gem	Can	Can	Leo	Leo	Leo	Vir	Vir	Lib	Lib	Lib	Sc
Aug 18	Can	Can	Can	Leo	Leo	Vir	Vir	Vir	Lib	Lib	Sc	Sc
Aug 27	Can	Can	Leo	Leo	Leo	Vir	Vir	Lib	Lib	Lib	Sc	Sc
Sept 4	Can	Can	Leo	Leo	Leo	Vir	Vir	Vir	Lib	Lib	Sc	Sc
Sept 12	Can	Leo	Leo	Leo	Vir	Vir	Lib	Lib	Lib	Sc	Sc	Sag
Sept 20	Leo	Leo	Leo	Vir	Vir	Vir	Lib	Lib	Sc	Sc	Sc	Sag
Sept 28	Leo	Leo	Leo	Vir	Vir	Lib	Lib	Lib	Sc	Sc	Sag	Sag
Oct 6	Leo	Leo	Vir	Vir	Vir	Lib	Lib	Sc	Sc	Sc	Sag	Sag
Oct 14	Leo	Vir	Vir	Vir	Lib	Lib	Lib	Sc	Sc	Sag	Sag	Cap
Oct 22	Leo	Vir	Vir	Lib	Lib	Lib	Sc	Sc	Sc	Sag	Sag	Cap
Oct 30	Vir	Vir	Vir	Lib	Lib	Sc	Sc	Sc	Sag	Sag	Cap	Cap
Nov 7	Vir	Vir	Lib	Lib	Lib	Sc	Sc	Sc	Sag	Sag	Cap	Cap
Nov 15	Vir	Vir	Lib	Lib	Sc	Sc	Sc	Sag	Sag	Cap	Cap	Aq
Nov 23	Vir	Lib	Lib	Lib	Sc	Sc	Sag	Sag	Sag	Cap	Cap	Aq
Dec 1	Vir	Lib	Lib	Sc	Sc	Sc	Sag	Sag	Cap	Cap	Aq	Aq
Dec 9	Lib	Lib	Lib	Sc	Sc	Sag	Sag	Sag	Cap	Cap	Aq	Pis
Dec 18	Lib	Lib	Sc	Sc	Sc	Sag	Sag	Cap	Cap	Aq	Aq	Pis
Dec 28	Lib	Lib	Sc	Sc	Sag	Sag	Sag	Cap	Aq	Aq	Pis	Ar

RISING SIGNS—P.M. BIRTHS

	1 PM	2 PM	3 PM	4 PM	5 PM	6 PM	7 PM	8 PM	9 PM	10 PM	11 PM	12 MID-NIGHT
Jan 1	Tau	Gem	Gem	Can	Can	Can	Leo	Leo	Vir	Vir	Vir	Lib
Jan 9	Tau	Gem	Gem	Can	Can	Leo	Leo	Leo	Vir	Vir	Vir	Lib
Jan 17	Gem	Gem	Can	Can	Can	Leo	Leo	Vir	Vir	Vir	Lib	Lib
Jan 25	Gem	Gem	Can	Can	Leo	Leo	Leo	Vir	Vir	Lib	Lib	Lib
Feb 2	Gem	Can	Can	Can	Leo	Leo	Vir	Vir	Vir	Lib	Lib	Sc
Feb 10	Gem	Can	Can	Leo	Leo	Leo	Vir	Vir	Lib	Lib	Lib	Sc
Feb 18	Can	Can	Can	Leo	Leo	Vir	Vir	Vir	Lib	Lib	Sc	Sc
Feb 26	Can	Can	Leo	Leo	Leo	Vir	Vir	Lib	Lib	Lib	Sc	Sc
Mar 6	Can	Leo	Leo	Leo	Vir	Vir	Vir	Lib	Lib	Sc	Sc	Sc
Mar 14	Can	Leo	Leo	Vir	Vir	Vir	Lib	Lib	Lib	Sc	Sc	Sag
Mar 22	Leo	Leo	Leo	Vir	Vir	Lib	Lib	Lib	Sc	Sc	Sc	Sag
Mar 30	Leo	Leo	Vir	Vir	Vir	Lib	Lib	Sc	Sc	Sc	Sag	Sag
Apr 7	Leo	Leo	Vir	Vir	Lib	Lib	Lib	Sc	Sc	Sc	Sag	Sag
Apr 14	Leo	Vir	Vir	Vir	Lib	Lib	Sc	Sc	Sc	Sag	Sag	Cap
Apr 22	Leo	Vir	Vir	Lib	Lib	Lib	Sc	Sc	Sc	Sag	Sag	Cap
Apr 30	Vir	Vir	Vir	Lib	Lib	Sc	Sc	Sc	Sag	Sag	Cap	Cap
May 8	Vir	Vir	Lib	Lib	Lib	Sc	Sc	Sag	Sag	Sag	Cap	Cap
May 16	Vir	Vir	Lib	Lib	Sc	Sc	Sc	Sag	Sag	Cap	Cap	Aq
May 24	Vir	Lib	Lib	Lib	Sc	Sc	Sag	Sag	Sag	Cap	Cap	Aq
June 1	Vir	Lib	Lib	Sc	Sc	Sc	Sag	Sag	Cap	Cap	Aq	Aq
June 9	Lib	Lib	Lib	Sc	Sc	Sag	Sag	Sag	Cap	Cap	Aq	Pis
June 17	Lib	Lib	Sc	Sc	Sc	Sag	Sag	Cap	Cap	Aq	Aq	Pis
June 25	Lib	Lib	Sc	Sc	Sag	Sag	Sag	Cap	Cap	Aq	Pis	Ar
July 3	Lib	Sc	Sc	Sc	Sag	Sag	Cap	Cap	Aq	Aq	Pis	Ar
July 11	Lib	Sc	Sc	Sag	Sag	Sag	Cap	Cap	Aq	Pis	Ar	Tau
July 18	Sc	Sc	Sc	Sag	Sag	Cap	Cap	Aq	Aq	Pis	Ar	Tau
July 26	Sc	Sc	Sag	Sag	Sag	Cap	Cap	Aq	Pis	Ar	Tau	Tau
Aug 3	Sc	Sc	Sag	Sag	Cap	Cap	Aq	Aq	Pis	Ar	Tau	Gem
Aug 11	Sc	Sag	Sag	Sag	Cap	Cap	Aq	Pis	Ar	Tau	Tau	Gem
Aug 18	Sc	Sag	Sag	Cap	Cap	Aq	Pis	Pis	Ar	Tau	Gem	Gem
Aug 27	Sag	Sag	Sag	Cap	Cap	Aq	Pis	Ar	Tau	Tau	Gem	Gem
Sept 4	Sag	Sag	Cap	Cap	Aq	Pis	Pis	Ar	Tau	Gem	Gem	Can
Sept 12	Sag	Sag	Cap	Aq	Aq	Pis	Ar	Tau	Tau	Gem	Gem	Can
Sept 20	Sag	Cap	Cap	Aq	Pis	Pis	Ar	Tau	Gem	Gem	Can	Can
Sept 28	Cap	Cap	Aq	Aq	Pis	Ar	Tau	Tau	Gem	Gem	Can	Can
Oct 6	Cap	Cap	Aq	Pis	Ar	Ar	Tau	Gem	Gem	Can	Can	Leo
Oct 14	Cap	Aq	Aq	Pis	Ar	Tau	Tau	Gem	Gem	Can	Can	Leo
Oct 22	Cap	Aq	Pis	Ar	Ar	Tau	Gem	Gem	Can	Can	Leo	Leo
Oct 30	Aq	Aq	Pis	Ar	Tau	Tau	Gem	Can	Can	Can	Leo	Leo
Nov 7	Aq	Aq	Pis	Ar	Tau	Tau	Gem	Can	Can	Can	Leo	Leo
Nov 15	Aq	Pis	Ar	Tau	Gem	Gem	Can	Can	Can	Leo	Leo	Vir
Nov 23	Pis	Ar	Ar	Tau	Gem	Gem	Can	Can	Leo	Leo	Leo	Vir
Dec 1	Pis	Ar	Tau	Gem	Gem	Can	Can	Can	Leo	Leo	Vir	Vir
Dec 9	Ar	Tau	Tau	Gem	Gem	Can	Can	Leo	Leo	Leo	Vir	Vir
Dec 18	Ar	Tau	Gem	Gem	Can	Can	Can	Leo	Leo	Vir	Vir	Vir
Dec 28	Tau	Tau	Gem	Gem	Can	Can	Leo	Leo	Vir	Vir	Vir	Lib

CHAPTER 7

The Keys to Reading Your Horoscope: The Glyphs

Are you ready to take your astrology knowledge to the next level and read your first horoscope chart? If so, you'll encounter a new language of symbols, because horoscope charts are written in glyphs, a centuries-old pictographic language. These little "pictures" are a type of shorthand used by astrologers around the world to indicate the planets and the signs.

There's no way to avoid learning the glyphs, if you want to get deeper into astrology. Whether you download your chart from one of the many Internet sites that offer free charts or you buy one of the many interesting astrology programs, you'll find charts are always written in glyph language. Some software makes it easier for beginners by listing the planets and their signs in English alongside the chart and other programs will pop up an English interpretation as your roll your mouse over the glyph. However, in the long run, it's much easier—and more fun—to learn the glyphs yourself.

There's an extra bonus to learning the glyphs: They contain a kind of visual code, with built-in clues that will tell you not only which sign or planet each represents, but what the symbol means in a deeper, more esoteric sense. Actually the physical act of writing the symbol is a mystical experience in itself, a way to invoke the deeper meaning of the sign or planet through age-old visual elements that have been with us since time began.

Since there are only twelve signs and ten planets (not counting a few asteroids and other space objects some astrologers use), it's a lot easier than learning to read a foreign language. Here's a code cracker for the glyphs, beginning with the glyphs for the planets. To those who already know their glyphs, don't just skim over the chapter. These familiar graphics have hidden meanings you will discover!

The Glyphs for the Planets

The glyphs for the planets are easy to learn. They're simple combinations of the most basic visual elements: the circle, the semicircle or arc, and the cross. However, each component of a glyph has a special meaning in relation to the other parts of the symbol.

The circle, which has no beginning or end, is one of the oldest symbols of spirit or spiritual forces. Early diagrams of the heavens—spiritual territory—are shown in circular form. The never-ending line of the circle is the perfect symbol for eternity. The semicircle or arc is an incomplete circle, symbolizing the receptive, finite soul, which contains spiritual potential in the curving line.

The vertical line of the cross symbolizes movement from heaven to earth. The horizontal line describes temporal movement, here and now, in time and space. Combined in a cross, the vertical and horizontal planes symbolize manifestation in the material world.

The Sun Glyph ☉

The sun is always shown by this powerful solar symbol, a circle with a point in the center. The center point is you, your spiritual center, and the symbol represents your infinite personality incarnating (the point) into the finite cycles of birth and death.

The sun has been represented by a circle or disk since ancient Egyptian times when the solar disk represented the sun god, Ra. Some archaeologists believe the great stone circles found in England were centers of sun worship. This particular version of the symbol was brought into common use in the sixteenth century after German occultist and scholar Cornelius Agrippa (1486–1535) wrote a book called *Die Occulta Philosophia,* which became accepted as the authority in the field. Agrippa collected many of the medieval astrological and magical symbols in this book, which have been used by astrologers since then.

The Moon Glyph ☽

The moon glyph is the most recognizable symbol on a chart, a left-facing arc stylized into the crescent moon. As part of a circle, the arc symbolizes the potential fulfillment of the entire circle, the life force that is still incomplete. Therefore, it is the ideal representation of the reactive, receptive, emotional nature of the moon.

The Mercury Glyph ☿

Mercury contains all three elemental symbols: the crescent, the circle, and the cross in vertical order. This is the "Venus with a hat" glyph (compare with the symbol of Venus). With another stretch of the imagination, can't you see the winged cap of Mercury the messenger? Think of the upturned crescent as antennae that tune in and transmit messages from the sun, reminding you that Mercury is the way you communicate, the way your mind works. The upturned arc is receiving energy into the spirit or solar circle, which will later be translated into action on the material plane, symbolized by the cross. All the elements are equally sized because Mercury is neutral; it doesn't play favorites! This planet symbolizes objective, detached, unemotional thinking.

The Venus Glyph ♀

Here the relationship is between two components: the circle of spirit and the cross of matter. Spirit is elevated over matter, pulling it upward. Venus asks, "What is beautiful? What do you like best? What do you love to have done to you?" Consequently, Venus determines both your ideal of beauty and what feels good sensually. It governs your own allure and power to attract, as well as what attracts and pleases you.

The Mars Glyph ♂

In this glyph, the cross of matter is stylized into an arrowhead pointed up and outward, propelled by the circle of spirit. With a little imagination, you can visualize it as the shield and spear of Mars, the ancient god of war. You can deduce that Mars embodies your spiritual energy projected into the outer world. It's your assertiveness, your initiative, your aggressive drive, what you like to do to others, your temper. If you know someone's Mars, you know whether they'll blow up when angry or do a slow burn. Your task is to use your outgoing Mars energy wisely and well.

The Jupiter Glyph ♃

Jupiter is the basic cross of matter, with a large stylized crescent perched on the left side of the horizontal, temporal plane. You might think of the crescent as an open hand, because one meaning of Jupiter is "luck," what's handed to you. You don't have to work for what you get from Jupiter; it comes to you, if you're open to it.

The Jupiter glyph might also remind you of a jumbo jet plane, with a huge tail fin, about to take off. This is the planet of travel, mental and spiritual, of expanding your horizons via new ideas, new spiritual dimensions, and new places. Jupiter embodies the optimism and enthusiasm of the traveler about to embark on an exciting adventure.

The Saturn Glyph ♄

Flip Jupiter over, and you've got Saturn. This might not be immediately apparent because Saturn is usually stylized into an "h" form like the one shown here. The principle it expresses is the opposite of Jupiter's expansive tendencies. Saturn pulls you back to earth: the receptive arc is pushed down underneath the cross of matter. Before there are any rewards or expansion, the duties and obligations of the material world must be considered. Saturn says, "Stop, wait, finish your chores before you take off!"

Saturn's glyph also resembles the sickle of old "Father Time."

Saturn was first known as Chronos, the Greek god of time, for time brings all matter to an end. When it was the most distant planet (before the discovery of Uranus), Saturn was believed to be the place where time stopped. After the soul departed from earth, it journeyed back to the outer reaches of the universe and finally stopped at Saturn, or at "the end of time."

The Uranus Glyph ♅

The glyph for Uranus is often stylized to form a capital *H* after Sir William Herschel, who discovered the planet. But the more esoteric version curves the two pillars of the H into crescent antennae, or "ears," like satellite disks receiving signals from space. These are perched on the horizontal material line of the cross of matter and pushed from below by the circle of the spirit. To many sci-fi fans, Uranus looks like an orbiting satellite.

Uranus channels the highest energy of all, the white electrical light of the universal spiritual force that holds the cosmos together. This pure electrical energy is gathered from all over the universe. Because Uranus energy doesn't follow any ordinary celestial drumbeat, it can't be controlled or predicted (which is also true of those who are strongly influenced by this eccentric planet). In the symbol, this energy is manifested through the balance of polarities (the two opposite arms of the glyph) like the two polarized wires of a lightbulb.

The Neptune Glyph ♆

Neptune's glyph is usually stylized to look like a trident, the weapon of the Roman god Neptune. However, on a more esoteric level, it shows the large upturned crescent of the soul pierced through by the cross of matter. Neptune nails down, or materializes, soul energy, bringing impulses from the soul level into manifestation. That is why Neptune is associated with imagination or "imagining in," making an image of the soul. Neptune works through feelings, sensitivity, and the mystical capacity to bring the divine into the earthly realm.

The Pluto Glyph ♇

Pluto is written two ways. One is a composite of the letters *PL,* the first two letters of the word Pluto and coincidentally the initials of Percival Lowell, one of the planet's discoverers. The other, more esoteric symbol is a small circle above a large open crescent that surmounts the cross of matter. This depicts Pluto's power to regenerate. Imagine a new little spirit emerging from the sheltering cup of the soul. Pluto rules the forces of life and death. After this planet has passed a sensitive point in your chart, you are transformed, reborn in some way.

Sci-fi fans might visualize this glyph as a small satellite (the circle) being launched. It was shortly after Pluto's discovery that we learned how to harness the nuclear forces that made space exploration possible. Pluto rules the transformative power of atomic energy, which totally changed our lives and from which there is no turning back.

The Glyphs for the Signs

On an astrology chart, the glyph for the sign will appear after that of the planet. For example, when you see the moon glyph followed first by a number and then by another glyph representing the sign, this means that the moon was passing over a certain degree of that astrological sign at the time of the chart. On the dividing lines between the houses on your chart, you'll find the symbol for the sign that rules the house.

Because sun sign symbols do not contain the same basic geometric components of the planetary glyphs, we must look elsewhere for clues to their meanings. Many have been passed down from ancient Egyptian and Chaldean civilizations with few modifications. Others have been adapted over the centuries.

In deciphering many of the glyphs, you'll often find that the symbols reveal a dual nature of the sign, which is not always apparent in the usual sun sign descriptions. For instance, the Gemini glyph is similar to the Roman numeral for two, and reveals this sign's longing to discover a twin soul. The Cancer glyph may be interpreted as resembling either the nurturing breasts or the self-protective claws of a crab, both symbols associated with the contrasting qualities of this sign. Libra's glyph embodies the duality of the spirit balanced with material reality. The Sagittarius glyph shows that the aspirant must also carry along the earthly animal nature in his quest. The Capricorn sea goat is another symbol with dual emphasis. The goat climbs high, yet is always pulled back by the deep waters of the unconscious. Aquarius embodies the double waves of mental detachment, balanced by the desire for connection with others, in a friendly way. Finally, the two fishes of Pisces, which are forever tied together, show the duality of the soul and the spirit that must be reconciled.

The Aries Glyph ♈

Since the symbol for Aries is the Ram, this glyph is obviously associated with a ram's horns, which characterize one aspect of the Aries personality—an aggressive, me-first, leaping-headfirst attitude. But the symbol can be interpreted in other ways as well. Some astrologers liken it to a fountain of energy, which Aries people also embody. The first sign of the zodiac bursts on the scene eagerly, ready to go. Another analogy is to the eyebrows and nose of the human head, which Aries rules, and the thinking power that is initiated by the brain.

One theory of this symbol links it to the Egyptian god Amun, represented by a ram in ancient times. As Amun-Ra, this god was believed to embody the creator of the universe, the leader of all the other gods. This relates easily to the position of Aries as the leader (or first sign) of the zodiac, which begins at the spring equinox, a time of the year when nature is renewed.

The Taurus Glyph ♉

This is another easy glyph to draw and identify. It takes little imagination to decipher the bull's head with long curving horns. Like its symbol the Bull, the archetypal Taurus is slow to anger but ferocious when provoked, as well as stubborn, steady, and sensual. Another association is the larynx (and thyroid) of the throat area (ruled by Taurus) and the eustachian tubes running up to the ears, which coincides with the relationship of Taurus to the voice, song, and music. Many famous singers, musicians, and composers have prominent Taurus influences.

Many ancient religions involved a bull as the central figure in fertility rites or initiations, usually symbolizing the victory of man over his animal nature. Another possible origin is in the sacred bull of Egypt, who embodied the incarnate form of Osiris, god of death and resurrection. In early Christian imagery, the Taurus Bull represented St. Luke.

The Gemini Glyph ♊

The standard glyph immediately calls to mind the Roman numeral for two (II) and the Twins symbol, as it is called, for Gemini. In almost all drawings and images used for this sign, the relationship between two persons is emphasized. Usually one twin will be touching the other, which signifies communication, human contact, the desire to share.

The top line of the Gemini glyph indicates mental communication, while the bottom line indicates shared physical space.

The most famous Gemini legend is that of the twin sons Castor and Pollux, one of whom had a mortal father while the other was the son of Zeus, king of the gods. When it came time for the mortal twin to die, his grief-stricken brother pleaded with Zeus, who agreed to let them spend half the year on earth in mortal form and half in immortal life, with the gods on Mount Olympus. This reflects a basic duality of humankind, which possesses an immortal soul yet is also subject to the limits of mortality.

The Cancer Glyph ♋

Two convenient images relate to the Cancer glyph. It is easiest to decode the curving claws of the Cancer symbol, the Crab. Like the crab's, Cancer's element is water. This sensitive sign also has a hard protective shell to protect its tender interior. The crab must be wily to escape predators, scampering sideways and hiding under rocks. The crab also responds to the cycles of the moon, as do all shellfish. The other image is that of two female breasts, which Cancer rules, showing that this is a sign that nurtures and protects others as well as itself.

In ancient Egypt, Cancer was also represented by the scarab beetle, a symbol of regeneration and eternal life.

The Leo Glyph ♌

Notice that the Leo glyph seems to be an extension of Cancer's glyph, with a significant difference. In the Cancer glyph, the lines curve inward protectively. The Leo glyph expresses energy outwardly. And there is no duality in the symbol, the Lion, or in Leo, the sign.

Lions have belonged to the sign of Leo since earliest times. It is not difficult to imagine the king of beasts with his sweeping mane and curling tail from this glyph. The upward sweep of the glyph easily describes the positive energy of Leo: the flourishing tail, the flamboyant qualities. Another analogy, perhaps a stretch of the imagination, is that of a heart leaping up with joy and enthusiasm, also very typical of Leo, which also rules the heart. In early Christian imagery, the Leo Lion represented St. Mark.

The Virgo Glyph ♍

You can read much into this mysterious glyph. For instance, it could represent the initials of "Mary Virgin," or a young woman holding a staff of wheat, or stylized female genitalia, all common interpretations. The M shape might also remind you that Virgo is ruled by Mercury. The cross beneath the symbol reveals the grounded, practical nature of this earth sign.

The earliest zodiacs link Virgo with the Egyptian goddess Isis, who gave birth to the god Horus after her husband Osiris had been killed, in the archetype of a miraculous conception. There are many ancient statues of Isis nursing her baby son, which are reminiscent of medieval Virgin and Child motifs. This sign has also been associated with the image of the Holy Grail, when the Virgo symbol was substituted with a chalice.

The Libra Glyph ♎

It is not difficult to read the standard image for Libra, the Scales, into this glyph. There is another meaning, however, that is equally relevant: the setting sun as it descends over the horizon. Libra's natural position on the zodiac wheel is the descendant, or sunset position (as the Aries natural position is the ascendant, or rising sign). Both images relate to Libra's personality. Libra is always weighing pros and cons for a balanced decision. In the sunset image, the sun (male) hovers over the horizontal earth (female) before setting. Libra is the space between these lines, harmonizing yin and yang, spiritual and material, male and female, ideal and real worlds. The glyph has also been linked to the kidneys, which are associated with Libra.

The Scorpio Glyph ♏

With its barbed tail, this glyph is easy to identify as the Scorpion for the sign of Scorpio. It also represents the male sexual parts, over which the sign rules. From the arrowhead, you can draw the conclusion that Mars was once its ruler. Some earlier Egyptian glyphs for Scorpio represent it as an erect serpent, so the Serpent is an alternate symbol.

Another symbol for Scorpio, which is not identifiable in this glyph, is the Eagle. Scorpios can go to extremes, either in soaring like the eagle or self-destructing like the scorpion. In early Christian imagery, which often used zodiacal symbols, the Scorpio Eagle was chosen to symbolize the intense apostle St. John the Evangelist.

The Sagittarius Glyph ♐

This is one of the easiest to spot and draw: an upward pointing arrow lifting up a cross. The arrow is pointing skyward, while the cross represents the four elements of the material world, which the arrow must convey. Elevating materiality into spirituality is an important Sagittarius quality, which explains why this sign is associated with higher learning, religion, philosophy, travel—the aspiring professions. Sagittarius can also send barbed arrows of frankness in the pursuit of truth, so the Archer symbol for Sagittarius is apt. (Sagittarius is also the sign of the supersalesman.)

Sagittarius is symbolically represented by the centaur, a mythological creature who is half man, half horse, aiming his arrow toward the skies. Though Sagittarius is motivated by spiritual aspiration, it also must balance the powerful appetites of the animal nature. The centaur Chiron, a figure in Greek mythology, became a wise teacher who, after many adventures and world travels, was killed by a poisoned arrow.

The Capricorn Glyph ♑

One of the most difficult symbols to draw, this glyph may take some practice. It is a representation of the sea goat: a mythical animal that is a goat with a curving fish's tail. The goat part of Capricorn wants to leave the waters of the emotions and climb to the elevated areas of life. But the fish tail is the unconscious, the deep chaotic psychic level that draws the goat back. Capricorn is often trying to escape the deep, feeling part of life by submerging himself in work, steadily ascending to the top. To some people, the glyph represents a seated figure with a bent knee, a reminder that Capricorn governs the knee area of the body.

An interesting aspect of this glyph is the contrast of the sharp pointed horns—which represent the penetrating, shrewd, conscious side of Capricorn—with the swishing tail—which represents its serpentine, unconscious, emotional force. One Capricorn legend, which dates from Roman times, tells of the earthy fertility god, Pan, who tried to save himself from uncontrollable sexual desires by jumping into the Nile. His upper body then turned into a goat, while the lower part became a fish. Later, Jupiter gave him a safe haven as a constellation in the skies.

The Aquarius Glyph ♒

This ancient water symbol can be traced back to an Egyptian hieroglyph representing streams of life force. Symbolized by the Water Bearer, Aquarius is distributor of the waters of life—the magic liquid of regeneration. The two waves can also be linked to the positive and negative charges of the electrical energy that Aquarius rules, a sort of universal wavelength. Aquarius is tuned in intuitively to higher forces via this electrical force. The duality of the glyph could also refer to the dual nature of Aquarius, a sign that runs hot and cold and that is friendly but also detached in the mental world of air signs.

In Greek legends, Aquarius is represented by Ganymede, who was carried to heaven by an eagle in order to become the cupbearer of Zeus and to supervise the annual flooding of the Nile. The sign later became associated with aviation and notions of flight. Like the other fixed signs (Taurus, Scorpio, and Leo), Aquarius is associated with an apostle, in this case St. Matthew.

The Pisces Glyph ♓

Here is an abstraction of the familiar image of Pisces, two Fishes swimming in opposite directions yet bound together by a cord. The Fishes represent the spirit—which yearns for the freedom of heaven—and the soul—which remains attached to the desires of the temporal world. During life on earth, the spirit and the soul are bound together. When they complement each other, instead of pulling in opposite directions, they facilitate the Pisces creativity. The ancient version of this glyph, taken from the Egyptians, had no connecting line, which was added in the fourteenth century.

In another interpretation, it is said that the left fish indicates the direction of involution or the beginning of a cycle, while the right fish signifies the direction of evolution, the way to completion of a cycle. It's an appropriate grand finale for Pisces, the last sign of the zodiac.

CHAPTER 8

Join the Astrology Community

Astrology fans love to share their knowledge and socialize. So why not join the community of astrologers online or at a conference? You might be surprised to find an astrology club in your local area. Connecting with other astrology fans and learning more about this fascinating subject has never been easier. In fact the many options available with just a click of your computer are mind-boggling.

You need only type the word *astrology* into any Internet search engine and watch hundreds of listings of astrology-related sites pop up. There are local meetings and international conferences where you can meet and study with other astrologers, and books and tapes to help you learn at home. You could even combine your vacation with an astrological workshop in an exotic locale, such as Bali or Mexico.

To help you sort out the variety of options available, here are our top picks of the Internet and the astrological community at large.

National Council for Geocosmic Research (NCGR)

Whether you'd like to know more about such specialties as financial astrology or techniques for timing events, or if you'd prefer the psychological or mythological approach, you'll meet the top astrologers at conferences sponsored by the National Council for Geocosmic Research. NCGR is dedicated to providing quality education, bringing astrologers and astrology fans together at conferences, and promoting fellowship. Their course structure provides a systematized study of the many facets of astrology. The organization sponsors educational workshops, taped lectures, conferences, and a directory of professional astrologers.

For an annual membership fee, you get their excellent publications and newsletters, plus the opportunity to network with other astrology buffs at local chapter events. At this writing there are chapters in twenty-six states and four countries.

To join NCGR and for the latest information on upcoming events and chapters in your city, consult their Web site: www.geocosmic.org.

American Federation of Astrologers (AFA)

Established in 1938, this is one of the oldest astrological organizations in the United States. AFA offers conferences, conventions, and a correspondence course. If you are looking for a reading, their interesting Web site will refer you to an accredited AFA astrologer.

6535 South Rural Road
Tempe, AZ 85283
Phone: (888) 301-7630 or (480) 838-1751
Fax: (480) 838-8293
Web site: www.astrologers.com

Association for Astrological Networking (AFAN)

Did you know that astrologers are still being harassed for practicing astrology? AFAN provides support and legal information, and works toward improving the public image of astrology. AFAN's network of local astrologers links with the international astrological community. Here are the people who will go to bat for astrology when it is attacked in the media. Everyone who cares about astrology should join!

8306 Wilshire Boulevard
PMB 537
Beverly Hills, CA 90211
Phone: (800) 578-2326
E-mail: info@afan.org
Web site: www.afan.org

International Society for Astrology Research (ISAR)

An international organization of professional astrologers dedicated to encouraging the highest standards of quality in the field of astrology with an emphasis on research. Among ISAR's benefits are quarterly journals, a weekly e-mail newsletter, and a free membership directory.

P.O. Box 38613
Los Angeles, CA 90038
Fax: (805) 933-0301
Web site: www.isarastrology.com

Astrology Magazines

In addition to articles by top astrologers, most have listings of astrology conferences, events, and local happenings.

Horoscope Guide
Kappa Publishing Group
6198 Butler Pike
Suite 200
Blue Bell, PA 19422-2600
Web site: www.kappapublishing.com/astrology

Dell Horoscope
Their Web site features a listing of local astrological meetings.

Customer Service
6 Prowitt Street
Norwalk, CT 06855
Phone: (800) 220-7443
Web site: www.dellhoroscope.com

The Mountain Astrologer
A favorite magazine of astrology fans, *The Mountain Astrologer* also has an interesting Web site featuring the latest news from an astrological point of view, plus feature articles from the magazine.

P.O. Box 970
Cedar Ridge, CA 95924
Web site: www.mountainastrologer.com

Astrology College

Kepler College of Astrological Arts and Sciences

A degree-granting college, which is also a center of astrology, has long been the dream of the astrological community and is a giant step forward in providing credibility to the profession. Therefore, the opening of Kepler College in 2000 was a historical event for astrology. It is the only college in the United States authorized to issue BA and MA degrees in astrological studies. Here is where to study with the best scholars, teachers, and communicators in the field. A long-distance study program is available for those interested.

Kepler College also offers online noncredit courses that anyone can take via the Kepler Community Learning Center. Classes range from two days to ten weeks in length, and the cost will vary depending upon the class taken. Students can access an online Web site to enroll in specific classes and interact with other students and instructors.

For more information, contact:

4630 200th Street SW
Suite P
Lynnwood, WA 98036
Phone: (425) 673-4292
Fax: (425) 673-4983
Web site: www.kepler.edu

Our Favorite Web sites

Of the thousands of astrological Web sites that come and go on the Internet, these have stood the test of time and are likely to still be operating when this book is published.

Astrodienst (www.astro.com)

Don't miss this fabulous international site, which has long been one of the best astrology resources on the Internet. It's a great place to view your own astrology chart. The world atlas on this site will give you the accurate longitude and latitude of your birthplace for setting up your horoscope. Then you can print out your free chart in a range of easy-to-read formats. Other attractions: a list of famous people born on your birth date, a feature that helps you choose the best vacation spot, and articles by world-famous astrologers.

AstroDatabank (www.astrodatabank.com)

When the news is breaking, you can bet this site will be the first to get accurate birthdays of the headliners. The late astrologer Lois Rodden was a stickler for factual information and her meticulous research is being continued, much to the benefit of the astrological community. The Web site specializes in charts of current newsmakers, political figures, and international celebrities. You can also participate in discussions and analysis of the charts and see what some of the world's best astrologers have to say about them. Their AstroDatabank program, which you can purchase at the site, provides thousands of birthdays sorted into categories. It's an excellent research tool.

StarIQ (www.stariq.com)

Find out how top astrologers view the latest headlines at the must-see StarIQ site. Many of the best minds in astrology comment on the latest news, stock market ups and downs, and political contenders. You can sign up to receive e-mail forecasts at the most important times keyed to your individual chart. (This is one of the best of the online forecasts.)

Astro-Noetics (www.astro-noetics.com)

For those who are ready to explore astrology's interface with politics, popular culture, and current events, here is a sophisticated site with in-depth articles and personality profiles. Lots of depth and content here for the astrology-savvy surfer.

Astrology Books (www.astroamerica.com)

The Astrology Center of America sells a wide selection of books on all aspects of astrology, from the basics to the most advanced, at this online bookstore. Also available are many hard-to-find and used books.

Astrology Scholars' Sites

See what Robert Hand, one of astrology's great teachers, has to offer on his site at www.robhand.com. A leading expert on the history of astrology, he's on the cutting edge of the latest research.

The Project Hindsight group of astrologers is devoted to restoring the astrology of the Hellenistic period, the primary source for all later Western astrology. There are fascinating articles for astrology fans on this site at www.projecthindsight.com.

Financial Astrology Sites

Financial astrology is a hot specialty, with many tipsters, players, and theorists. There are online columns, newsletters, specialized financial astrology software, and mutual funds run by astrology seers. One of the more respected financial astrologers is Ray Merriman, whose market comments on www.mmacycles.com are a must for those following the bulls and bears.

Explore Your Relationships (www.topsynergy.com)

Ever wondered how you'd get along with Brad Pitt, Halle Berry, or another famous hottie? TopSynergy offers a clever tool called a relationship analyst that will help you use astrology to analyze past, present, or possible future relationships. There's a database of celebrity horoscopes for you to partner with your own as well. It's free for unlimited use.

How to Zoom Around the Sky

If you haven't already discovered the wonders of Google Earth (www.earth.google.com), then you've been missing close-up aerial views of anyplace on the planet from your old hometown to the beaches of Hawaii. Even more fascinating for astrology buffs is the newest feature called Google Sky, a marvel of computer technology that lets you view the sky overhead from anyplace you choose. Want to see the stars over Paris at the moment? A few clicks of your mouse will take you there. Then you can follow the tracks of the sun, moon, and planets or check astronomical information and beautiful Hubble images. Go to the Google Web site to download this free program. Then get ready to take a cosmic tour around the earth and sky.

Listen to the Sounds of Your Sign

Astrology Weekly (www.astrologyweekly.com) is a Web site from Romania, with lots to offer astro surfers. Here you can check all the planetary placements for the week, get free charts, join an international discussion group, and check out charts for countries and world leaders. Of special interest is the chart generator, an easy-to-use feature that will create a natal chart. Just click on *new chart* and enter the year, month, day, time, longitude, and latitude of your birth place. Select the Placidus or Koch house system and click on *show it.* Your chart should come right up on the screen. You can then copy the link to your astrology chart, store it, and later share your chart with friends. If you don't have astrology software, this is a good way to view charts instantly. This site also has some fun ways to pass the time, such as listening to music especially chosen for your sun sign.

Stellar Gifts

If you've ever wondered what to give your astrology buddies, here's the place to find foolproof gifts. How about a mug, mouse pad, or plaque decorated with someone's chart? Would a special person like a pendant personalized with their planets? Check out www.milestonegifts.co.uk for some great ideas for putting those astrology charts to decorative use.

CHAPTER 9

The Best Astrology Software: Take Your Knowledge to the Next Level

Are you ready to begin looking at charts of friends and family? Would you like to call up your favorite celebrity's chart or check the aspects every day on your BlackBerry? Perhaps you'd like to study astrology in depth and would prefer a more comprehensive program that adapts to your needs as you learn. If you haven't discovered the wonders of astrology software, you're missing out!

Astrology technology has advanced to the point where even a computerphobe can call up a Web site on a BlackBerry browser and put a chart on the screen in seconds. It does help to have some basic knowledge of the signs, houses, planets, and especially the glyphs for the planets and the signs. Then you can practice reading charts and relating the planets to the lives of friends, relatives, and daily events, the ideal way to get more involved with astrology.

There's a program for every level of interest at all price points—starting with free. For the dabbler, there are the affordable Winstar Express, Know, and Time Passages. For the serious student, there are Astrology (free), Solar Fire, Kepler, Winstar Plus—software that does every technique on the planet and gives you beautiful chart printouts. If you're a MAC user, you'll be satisfied with the wonderful IO and Time Passages software.

However, since all the programs use the astrology symbols, or glyphs, for planets and signs, rather than written words, you should learn the glyphs before you purchase your software. Chapter 7 will help you do just that. Here are some software options for you to explore.

Easy for Beginners

Time Passages

Designed for either a Macintosh or Windows computer, Time Passages is straightforward and easy to use. It allows you to generate charts and interpretation reports for yourself or friends and loved ones at the touch of a button. If you haven't yet learned the astrology symbols, this might be the program for you. Just roll your mouse over any symbols of the planets, signs, or house cusps, and you'll be shown a description in plain English below the chart. Then click on the planet, sign, or house cusp and up pops a detailed interpretation. Couldn't be easier. A new Basic Edition, under fifty dollars at this writing, is bargain priced and ideal for beginners.

Time Passages
(866) 772-7876 (866-77-ASTRO)
Web site: www.astrograph.com

The "Know Thru Astrology" Series

This new series is designed especially for the nonastrologer. There are four programs in the series: KNOW Your Self, KNOW Your Future, KNOW Your Lover, and KNOW Your Child, each priced at an affordable $49.95 (at this writing). Though it is billed as beginner software, the KNOW series offers many sophisticated options, such as a calendar to let you navigate future or past influences, detailed chart interpretations, built-in pop-ups to show you what everything means. You'll need a PC running current Windows versions starting with Windows 98 SE, with 512 Mb RAM, and a hard drive with 170–300 Mb free space.

Matrix Software
126 South Michigan Avenue
Big Rapids, MI 49307
(800) 752-6387
Web site: www.astrologysoftware.com

Growth Opportunities

Astrolabe

Astrolabe is one of the top astrology software resources. Check out the latest version of their powerful Solar Fire software for Windows. It's a breeze to use and will grow with your increasing knowledge of astrology to the most sophisticated levels. This company also markets a variety of programs for all levels of expertise and a wide selection of computer-generated astrology readings. This is a good resource for innovative software as well as applications for older computers.

The Astrolabe Web site is a great place to start your astrology tour of the Internet. Visitors to the site are greeted with a chart of the time you log on. And you can get your chart calculated, also free, with a mini interpretation e-mailed to you.

Astrolabe
Box 1750-R
Brewster, MA 02631
Phone: (800) 843-6682
Web site: www.alabe.com

Matrix Software

You'll find a wide variety of software at student and advanced levels in all price ranges, demo disks, lots of interesting readings. Check out Winstar Express, a powerful but reasonably priced program suitable for all skill levels. The Matrix Web site offers lots of fun activities for Web surfers, such as free readings from the I Ching, the runes, and the tarot. There are many free desktop backgrounds with astrology themes.

Matrix Software
126 South Michigan Avenue
Big Rapids, MI 49307
Phone: (800) 752-6387
Web site: www.astrologysoftware.com

Astro Computing Services (ACS)

Books, software, individual charts, and telephone readings are offered by this company. Their freebies include astrology greeting cards and new moon reports. Find technical astrology materials here such as *The American Ephemeris* and PC atlases. ACS will calculate and send charts to you, a valuable service if you do not have a computer.

Starcrafts Publishing
334 Calef Hwy.
Epping, NH 03042
Phone: (866) 953-8458
Web site: www.astrocom.com

Air Software

Here you'll find powerful, creative astrology software, plus current stock market analysis. Financial astrology programs for stock market traders are a specialty. There are some interesting freebees at this site. Check out the maps of eclipse paths for any year and a free astrology clock program.

Air Software
115 Caya Avenue
West Hartford, CT 06110
Phone: (800) 659-1247
Web site: www.alphee.com

Kepler: State of the Art

Here's a program that's got everything. Gorgeous graphic images, audio-visual effects, and myriad sophisticated chart options are built into this fascinating software. It's even got an astrological encyclopedia, plus diagrams and images to help you understand advanced concepts. This program is pricey, but if you're serious about learning astrology, it's an investment that will grow with you! Check out its features at www.astrosoftware.com.

Timecycles Research: For Mac Users

Here's where Mac users can find astrology software that's as sophisticated as it gets. If you have a Mac, you'll love their beautiful graphic IO Series programs.

Time Cycles Research
P.O. Box 797
Waterford, CT 06385
(800) 827-2240
Web site: www.timecycles.com

Shareware and Freeware: The Price Is Right!

Halloran Software: A Super Shareware Program

Check out Halloran Software's Web site, which offers several levels of Windows astrology software. Beginners should consider their Astrology for Windows shareware program, which is available in unregistered demo form as a free download and in registered form for a very reasonable price.

Halloran Software
P.O. Box 75713
Los Angeles, CA 90075
(800) 732-4628
Web site: www.halloran.com

ASTROLOG

If you're computer-savvy, you can't go wrong with Walter Pullen's amazingly complete Astrology program, which is offered absolutely free at the site. The Web address is www.astrolog.org/astrolog.htm.

Astrolog is an ultrasophisticated program with all the features of much more expensive programs. It comes in versions for all formats: DOS, Windows, Mac, and UNIX. It has some cool features, such as a revolving globe and a constellation map. If you are looking for astrology software with all the bells and whistles that doesn't cost big bucks, this program has it all!

Buying a Computer with Astrology in Mind?

The good news is that astrology software is becoming more sophisticated and fun to use. However, if you've inherited an old computer, don't despair. You don't need the fastest processor and all the newest bells and whistles to run perfectly adequate astrology software. It is still possible to find programs for elder systems, including many new exciting programs.

To take full advantage of all the options, it is best to have a system that runs versions of Windows starting with Windows 98 SE. If you're buying a new computer, invest in one with as much RAM as possible, at least 1 GB. A CD drive will be necessary to load programs or an Internet connection, if you prefer to download programs online.

Mac fans who want to run Windows astrology software should invest in dual boot computers that will operate both the Mac and the Windows XP and Vista platforms.

CHAPTER 10

Ask the Expert: A Personal Reading Could Help

In these changing times, preparing ourselves for challenges ahead becomes a top priority as new issues surface in our lives. This could be the ideal time to add an astrologer to your dream team of advisers. Horoscopes can offer general advice to all members of your sign, but a personal reading can deal with what matters most to you. It can help you sort out a problem, find and use the strengths in your horoscope, set you on a more fulfilling career path, give you insight into your romantic life, or help you decide where to relocate. Many people consult astrologers to find the optimum time to schedule an important event, such as a wedding or business meeting.

Another good reason for a reading is to refine your knowledge of astrology by consulting with someone who has years of experience analyzing charts. You might choose an astrologer with a specialty that intrigues you. Armed with the knowledge of your chart that you have acquired so far, you can then learn to interpret subtle nuances or gain insight into your talents and abilities.

How do you choose when there are so many different kinds of readings available, especially since the Internet has brought astrology into the mainstream? Besides individual one-on-one readings with a professional astrologer, there are personal readings by mail, telephone, Internet, and tape. Well-advertised computer-generated reports and celebrity-sponsored readings are sure to attract your attention on commercial Web sites and in magazines. You can even purchase a reading that is incorporated into an expensive handmade fine art book. Then there are astrologers who specialize in specific areas such as finance or medical astrology. And unfortunately, there are many questionable practitioners who range from streetwise Gypsy fortune-tellers to unscrupulous scam artists.

The following basic guidelines can help you sort out your options to find the reading that's right for you.

One-on-One Consultations with a Professional Astrologer

Nothing compares to a one-on-one consultation with a professional astrologer who has analyzed thousands of charts and can pinpoint the potential in yours. During your reading, you can get your specific questions answered and discuss possible paths you might take. There are many astrologers who now combine their skills with training in psychology and are well-suited to help you examine your alternatives.

To give you an accurate reading, an astrologer needs certain information from you: the date, time, and place where you were born. (A horoscope can be cast about anyone or anything that has a specific time and place.) Most astrologers will then enter this information into a computer, which will calculate a chart in seconds, and interpret the resulting chart.

If you don't know your exact birth time, you can usually locate it at the Bureau of Vital Statistics at the city hall of the town or the county seat in the state where you were born. If you still have no success in getting your time of birth, some astrologers can estimate an approximate birth time by using past events in your life to determine the chart. This technique is called rectification.

How to Find an Astrologer

Choose your astrologer with the same care as you would any trusted adviser, such as a doctor, lawyer, or banker. Unfortunately, anyone can claim to be an astrologer—to date, there is no licensing of astrologers or universally established professional criteria. However, there are nationwide organizations of serious, committed astrologers that can help you in your search.

Good places to start your investigation are organizations such as the American Federation of Astrologers (AFA) or the National Council for Geocosmic Research (NCGR), which offer a program of study and certification. If you live near a major city, there is sure to be an active NCGR chapter or astrology club in your area; many are listed in astrology magazines available at your local newsstand. In response to many requests for referrals, both the AFA and the NCGR have directories of professional astrologers listed on their Web sites; these directories include a glossary of terms and an explanation of specialties within the astrological field. Contact the NCGR and AFA headquarters for information. (See also Chapter 8.)

What Happens in a Reading

As a potentially lucrative freelance business, astrology has always attracted self-styled experts who may not have the knowledge or the counseling experience to give a helpful reading. These astrologers can range from the well-meaning amateur to the charlatan or street-corner Gypsy who has for many years given astrology a bad name. Be very wary of astrologers who claim to have occult powers or who make pretentious claims of celebrated clients or miraculous achievements. You can often tell from the initial phone conversation if the astrologer is legitimate. He or she should ask for your birthday time and place and then conduct the conversation in a professional manner. Any astrologer who gives a reading based only on your sun sign is highly suspect.

When you arrive at the reading, the astrologer should be prepared. The consultation should be conducted in a private, quiet place. The astrologer should be interested in your problems of the moment. A good reading is interactive and involves feedback on your part, so if the reading is not relating to your concerns, you should let the astrologer know. You should feel free to ask questions and get clarifications of any technical terms. The more you actively participate, rather than expecting the astrologer to carry the reading or come forth with oracular predictions, the more meaningful your experience will be. An astrologer should help you validate your current experience and be frank about possible negative happenings, but also suggest a positive course of action.

In their approach to a reading, some astrologers may be more literal and others more intuitive. Those who have had counseling training may take a more psychological approach. Though some astrologers may seem to have an almost psychic ability, extrasensory perception or any other parapsychological talent is not essential. A very accurate picture can be drawn from the data in your horoscope chart.

An astrologer may do several charts for each client, including one for the time of birth and a progressed chart, showing the evolution from birth to the present time. According to your individual needs, there are many other possibilities, such as a chart for a different location if you are contemplating a change of place. Relationships between any two people, things, or events can be interpreted with a chart that compares one partner's horoscope with the other's. A composite chart, which uses the midpoint between planets in two individual charts to describe the relationship, is another commonly used device.

An astrologer will be particularly interested in transits, those times when cycling planets activate the planets or sensitive points in your birth chart. These indicate important events in your life.

Many astrologers offer readings recorded on tape or CD, which is another option to consider, especially if the astrologer you choose lives at a distance from you. In this case, you'll be mailed a recorded reading based on your birth chart. This type of reading is more personal than a computer printout and can give you valuable insights, though it is not equivalent to a live dialogue with the astrologer when you can discuss your specific interest and issues of the moment.

The Telephone Reading

Telephone readings come in two varieties: a dial-in taped reading, usually recorded in advance by an astrologer, or a live consultation with an "astrologer" on the other end of the line. The recorded readings are general daily or weekly forecasts, applied to all members of your sign and charged by the minute. The quality depends on the astrologer. Be aware that these readings can run up quite a telephone bill, especially if you get into the habit of calling every day. Be sure that you are aware of the per-minute cost of each call beforehand.

Live telephone readings also vary with the expertise of the astrologer. Ideally, the astrologer at the other end of the line enters your birth data into a computer, which then quickly calculates your chart. This chart will be referred to during the consultation. The advantage of a live telephone reading is that your individual chart is used and you can ask about a specific problem. However, before you invest in any reading, be sure that your astrologer is qualified and that you fully understand in advance how much you will be charged. There should be no unpleasant financial surprises later. The best astrologer is one who is recommended to you by a friend or family member.

Computer-Generated Reports

Companies that offer computer programs (such as ACS, Matrix, and Astrolabe) also offer a variety of computer-generated horoscope readings. These can be quite comprehensive, offering a beautiful printout of the chart plus many pages of detailed information about each planet and aspect of the chart. You can then study it at your convenience. Of course, the interpretations will be general, since there is no personal input from you, and might not cover your immediate concerns. Since computer-generated horoscopes are much lower in cost than live consultations, you might consider them as either a supplement or a preparation for an eventual live reading. You'll then be more familiar with your chart and able to plan specific questions in advance. They also make a terrific gift for astrology fans. In chapter 9, there are listed several companies that offer computerized readings prepared by reputable astrologers.

Whichever option you decide to pursue, may your reading be an empowering one!

CHAPTER 11

Loving Every Sign in the Zodiac

In times of change, we crave the comfort of a loving partner more than ever. If we don't have love, we want to know how and where to find it; and if we already have a loving relationship, we want to know how to make it last forever. You can use astrology to find a lover, understand the one you have, or add excitement to your current relationship. Here are sun-sign seduction tips for romancing every sign in the zodiac.

Aries: Play Hard to Get

This highly physical sign is walking dynamite with a brief attention span. Don't be too easy to get, ladies. A little challenge, a lively debate, and a merry chase only heat them up. They want to see what you're made of. Once you've lured them into your lair, be a challenge and a bit of a daredevil. Pull out your X-rated tricks. Don't give your all—let them know there's more where that came from. Make it exciting; show you're up for adventure. Wear bright red somewhere interesting. Since Aries rules the head and face, be sure to focus on these areas in your lovemaking. Use your lips, tongue, breath, and even your eyelashes to the max. Practice scalp massages and deep kissing techniques. Aries won't wait, so when you make your move, be sure you're ready to follow through. No head games or teasing!

To keep you happy, you've got to voice your *own* needs, because this lover will be focused on *his*. Teach him how to please, or this could be a one-sided adventure.

Taurus: Appeal to All Their Senses

Taurus wins as the most sensual sign, with the most sexual stamina. This man is earthy and lusty in bed; he can go on all night. This is not a sign to tease. Like a bull, he'll see red, not bed. So make him comfortable, and then bombard all his senses. Good food gets Taurus in the mood. So do the right music, fragrance, revealing clothes, and luxurious bedlinens. Give him a massage with delicious-smelling and -tasting oils; focus on the neck area.

Don't forget to turn off the phone! Taurus hates interruptions. Since they can be very vocal lovers, choose a setting where you won't be disturbed. And don't ever rush; enjoy a long, slow, delicious encounter.

Gemini: Be a Playmate

Playful Gemini loves games, so make your seduction fun. Be their lost twin soul or confidante. Good communication is essential, so share deep secrets and live out fantasies. This sign adores variety. Nothing bores Gemini more than making love the same way all the time, or bringing on the heavy emotions. So trot out all the roles you've been longing to play. Here's the perfect partner. But remember to keep it light and fun. Gemini's turn-on zone is the hands, and this sign gives the best massages. Gadgets that can be activated with a touch amuse Gemini. This sign is great at doing two things at once, like making love while watching an erotic film. Turn the cell phone off unless you want company. On the other hand, Gemini is your sign for superhot phone sex.

Gemini loves a change of scene. So experiment on the floor, in the shower, or on the kitchen table. Borrow a friend's apartment or rent a hotel room for variety.

Cancer: Use the Moon

The key to Cancer is to get this moon child in the mood. Consult the moon—a full moon is best. Wining, dining, old-fashioned courtship, and breakfast in bed are turn-ons. Whatever makes your Cancer feel secure will promote shedding inhibitions in the sack. (Don't try any of your Aries daredevil techniques here!) Cancer prefers familiar, comfortable, homey surroundings. Cancer's turn-on zone is the breasts. Cancer women often have naturally inflated chests. Cancer men may fantasize about a well-endowed playmate. If your breasts are enhanced, show them off. Cancer will want to know all your deepest secrets, so invent a few good ones. But lots of luck delving into *their* innermost thoughts!

Take your Cancer near water. The sight and sound of the sea can be their aphrodisiac. A moonlit beach, a deserted swimming pool, a Jacuzzi, or a bubble bath are good seduction spots. Listen to the rain patter on the roof in a mountain cabin.

Leo: Offer the Royal Treatment

Leo must be the best and hear it from you often. In return, they'll perform for you, telling you just what you want to hear (true or not). They like a lover with style and endurance, and to be swept off their feet and into bed. Leos like to go first-class all the way, so build them up with lots of attention, wining and dining, and special gifts.

Never mention other lovers or make them feel second-best. A sure signal for Leo to look elsewhere is a competitive spouse. Leos take great pride in their bodies, so you should pour on the admiration. A few well-placed mirrors could inspire them. So would a striptease with beautiful lingerie, expensive fragrance on the sheets, and, if female, an occasional luxury hotel room, with champagne and caviar delivered by room service. Leo's erogenous zone is the lower back, so a massage with expensive oils would make your lion purr with pleasure.

Virgo: Let Them Be the Teacher

Virgo's standards are so sky-high that you may feel intimidated at first. The key to pleasing fussy Virgo lovers is to look for the hot fantasy beneath their cool surface. They're really looking for someone to make over. So let Virgo play teacher, and you play the willing student; the doctor-patient routine works as well. Be Eliza Doolittle to his Henry Higgins.

Let Virgo help you improve your life, quit smoking, learn French, and diet. Read an erotic book together, and then practice the techniques. Or study esoteric, erotic exercises from the Far East.

The Virgo erogenous zone is the tummy area, which should be your base of operations. Virgo likes things pristine and clean. Fall onto crisp, immaculate white sheets. Wear a sheer virginal white nightie. Smell shower-fresh with no heavy perfume. Be sure your surroundings pass the hospital test. A shower together afterward (with great-smelling soap) could get the ball rolling again.

Libra: Look Your Best

Libra must be turned on aesthetically. Make sure you look as beautiful as possible, and wear something stylishly seductive but never vulgar. Have a mental affair first, as you flirt and flatter this sign. Then proceed to the physical. Approach Libra like a dance partner, ready to waltz or tango.

Libra must be in the mood for love; otherwise, forget it. Any kind of ugliness is a turnoff. Provide an elegant and harmonious atmosphere, with no loud noise, clashing colors, or uncomfortable beds. Libra is not an especially spontaneous lover, so it is best to spend time warming them up. Libra's back is his erogenous zone, your cue to provide back rubs with scented potions. Once in bed, you can be a bit aggressive sexually. Libra loves strong, decisive moves. Set the scene, know what you want, and let Libra be happy to provide it.

Scorpio: Be an All-or-Nothing Lover

Scorpio is legendary in bed, often called the sex sign of the zodiac. But seducing them is often a power game. Scorpio likes to be in control, even the quiet, unassuming ones. Scorpio loves a mystery, so don't tell all. Keep them guessing about you, offering tantalizing hints along the way. The hint of danger often turns Scorpio on, so you'll find members of this sign experimenting with the exotic and highly erotic forms of sex. Sadomasochism, bondage, or anything that tests the limits of power could be a turn-on for Scorpio.

Invest in some sexy black leather and some powerful music. Clothes that lace, buckle, or zip tempt Scorpio to untie you. Present yourself as a mysterious package just waiting to be unwrapped.

Once in bed, there are no holds barred with Scorpio. They'll find your most pleasurable pressure points, and touch you as you've never been touched before. They are quickly aroused (the genital area belongs to this sign) and are willing to try anything. But they can be possessive. Don't expect your Scorpio to share you with anyone. It's all or nothing for them.

Sagittarius: Be a Happy Wanderer

Sagittarius men are the Don Juans of the zodiac—love-'em-and-leave-'em types who are difficult to pin down. Your seduction strategy is to join them in their many pursuits, and then hook them with love on the road. Sagittarius enjoys sex in venues that suggest movement; planes, SUVs, or boats. But a favorite turn-on place is outdoors, in nature. A deserted hiking path, a field of tall grass, or a remote woodland glade—all give the centaur sexy ideas. Athletic Sagittarius might go for some personal training in an empty gym. Join your Sagittarius for amorous aerobics, meditate together, and explore the tantric forms of sex. Lovemaking after hiking and skiing would be healthy fun.

Sagittarius enjoys lovers from exotic ethnic backgrounds, or lovers met in spiritual pursuits or on college campuses. Sagittarius are great cheerleaders and motivators, and will enjoy feeling that they have inspired you to be all that you can be.

There may be a canine or feline companion sharing your Sagittarius lover's bed with you, so check your allergies. And bring Fido or Felix a toy to keep them occupied.

Capricorn: Take Their Mind off Business

The great news about Capricorn lovers is that they improve with age. They are probably the sexiest seniors. So stick around, if you have a young one. They're lusty in bed (it's not the sign of the goat for nothing), and can be quite raunchy and turned on by X-rated words and deeds. If this is not your thing, let them know. The Capricorn erogenous zone is the knees. Some discreet fondling in public places could be your opener. Capricorn tends to think of sex as part of a game plan for the future. They are well-organized, and might regard lovemaking as relaxation after a long day's work. This sign often combines business with pleasure. So look for a Capricorn where there's a convention, trade show, or work-related conference.

Getting Capricorn's mind off his agenda and onto yours could take some doing. Separate him from his buddies by whispering sexy secrets in his ear. Then convince him you're an asset to his image and a boon to his health. Though he may seem uptight at first, you'll soon discover he's a love animal who makes a wonderful and permanent pet.

Aquarius: Give Them Enough Space

This sign really does not want an all-consuming passion or an all-or-nothing relationship. Aquarius needs space. But once they feel free to experiment with a spontaneous and exciting partner, Aquarius can give you a far-out sexual adventure.

Passion begins in the mind, so a good mental buildup is key. Aquarius is an inventive sign who believes love is a playground without rules. Plan surprise, unpredictable encounters in unusual places. Find ways to make love transcendental, an extraordinary and unique experience. Be ready to try anything Aquarius suggests, if only once. Calves and ankles are the special Aquarius erogenous zone, so perfect your legwork.

Be careful not to be too possessive. Your Aquarius needs lots of space and tolerance for friends (including old lovers) and their many outside interests.

Pisces: Live Their Fantasies

Pisces is the sign of fantasy and imagination. This sign has great theatrical talent. Pisces looks for lovers who will take care of them. Pisces will return the favor! Here is someone who can psych out your deepest desires without mentioning them. Pisces falls for sob stories and is always ready to empathize. It wouldn't hurt to have a small problem for Pisces to help you overcome. It might help if you cry on his shoulder, for this sign needs to be needed. Use your imagination when setting the scene for love. A dramatic setting brings out Pisces theatrical talents. Or creatively use the element of water. Rain on the roof, waterfalls, showers, beach houses, water beds, and Jacuzzis could turn up the heat. Experiment with pulsating jets of water. Take midnight skinny-dips in deserted pools.

The Pisces erogenous zone is the feet. This is your cue to give a sensuous foot massage using scented lotions. Let him paint your toes. Beautiful toenails in sexy sandals are a special turn-on.

Your Hottest Love Match

Here's a tip for finding your hottest love match. If your lover's Mars sign makes favorable aspects to your Venus, is in the same element (earth, air, fire, water), or is in the same sign, your lover will do what you want done! Mars influences how we act when we make love, while Venus shows what we like done to us. Sometimes fighting and making up is the sexiest fun of all. If you're the type who needs a spark to keep lust alive (you know who you are!), then look for Mars and Venus in different signs of the same quality (fixed or cardinal or mutable). For instance, a fixed sign (Taurus, Leo, Scorpio, Aquarius) paired with another fixed sign can have a sexy tug-of-war before you finally surrender. Two cardinal signs (Aries, Cancer, Libra, Capricorn) set off passionate fireworks when they clash. Mutable signs (Gemini, Virgo, Sagittarius, Pisces) play a fascinating game of cat and mouse, never quite catching each other.

Your Most Seductive Time

The best time for love is when Venus is in your sign, making you the most desirable sign in the zodiac. This only lasts about three weeks (unless Venus is retrograde) so don't waste time! And find out the time this year when Venus is in your sign by consulting the Venus chart at the end of chapter 5.

What's the Sexiest Sign?

It depends on what sign you are. Astrology has traditionally given this honor to Scorpio, the sign associated with the sex organs. However, we are all a combination of different signs (and turn-ons). Gemini's communicating ability and manual dexterity could deliver the magic touch. Cancer's tenderness and understanding could bring out your passion more than regal Leo.

Which Is the Most Faithful Sign?

The earth signs of Capricorn, Taurus, and Virgo are usually the most faithful. They tend to be more home- and family-oriented, and they are usually choosy about their mates. It's impractical, inconvenient, and probably expensive to play around, or so they think.

Who'll Play Around?

The mutable signs of Gemini, Pisces, and Sagittarius win the playboy or playgirl sweepstakes. These signs tend to be changeable, fickle, and easily bored. But they're so much fun!

CHAPTER 12

Financial Tips from the Stars

Getting the most bang from our buck will be our personal challenge this year, as we continue to learn to live within our means and balance our budgets. One of the advantages of astrology is that we can know the natural direction of the cosmic forces in advance and make financial plans accordingly.

Over the past few years, we've experienced a dramatic shift from the expansive risk taking of Pluto in Sagittarius to the conservative, thrift-promoting Pluto in Capricorn. This influence should continue for several years. Financially savvy astrologers also look to the movement of Jupiter, the planet of luck and expansion, for growth opportunities. Jupiter gives an extra boost to the sign it is passing through. Jupiter moves through Pisces, a sign that Jupiter especially favors, so Pisces and fellow water signs, Cancer and Scorpio, receive extra-lucky rays. Most of us could benefit from using some Pisces-inspired creativity, insight, and imagination especially in the area of our horoscope where Jupiter will be giving us growth opportunities. Pisces will give us the imaginative ideas; then Jupiter enters Aries briefly over the summer and for a lengthy stay next year, which should give us the courage and pioneering spirit to pursue them.

Aries

You've got a taste for fast money, quick turnover, and edgy investments, with no patience for gradual, long-term gains.

You're an impulse buyer with the nerve for risky tactics that could backfire. On the other hand, you're a pioneer who can see into the future, who dares to take a gamble on a new idea or product that could change the world . . . like Sam Walton of the Wal-Mart stores, who changed the way we shop. You need a backup plan in case one of your big ideas burns out. To protect your money, get a backup plan you can follow without thinking about it. Have a percentage of your income automatically put into a savings or retirement account. Then give yourself some extra funds to play with. Your weak point is your impatience; so you're not one to wait out a slow market or watch savings slowly accumulate. When Jupiter moves into Aries temporarily this summer, you'll want to move full steam ahead. However, you may have to reevaluate your goals in the fall. Save your big moves for next year, when Jupiter reenters Aries and you can make real progress.

Taurus

You're a saver who loves to see your cash, as well as your possessions, accumulate. You have no qualms about steadily increasing your fortune. You're a savvy trader and a shrewd investor, in there for long-term gains. You have low toleration for risk; you hate to lose anything. But you do enjoy luxuries, and may need to reward yourself frequently. You might pass up an opportunity because it seems too risky, but you should take a chance once in a while. Since you're inspired by Jupiter in Pisces and Aries this year, it's time to support your long-range goals and ideals by exploring socially conscious investments, especially in the clean-energy field and the creative arts. You're especially lucky in real estate or any occupation that requires appraising and trading, as well as earth-centered businesses like organic farming and conservation.

Gemini

With Gemini, the cash can flow in and then out just as quickly. You naturally multi-task, and you are sure to have several projects going at once, as well as several credit cards, which can easily get out of hand. Saving is not one of your strong points—too boring. You fall in and out of love with different ideas; you have probably tried a round of savings techniques. Diversification is your best strategy. Have several different kinds of investments—at least one should be a long-term plan. Set savings goals and then regularly deposit small amounts into your accounts. Follow the lead of Gemini financial adviser Suze Orman and get a good relationship going with your money! With lucky Jupiter accenting your public image, there should be new career opportunities this year. Investigate careers in communications and the media.

Cancer

You can be a natural moneymaker with your peerless intuition. You can spot a winner that everyone else misses. Consider Cancer success stories like those of cosmetics queen Estee Lauder and Roxanne Quimby, of Burt's Bees, who turned her friend's stash of beeswax into a thriving cosmetics business. Who knew? So trust your intuition. You are a saver who always has a backup plan, just in case. Remember to treat and nurture yourself as well as others. Investments in the food industry, restaurants, hotels, shipping, and water-related industries are Cancer territory. You're one of the luckiest signs this year, so keep your antennae tuned for new investment opportunities.

Leo

You love the first-class lifestyle, but may not always have the resources to support it. Finding a way to fund your extravagant tastes is the Leo challenge. Some courses in money management or an expert financial coach could set you on the right track. However, you're also a terrific salesperson, and you're fabulous in high-profile jobs that pay a lot. You're the community tastemaker; you satisfy your appetite for "the best" by working for a quality company that sells luxury goods, splendid real estate, dream vacations, and first-class travel—that way you'll have access to the lifestyle without having to pay for it. This year, Jupiter brings luck through fortunate partnerships and travel.

Virgo

Your sign is a stickler for details, which includes your money management. You like to follow your spending and saving closely; you enjoy planning, budgeting, and price comparison. Your sign usually has no problem sticking to a savings or investment plan. You have a critical eye for quality, and you like to bargain and to shop to get the best value. In fact, Warren Buffet, a Virgo billionaire, is known for value investing. You buy cheap and sell at a profit. Investing in health care, organic products, and food could be profitable for you. With Jupiter in Pisces accenting partnerships, you might want to team up for investing purposes this year.

Libra

Oh, do you ever love to shop! And you often have an irresistible urge to acquire an exquisite object or a designer dress you can't really afford or to splurge on the perfect antique armoire. You don't like to settle for second-rate or bargain buys. Learning to prioritize your spending is especially difficult for your sign, so try to find a good money manager to do it for you. Following a strictly balanced budget is your key to financial success. With Libra's keen eye for quality and good taste, you are a savvy picker at auctions and antiques fairs, so you might be able to turn around your purchase for a profit. With Jupiter accenting the care and maintenance part of your life, this is an excellent year to put your finances in order and balance the budget.

Scorpio

Scorpios prefer to stay in control of their finances at all times. You're sure to have a financial-tracking program on your computer. You're not an impulse buyer, unless you see something that immediately turns you on. Rely on your instincts! Scorpio is the sign of credit cards, taxes, and loans, so you are able to use these tools cleverly. Investing for Scorpio is rarely casual. You'll do extensive research and track your investments by reading the financial pages, annual reports, and profit-loss statements. Investigate the arts, media, and oil and water projects for Jupiter-favored investments this year.

Sagittarius

Sagittarius is a natural gambler, with a high tolerance for risk. It's important for you to learn when to hold 'em, and when to fold 'em, as the song goes, by setting limits on your risk taking and covering your assets. You enjoy the thrill of playing the stock market, where you could win big and lose big. Money itself is rarely the object for Sagittarius—it's the game that counts. Since your sign rarely saves for a rainy day, your best strategy might be a savings plan that transfers a certain amount into a savings account. Regular bill-paying plans are another strategy to keep you on track. Jupiter favors investing in home improvements and family-related businesses this year.

Capricorn

You're one of the strongest money managers in the zodiac, which should serve you well this year when Jupiter, the planet of luck and expansion, is blessing your house of finance. You're a born bargain hunter and clever negotiator—a saver rather than a spender. You are the sign of self-discipline, which works well when it comes to sticking with a budget and living frugally while waiting for resources to accumulate. You are likely to plan carefully for your elder years, profiting from long-term investments. You have a keen sense of value, and you will pick up a bargain and then turn it around at a nice profit. Jupiter favors the communications industry and opportunities in your local area this year.

Aquarius

There should be many chances to speculate on forward-looking ventures this year. The Aquarius trait of unpredictability extends to your financial life, where you surprise us all with your ability to turn something totally unique into a money spinner. Consider your wealthy sign mates Oprah Winfrey and Michael Bloomberg, who have been able to intuit what the public will buy at a given moment. Some of your ideas might sound far-out, but they turn out to be right on the money. Investing in high-tech companies that are on the cutting edge of their field is good for Aquarius. You'll probably intuit which ones will stay the course. You'll feel good about investing in companies that improve the environment, such as new types of fuel, or ones that are related to your favorite cause.

Pisces

Luck is with you this year! The typical Pisces is probably the sign least interested in money management. However, there are many billionaires born under your sign, such as Michael Dell, David Geffen, and Steve Jobs. Generally they have made money from innovative ideas and left the details to others. That might work for you. Find a Scorpio, Capricorn, or Virgo to help you set a profitable course and systematically save (which is not in your nature). Sign up for automatic bill paying so you won't have to think about it. If you keep in mind how much less stressful life will be and how much more you can do when you're not worried about paying bills, you might be motivated enough to stick to a sensible budget. Investment-wise, consider anything to do with water—off-shore drilling, water conservation and purifying, shipping, and seafood. Petroleum is also ruled by your sign, as are institutions related to hospitals.

CHAPTER 13

Children of 2010

Parents of several children may see a marked difference between children born in 2010 and those born more than two years ago, because the cosmic atmosphere has changed, which should imprint the personalities of this year's children.

Astrologers look to the slow-moving outer planets—Uranus, Neptune, and Pluto—to describe a generation. When an outer planet changes signs, this indicates a significant shift in energy, which is the case in 2010. In the first half of the year, Uranus and Jupiter in Pisces continue the visionary and creative influence of that sign, which will be reflected in the children born then. However, Uranus moves briefly into fiery Aries in June, which will be accompanied by Jupiter, the planet of expansion, indicating a very astrologically active summer of 2010. Children born during the warm months will reflect this with more drive and energy. After Uranus retrogrades back into Pisces in mid-August for the remainder of the year, the atmosphere becomes somewhat calmer. Neptune still passing through Aquarius and Pluto in Capricorn should add vision and practicality to the personality of this year's children. This generation will be focused on saving the planet and on making things work in order to clear the path for the future. Saturn in Libra will enter the mixture, teaching them diplomacy in getting along with others.

Astrology can be an especially helpful tool when used to design an environment that enhances and encourages each child's positive qualities. Some parents start before conception, planning the birth of their child as far as possible to harmonize with the signs of other family members. However, each baby has its own schedule, so if yours arrives a week early or late, or elects a different sign than you'd planned, recognize that the new sign may be more in line with the mission your child is here to accomplish. In other words, if you were hoping for a Libra child and he arrives during Virgo, that Virgo energy may be just what is needed to stimulate or complement your family. Remember that there are many astrological elements besides the sun sign that indicate strong family ties. Usually each child will share a particular planetary placement, an emphasis on a particular sign or house, or a certain chart configuration with his parents and other family members. Often there is a significant planetary angle that will define the parent-child relationship, such as family sun signs that form a T-square or a triangle.

One important thing you can do is to be sure the exact moment of birth is recorded. This will be essential in calculating an accurate astrological chart. The following descriptions can be applied to the sun or moon sign (if known) of a child—the sun sign will describe basic personality and the moon sign indicates the child's emotional needs.

The Aries Child

Baby Aries is quite a handful. This energetic child will walk—and run—as soon as possible, and perform daring feats of exploration. Caregivers should be vigilant. Little Aries seems to know no fear (and is especially vulnerable to head injuries). Many Aries children, in their rush to get on with life, seem hyperactive, and they are easily frustrated when they can't get their own way. Violent temper tantrums and dramatic physical displays are par for the course with this child, requiring a time-out mat or naughty chair.

The very young Aries should be monitored carefully, since he is prone to take risks and may injure himself. Aries love to take things apart and may break toys easily, but with encouragement, the child will develop formidable coordination. Aries's bossy tendencies should be molded into leadership qualities, rather than bullying, which should be easy to do with this year's babies. Encourage these children to take out aggressions and frustrations in active, competitive sports, where they usually excel. When young Aries learns to focus energies long enough to master a subject and learns consideration for others, the indomitable Aries spirit will rise to the head of the class.

Aries born in 2010 will be a more subdued version of this sign, but still loaded with energy. The Capricorn effect should make little Aries easier to discipline and more focused on achievement. A natural leader!

The Taurus Child

This is a cuddly, affectionate child who eagerly explores the world of the senses, especially the senses of taste and touch. The Taurus child can be a big eater and will put on weight easily if not encouraged to exercise. Since this child likes comfort and gravitates to beauty, try coaxing little Taurus to exercise to music, or take him or her out of doors, with hikes or long walks. Though Taurus may be a slow learner, this sign has an excellent retentive memory and generally masters a subject thoroughly. Taurus is interested in results and will see each project patiently through to completion, continuing long after others have given up. This year's earth sign planets will give him a wonderful sense of support and accomplishment.

Choose Taurus toys carefully to help develop innate talents. Construction toys, such as blocks or erector sets, appeal to their love of building. Paints or crayons develop their sense of color. Many Taurus have musical talent and love to sing, which is apparent at a young age.

This year's Taurus will want a pet or two, and a few plants of his own. Give little Taurus a small garden, and watch the natural green thumb develop. This child has a strong sense of acquisition and an early grasp of material value. After filling a piggy bank, Taurus graduates to a savings account, before other children have started to learn the value of money.

Little Taurus gets a bonanza of good luck from Jupiter in compatible Pisces, supported by Pluto in Capricorn and Saturn retrograding back into Virgo, a compatible earth sign. These should give little Taurus an especially easygoing disposition and provide many opportunities to live up to his sign's potential.

The Gemini Child

Little Gemini will talk as soon as possible, filling the air with questions and chatter. This is a friendly child who enjoys social contact, seems to require company, and adapts quickly to different surroundings. Geminis have quick minds that easily grasp the use of words, books, and telephones, and will probably learn to talk and read at an earlier age than most. Though they are fast learners, Gemini may have a short attention span, darting from subject to subject. Projects and games that help focus the mind could be used to help them concentrate. Musical instruments, typewriters, and computers help older Gemini children combine mental with manual dexterity. Geminis should be encouraged to finish what they start before they go on to another project. Otherwise, they can become jack-of-all-trade types who have trouble completing anything they do. Their disposition is usually cheerful and witty, making these children popular with their peers and delightful company at home.

This year's Gemini baby is impulsive and full of energy, with a strong Aries influence in his life. He will be highly independent and original, a go-getter. When he grows up, Gemini may change jobs several times before he finds a position that satisfies his need for stimulation and variety.

The Cancer Child

This emotional, sensitive child is especially influenced by patterns set in early life. Young Cancers cling to their first memories as well as their childhood possessions. They thrive in calm emotional waters, with a loving, protective mother, and usually remain close to her (even if their relationship with her was difficult) throughout their lives. Divorce and death—anything that disturbs the safe family unit—are devastating to Cancers, who may need extra support and reassurance during a family crisis.

They sometimes need a firm hand to push the positive, creative side of their personality and discourage them from getting swept away by emotional moods or resorting to emotional manipulation to get their way. If this child is praised and encouraged to find creative expression, Cancers will be able to express their positive side consistently, on a firm, secure foundation.

This year's Cancer baby may run against type, thanks to a meeting of Jupiter and Uranus in hyperactive Aries, which might make him much more outgoing and energetic than usual. He should have natural leadership tendencies, which should be encouraged, and the parents' challenge will be to find positive outlets for his energy.

The Leo Child

Leo children love the limelight and will plot to get the lion's share of attention. These children assert themselves with flair and drama, and can behave like tiny tyrants to get their way. But in general, they have a sunny, positive disposition and are rarely subject to blue moods.

At school, they're the types voted most popular, head cheerleader, or homecoming queen. Leo is sure to be noticed for personality, if not for stunning looks or academic work; the homely Leo will be a class clown, and the unhappy Leo can be the class bully.

Above all, a Leo child cannot tolerate being ignored for long. Drama or performing-arts classes, sports, and school politics are healthy ways for Leo to be a star. But Leos must learn to take lesser roles occasionally, or they will have some painful putdowns in store. Usually, their popularity is well earned; they are hard workers who try to measure up to their own high standards—and usually succeed.

This year's Leo should be a highly active version of the sign, with Saturn in Libra teaching lessons of balance and diplomacy in relationships, while Jupiter and Uranus in Aries amp up the energy level and Pluto in Capricorn demands focus and results. Good use of this energy could produce pioneers, fearless natural leaders who could change the world for the better.

The Virgo Child

The young Virgo can be a quiet, rather serious child, with a quick, intelligent mind. Early on, little Virgo shows far more attention to detail and concern with small things than other children. Little Virgo has a built-in sense of order and a fascination with how things work. It is important for these children to have a place of their own, which they can order as they wish and where they can read or busy themselves with crafts and hobbies. This child's personality can be very sensitive. Little Virgo may get hyper and overreact to seemingly small irritations, which can take the form of stomach upsets or delicate digestive systems. But this child will flourish where there is mental stimulation and a sense of order. Virgos thrive in school, especially in writing or language skills, and they seem truly happy when buried in books. Chances are, young Virgo will learn to read ahead of classmates. Hobbies that involve detail work or that develop fine craftsmanship are especially suited to young Virgos.

Baby Virgo of 2010 is likely to be an early talker, and will show concern for the welfare of others. This child should be a natural communicator and may show an interest in the arts or the legal profession.

The Libra Child

The Libra child learns early about the power of charm and appearance. This is often a very physically appealing child with an enchanting dimpled smile, who is naturally sociable and enjoys the company of both children and adults. It is a rare Libra child who is a discipline problem, but when their behavior is unacceptable, they respond better to calm discussion than displays of emotion, especially if the discussion revolves around fairness. Because young Libras without a strong direction tend to drift with the mood of the group, these children should be encouraged to develop their unique talents and powers of discrimination, so they can later stand on their own.

In school, this child is usually popular and will often have to choose between social invitations and studies. In the teen years, social pressures mount as the young Libra begins to look for a partner. This is the sign of best friends, so Libra's choice of companions can have a strong effect on his future direction. Beautiful Libra girls may be tempted to go steady or have an unwise early marriage. Chances are, both sexes will fall in and out of love several times in their search for the ideal partner.

Little Libra of 2010 is an especially creative, expressive child, who may have strong artistic talents. This child is endowed with much imagination, as well as social skills.

The Scorpio Child

The Scorpio child may seem quiet and shy, but will surprise others with intense feelings and formidable willpower. Scorpio children are single-minded when they want something and intensely passionate about whatever they do. One of a caregiver's tasks is to teach this child to balance activities and emotions, yet at the same time to make the most of his great concentration and intense commitment.

Since young Scorpios do not show their depth of feelings easily, parents will have to learn to read almost imperceptible signs that troubles are brewing beneath the surface. Both Scorpio boys and girls enjoy games of power and control on or off the playground. Scorpio girls may take an early interest in the opposite sex, masquerading as tomboys, while Scorpio boys may be intensely competitive and loners. When her powerful energies are directed into work, sports, or challenging studies, Scorpio is a superachiever, focused on a goal. With trusted friends, young Scorpio is devoted and caring—the proverbial friend through thick and thin, loyal for life.

Scorpio 2010 has a strong emphasis on achievement and success. Uranus and lucky Jupiter in Pisces in their house of creativity should put them on the cutting edge of whichever field they choose.

The Sagittarius Child

This restless, athletic child will be out of the playpen and off on explorative adventures as soon as possible. Little Sagittarius is remarkably well-coordinated, attempting daredevil feats on any wheeled vehicle from scooters to skateboards. These natural athletes need little encouragement to channel their energies into sports. Their cheerful friendly dispositions earn them popularity in school, and once they have found a subject where their talent and imagination can soar, they will do well academically. They love animals, especially horses, and will be sure to have a pet or two, if not a home zoo. When they are old enough to take care of themselves, they'll clamor to be off on adventures of their own, away from home, if possible.

This is a child who loves to travel, who will not get homesick at summer camp, and who may sign up to be a foreign-exchange student or spend summers abroad. Outdoor adventure appeals to little Sagittarius, especially if it involves an active sport, such as skiing, cycling or mountain climbing. Give them enough space and encouragement, and their fiery spirit will propel them to achieve high goals.

Baby Sagittarius of 2010 has a natural generosity of spirit and an optimistic, social nature. Home and family will be especially important to him, though he may have an unconventional family life. He'll have an ability to look past the surface of things to seek out what has lasting value.

The Capricorn Child

These purposeful, goal-oriented children will work to capacity if they feel this will bring results. They're not ones who enjoy work for its own sake—there must be a goal in sight. Authority figures can do much to motivate these children, but once set on an upward path, young Capricorn will mobilize his energy and talent and work harder, and with more perseverance, than any other sign. Capricorn has built-in self-discipline that can achieve remarkable results, even if lacking the flashy personality, quick brainpower, or penetrating insight of others. Once involved, young Capricorn will stick to a task until it is mastered. This child also knows how to use others to his advantage and may well become the team captain or class president.

A wise parent will set realistic goals for the Capricorn child, paving the way for the early thrill of achievement. Youngsters should be encouraged to express their caring, feeling side to others, as well as their natural aptitude for leadership. Capricorn children may be especially fond of grandparents and older relatives, and will enjoy spending time with them and learning from them. It is not uncommon for young Capricorns to have an older mentor or teacher who guides them. With their great respect for authority, Capricorn children will take this influence very much to heart.

The Capricorn born in 2010 should be a good talker, with sharp mental abilities. He is likely to be social and outgoing, with lots of friends and closeness to brothers and sisters.

The Aquarius Child

The Aquarius child has a well-focused, innovative mind that often streaks so far ahead of peers that this child seems like an oddball. Routine studies never hold the restless youngster for long; he or she will look for another, more experimental place to try out his ideas and develop his inventions. Life is a laboratory to the inquiring Aquarius mind. School politics, sports, science, and the arts offer scope for their talents. But if there is no room for expression within approved social limits, Aquarius is sure to rebel. Questioning institutions and religions comes naturally, so these children may find an outlet elsewhere, becoming rebels with a cause. It is better not to force these children to conform, but rather to channel forward-thinking young minds into constructive group activities.

This year's Aquarius will have special financial talent. Luck and talent are his and fame could be in the stars!

The Pisces Child

Give young Pisces praise, applause, and a gentle, but firm, push in the right direction. Lovable Pisces children may be abundantly talented, but may be hesitant to express themselves, because they are quite sensitive and easily hurt. It is a parent's challenge to help them gain self-esteem and self-confidence. However, this same sensitivity makes them trusted friends who'll have many confidants as they develop socially. It also endows many Pisces with spectacular creative talent.

Pisces adores drama and theatrics of all sorts; therefore, encourage them to channel their creativity into art forms rather than indulging in emotional dramas. Understand that they may need more solitude than other children may as they develop their creative ideas. But though daydreaming can be creative, it is important that these natural dreamers not dwell too long in the world of fantasy. Teach them practical coping skills for the real world.

Since Pisces are sensitive physically, parents should help them build strong bodies with proper diet and regular exercise. Young Pisces may gravitate to more individual sports, such as swimming, sailing, and skiing, rather than to team sports. Or they may prefer more artistic physical activities, like dance or ice-skating.

Born givers, these children are often drawn to the underdog (they quickly fall for sob stories) and attract those who might take advantage of their empathic nature. Teach them to choose friends wisely, to set boundaries in relationships, and to protect their emotional vulnerability—invaluable lessons in later life.

With the planet Uranus now in Pisces along with lucky Jupiter, the 2010 baby belongs to a generation of Pisces movers and shakers. This child may have a rebellious streak that rattles the status quo. But this generation also has a visionary nature, which will be much concerned with the welfare of the world at large.

CHAPTER 14

Give the Perfect Gift to Every Sign

So often we're in a quandary about what to give a loved one, someone who has everything, that hard-to-please friend, or a fascinating new person in your life, or about the right present for a wedding, birthday, or hostess gift. Why not let astrology help you make the perfect choice by appealing to each sun sign's personality. When you're giving a gift, you're also making a memory, so it should be a special occasion. The gift that's most appreciated is one that touches the heart, reminds you both of a shared experience, or shows that the giver has really cared enough to consider the recipient's personality.

In general, the water signs (Cancer, Pisces, Scorpio) enjoy romantic, sentimental, and imaginative gifts given in a very personal way. Write your loved one a poem or a song to express your feelings. Assemble an album of photos or mementos of all the good times you've shared. Appeal to their sense of fantasy. Scorpio Richard Burton had the right idea when he gave Pisces Elizabeth Taylor a diamond bracelet hidden in lavender roses (her favorite color).

Fire signs (Aries, Leo, Sagittarius) appreciate a gift presented with lots of flair. Pull out the drama, like the actor who dazzled his Aries sweetheart by presenting her with trash cans overflowing with daisies.

Air signs (Gemini, Libra, Aquarius) love to be surprised with unusual gifts. The Duke of Windsor gave his elegant Gemini duchess, Wallis Windsor, fabulous jewels engraved with love notes and secret messages in their own special code.

Earth signs (Taurus, Virgo, Capricorn) value solid, tangible gifts or ones that appeal to all the senses. Delicious gourmet treats, scented body lotions, the newest CDs, the gift of a massage, or stocks and bonds are sure winners! Capricorn Elvis Presley once received a gold-plated piano from his wife.

Here are some specific ideas for each sign:

Aries

These are the trendsetters of the zodiac, who appreciate the latest thing! For Aries, it's the excitement that counts, so present your gift in a way that will knock their socks off. Aries is associated with the head, so a jaunty hat, hair ornaments, chandelier earrings, sunglasses, and hair-taming devices are good possibilities. Aries love games of any kind that offer a real challenge, like war video games, military themes, or rousing music with a beat. Anything red is a good bet: red flowers, red gems, and red accessories. How about giving Aries a way to let off steam with a gym membership or aerobic-dancing classes? Monogram a robe with a nickname in red.

Taurus

These are touchy-feely people who love things that appeal to all their senses. Find something that sounds, tastes, smells, feels, or looks good. And don't stint on quality or comfort. Taurus know the value of everything and will be aware of the price tag. Taurus foodies will appreciate chef-worthy kitchen gadgets, the latest cookbook, and gourmet treats. Taurus is a great collector. Find out what their passion is and present them with a rare item or a beautiful storage container such as an antique jewelry box. Green-thumb Taurus would love some special plants or flowers, garden tools, beautiful plant containers. Appeal to their sense of touch with fine fabrics—high-thread-count sheets, cashmere, satin, and mohair. One of the animal-loving signs, Taurus might appreciate a retractable leash or soft bed for the dog or cat. Get them a fine wallet or checkbook cover. They'll use it often.

Gemini

Mercury-ruled Gemini appreciates gifts that appeal to their mind. The latest book or novel, a talked-about film, a CD from a hot new singer, or a high-tech gadget might appeal. A beautiful diary or a tape recorder would record their adventures. Since Geminis often do two things at once, a telephone gadget that leaves their hands free would be appreciated. In fact, a new telephone device or superphone would appeal to these great communicators. Gloves, rings, and bracelets accent their expressive hands. Clothes from an interesting new designer appeal to their sense of style. You might try giving Gemini a variety of little gifts in a beautiful box or a Christmas stocking. A tranquil massage at a local spa would calm Gemini's sensitive nerves. Find an interesting way to wrap your gift. Nothing boring, please!

Cancer

Cancer is associated with home and family, so anything to do with food, entertaining at home, and family life is a good bet. Beautiful dishes or serving platters, silver items, fine crystal and linen, gourmet cookware, cooking classes or the latest DVD from a cooking teacher might be appreciated. Cancer designers Vera Wang and Giorgio Armani have perfected the Cancer style and have many home products available, as well as their elegant designer clothing. Naturally, anything to do with the sea is a possibility: pearls, coral, or shell jewelry. Boat and water-sports equipment might work. Consider cruise wear for traveling Cancers. Sentimental Cancer loves antiques and silver frames for family photos. Cancer people are often good photographers, so consider frames, albums, and projectors to showcase their work. Present your gift in a personal way with a special note.

Leo

Think big with Leo and appeal to this sign's sense of drama. Go for the gold (Leo's color) with gold jewelry, designer clothing, or big attention-getting accessories. Follow their signature style, which could be superelegant, like Jacqueline Onassis, or superstar, like Madonna or Jennifer Lopez. This sign is always ready for the red carpet and stays beautifully groomed, so stay within these guidelines when choosing your gift. Feline motifs and animal prints are usually a hit. The latest grooming aids, high-ticket cosmetics, and mirrors reflect their best image. Beautiful hairbrushes tame their manes. Think champagne, high-thread-count linens, and luxurious loungewear or lingerie. Make Leo feel special with a custom portrait or photo shoot with your local star photographer. Be sure to go for spectacular wrapping, with beautiful paper and ribbons. Present your gift with a flourish!

Virgo

Virgo usually has a special subject of interest and would appreciate relevant books, films, lectures, or classes. Choose health-oriented things: gifts to do with fitness and self-improvement. Virgo enjoys brainteasers, crossword puzzles, computer programs, organizers, and digital planners. Fluffy robes, bath products, and special soaps appeal to Virgo's sense of cleanliness. Virgo loves examples of good, practical design: efficient telephones, beautiful briefcases, computer cases, desk accessories. Choose natural fibers and quiet colors when choosing clothes for Virgo. Virgo has high standards, so go for quality when choosing a gift.

Libra

Whatever you give this romantic sign, go for beauty and romance. Libra loves accessories, decorative objects, whatever makes him or his surroundings more aesthetically pleasing. Beautiful flowers in pastel colors are always welcome. Libras are great hosts and hostesses, who might appreciate a gift related to fine dining: serving pieces, linens, glassware, flower vases. Evening or party clothes please since Libra has a gadabout social life. Interesting books, objets d'art, memberships to museums, and tickets to cultural events are good ideas. Fashion or home-decorating magazine subscriptions usually please Libra women. Steer away from anything loud, garish, or extreme. Think pink, one of their special colors, when giving Libra jewelry, clothing, or accessories. It's a very romantic sign, so be sure to remember birthdays, holidays, and anniversaries with a token of affection.

Scorpio

Scorpios love mystery, so bear that in mind when you buy these folks a present. You could take this literally and buy them a good thriller DVD, novel, or video game. Scorpios are power players, so a book about one of their sign might please. Bill Gates, Jack Welch, Condoleezza Rice, and Hillary Clinton are hot Scorpio subjects. Scorpios love black leather, suede, fur, anything to do with the sea, power tools, tiny spy tape recorders, and items with secret compartments or intricate locks. When buying a handbag for Scorpio, go for simple shapes with lots of interior pockets. Sensuous Scorpios appreciate hot lingerie, sexy linens, body lotions, and perfumed candles. Black is the favored color for Scorpio clothing—go for sexy textures like cashmere and satin in simple shapes by designers like Calvin Klein. This sign is fascinated with the occult, so give them an astrology or tarot-card reading, beautiful crystals, or an astrology program for the computer.

Sagittarius

For these outdoor people, consider adventure trips, designer sportswear, gear for their favorite sports. A funny gift or something for their pets pleases Sagittarius. For clothing and accessories, the fashionista of this sign tends to like bright colors and dramatic innovative styles. Otherwise, casual sportswear is a good idea. These travelers usually have a favorite getaway place; give them a travel guide, DVD, novel, or history book that would make their trip more interesting. Luggage is also a good bet. Sleek carry-ons, travel wallets, ticket holders, business-card cases, and wheeled computer bags might please these wanderers. Anything that makes travel more comfortable and pleasant is good for Sagittarius, including a good book to read en route. This sign is the great gambler of the zodiac, so gifts related to their favorite gambling venue would be appreciated.

Capricorn

For this quality-conscious sign, go for a status label from the best store in town. Get Capricorns something good for their image and career. They could be fond of things Spanish, like flamenco or tango music, or of country-and-western music and motifs. In the bookstore, go for biographies of the rich and famous, or advice books to help Capricorn get to the top. Capricorns take their gifts seriously, so steer away from anything too frivolous. Garnet, onyx, or malachite jewelry, Carolina Herrera fragrance and clothing, and beautiful briefcases and wallets are good ideas. Glamorous status tote bags carry business gear in style. Capricorns like golf, tennis, and sports that involve climbing, cycling, or hiking, so presents could be geared to their outdoor interests. Elegant evening accessories would be fine for this sign, which often entertains for business.

Aquarius

Give Aquarius a surprise gift. This sign is never impressed with things that are too predictable. So use your imagination to present the gift in an unusual way or at an unexpected time. With Aquarius, originality counts. When in doubt, give them something to think about, a new electronic gadget, perhaps a small robot, or an advanced computer game. Or something New Age, like an amethyst-crystal cluster. Aquarius like innovative materials with a space-age look. They are the ones with the wraparound glasses, the titanium computer cases. This air sign loves to fly—an airplane ticket always pleases. Books should be on innovative subjects, politics, or adventures of the mind. Aquarius goes for unusual color combinations—especially electric blue or hot pink—and abstract patterns. They like the newest, coolest looks on the cutting edge of fashion and are not afraid to experiment. Think of Paris Hilton's constantly changing looks. Look for an Aquarius gift in an out-of-the-way boutique or local hipster hangout. They'd be touched if you find out Aquarius's special worthy cause and make a donation. Spirit them off to hear their favorite guru.

Pisces

Pisces respond to gifts that have a touch of fantasy, magic, and romance. Look for mystical gifts with a touch of the occult. Romantic music (a customized CD of favorite love songs) and love stories appeal to Pisces sentimentalists. Pisces is associated with perfume and fragrant oils, so help this sign indulge with their favorite scent in many forms. Anything to do with the ocean, fish, and water sports appeals to Pisces. How about a whirlpool, a water-therapy spa treatment, or a sea salt rub. Appeal to this sign with treats for the feet: foot massages, pedicures, ballet tickets, and dance lessons. Cashmere socks and metallic evening sandals are other Pisces pleasers. A romantic dinner overlooking the water is Pisces paradise. A case of fine wine or another favorite liquid is always appreciated. Write a love poem and enclose it with your gift.

CHAPTER 15

Your Pet-Scope for 2010: How to Choose Your Best Friend for Life

With Jupiter, the planet of luck and expansion, in compassionate Pisces, this is a great time to bring joy into your life by adopting an animal friend. At this writing, 63 percent of all American households have at least one pet, according to a recent survey by the American Pet Product Manufacturers Association. And we spend billions of dollars on the care and feeding of our beloved pets. Our pets are counted as part of the family, often sharing our beds and accompanying us on trips.

Whether you choose to adopt an animal from a local shelter or buy a Thoroughbred from a breeder, try for an optimal time of adoption and sun sign of your new friend. If you're rescuing an animal, however, it's difficult to know the sun sign of the animal, but you can adopt on a day when the moon is compatible with yours, which should bless the emotional relationship. Using the moon signs listed in the daily forecasts in this book, choose a day when the moon is in your sign, a sign of the same element, or a compatible element. This means fire and air signs should go for a day when the moon is in fire signs Aries, Leo, Sagittarius or air signs Gemini, Libra, or Aquarius. Water and earth signs should choose a day when the moon is in water signs Cancer, Scorpio, or Pisces or earth signs Taurus, Virgo, or Capricorn. If possible, aim for a new moon, good for beginning a new relationship.

Here are some sign-specific tips for adopting an animal that will be your best friend for life.

Aries: The Rescuer

Aries gets special pleasure from rescuing animals in distress and rehabbing them, so do check your local shelters if you're thinking of adopting an animal. As an active fire sign, you'd be happiest with a lively animal that can accompany you, and you might do well with a rescue animal such as a German shepherd or Labrador retriever. You'd also enjoy training such an animal. Otherwise look for intelligence, alertness, playfulness and obedience in your friend. Since Aries tend to have an active life, look for a sleek, low maintenance coat on your dog or cat. Cat lovers would enjoy the more active breeds such as the Siamese or Abyssinian.

An Aries sun-sign dog or cat would be ideal. Aries animals have a brave, energetic, rather combative nature. They can be mischievous, so the kittens and puppies should be monitored for safety. They'll dare to jump higher, run faster, and chase more animals than their peers. They may require stronger words and more obedience training than other signs. Give them plenty of toys and play active games with them often.

Taurus: The Toucher

Taurus is a touchy-feely sign, and this extends to your animal relationships. Look for a dog or cat that enjoys being petted and groomed, is affectionate, and adapts well to family life. As one of the great animal-loving signs, Taurus is likely to have several pets, so it is important that they all get along together. Give each one its own special safe space to minimize turf wars.

Taurus animals are calm and even tempered, but do not like being teased and could retaliate, so be sure to instruct children in the proper way to handle and play with their pet. Since this sign has strong appetites and tends to put on weight easily, be careful not to overindulge them in caloric treats and table snacks. Sticking to a regular feeding schedule could help eliminate between-meal snacking.

Taurus female animals are excellent mothers and make good breeders. They tend to be clean and less destructive of home furnishings than other animals.

Gemini: The Companion

A bright, quick-witted sign like yours requires an equally interesting and communicative pet. Choose a social animal that adapts well to different environments, since you may travel or have homes in different locations.

Gemini animals can put up with noise, telephones, music, and different people coming and going. They'll want to be part of the action, so place a pillow or roost in a public place. They do not like being left alone, however, so, if you will be away for long periods, find them an animal companion to play with. You might consider adopting two Gemini pets from the same litter.

Animals born under this sign are easy to teach and some enjoy doing tricks or retrieving. They may be more vocal than other animals, especially if they are confined without companionship.

Cancer: The Nurturer

Cancer enjoys a devoted, obedient animal who demonstrates loyalty to its master. An affectionate, home-loving dog or cat who welcomes you and sits on your lap would be ideal. The emotional connection with your pet is most important; therefore, you may depend on your powerful psychic powers when choosing an animal. Wait until you feel that strong bond of psychic communication between you both. The moon sign of the day you adopt is very important for moon-ruled Cancer, so choose a water sign, if possible.

Cancer animals need a feeling of security; they don't like changes of environment or too much chaos at home. If you intend to breed your animal, the Cancer pet makes a wonderful and fertile mother.

Leo: The Prideful Owner

The Leo owner may choose a pet that reminds you of your own physical characteristics, such as similar coloring or build. You'll be proud of your pet, keep the animal groomed to perfection, and choose the most spectacular example of the breed. Noble animals with a regal attitude, beautiful fur, or striking markings are often preferred, such as the Himalayan or red tabby Persian cat, the standard poodle, the chow chow dog. An attention getter is a must.

Under the sign of the King of Beasts, Leo-born animals have proud noble natures. They usually have a cheerful, magnanimous disposition and rule their domains regardless of their breed, holding their heads with pride and walking with great authority. They enjoy grooming, like to show off and be the center of attention. Leo animals are naturals for the show ring, thriving in the spotlight and applause. They'll thrive with plenty of petting, pampering, and admiration.

Virgo: The Caregiver

Virgo owners will be very particular about their pets, paying special attention to requirements for care and maintenance. You need a pet who is clean, obedient, intelligent, yet rather quiet. A highly active, barking or meowing pet that might get on your nerves is a no-no.

Cats are usually very good pets for Virgo. Choose one of the calm breeds, such as a Persian. Though this is a high-maintenance cat, its beauty and personality will be rewarding.

You are compassionate with animals in need, and you might find it rewarding to volunteer at a local shelter or veterinary clinic or to train service dogs.

Virgo animals can be fussy eaters, very particular about their environment. They are gentle and intelligent, and respond to kind words and quiet commands, never harsh treatment.

Virgo is an excellent sign for dogs that are trained to do service work, since they seem to enjoy being useful and are intelligent enough to be easily trained.

Libra: The Beautifier

The Libra owner responds to beauty and elegance in your pet. You require a well-mannered, but social companion, who can be displayed in all of nature's finery. An exotic variety such as a graceful curly-haired Devon Rex cat would be a showstopper. Libra often prefers the smaller varieties, such as a miniature schnauzer, a mini-greyhound or a teacup poodle.

Pets born under Libra are usually charming, well-mannered gentlemen who love the comforts of home life. They tend to be more careful than other signs, not rushing willfully into potentially dangerous situations. They'll avoid confrontations and harsh sounds, responding to words of love and gentle corrections.

Scorpio: The Powerful

Scorpios enjoy a powerful animal with a strong character. They enjoy training animals in obedience, would do well with service dogs, guard dogs, or police animals. Some Scorpios enjoy the more exotic, edgy pets, such as hairless Sphynx cats or Chinese chin dogs. Scorpios could find rescuing animals in dire circumstances and finding them new homes especially rewarding, as Matthew McConaughey did during Hurricane Katrina.

Animals born under this sign tend to be one-person pets, very strongly attached to their owners and extremely loyal and possessive. They are natural guard animals who will take extreme risks to protect their owners. They are best ruled by love and with consistent behavior training. They need to respect their owners and will return their love with great devotion.

Sagittarius: The Jovial Freedom Lover

Sagittarius is a traveler and one of the great animal lovers of the zodiac. The horse is especially associated with your sign, and you could well be a "horse whisperer." You generally respond most to large, active animals. If a small animal, like a Chihuahua, steals your heart, be sure it's one that travels well or tolerates your absence. Outdoor dogs like hunting dogs, retrievers, and border collies would be good companions on your outdoor adventures.

Sagittarius animals are freedom-loving, jovial, happy-go-lucky types. They may be wanderers, however, so be sure they have the proper identification tags and consider embedded microchip identification. These animals tend to be openly affectionate, companionable, untemperamental. They enjoy socializing and playing with humans and other animals and are especially good with active children.

Capricorn: The Thoroughbred

Capricorn is a discriminating owner, with a great sense of responsibility toward your animal. You will be concerned with maintenance and care, will rarely neglect or overlook any health issues with your pet. You will also discipline your pet wisely, not tolerating any destructive or outrageous antics. You will be attracted to good breeding, good manners, and deep loyalty from your pet.

The Capricorn pet tends to be more quiet and serious than other pets, perhaps a lone wolf who prefers the company of its owner, rather than a sociable or mischievous type. This is another good sign for a working dog, such as a herder, as Capricorn animals enjoy this outlet for their energy.

Aquarius: The Independent Original

Aquarius owners tend to lead active, busy lives and need an animal who can either accompany them cheerfully or who won't make waves. Demanding or high-maintenance dogs are not for you. You might prefer unusual or oddball types of pets, such as dressed-up Chihuahuas who travel in your tote bag or scene-stealing, rather shocking hairless cats. Or you will acquire a group of animals who can play with one another when you are pursuing outside activities, as Oprah Winfrey does. You can relate to the independence of cats, who require relatively little care and maintenance.

Aquarius animals are not loners—they enjoy the companionship of humans or groups of other animals. They tend to be more independent and may require more training to follow the house rules. However, they can have unique personalities and endearing oddball behavior.

Pisces: The Soul Mate

This is the sign that can "talk to the animals." Pisces owners enjoy a deep communication with their pets, love having their animals accompany them, sleep with them, and show affection. Tenderhearted Pisces will often rescue an animal in distress or adopt an animal from a shelter.

Tropical fish are often recommended as a Pisces pet, and seem to have a natural tranquilizing effect on this sign. However, Pisces may require an animal that shows more affection than their fish friends.

Pisces animals are creative types, can be sensually seductive and mysterious, mischievous and theatrical. They make fine house pets, do not usually like to roam far from their owners, and have a winning personality, especially with the adults in the home. Naturally sensitive and seldom vicious, they should be treated gently and given much praise and encouragement.

CHAPTER 16

Your Scorpio Personality and Potential: The Roles You Play in Life

The more you understand your Scorpio personality and potential, the more you'll benefit from using your special solar power to help create the life you want. There's a life coach, personal trainer, career adviser, fashion expert, and matchmaker all built into your Scorpio sun sign. Whether you want to make a radical change in your life or simply choose a new wardrobe or paint a room, your sun sign can help you discover new possibilities and make good decisions. You could tap into your Scorpio power to deal with relationship issues, such as getting along with your boss or spicing up your love life. Maybe you'll be inspired by a celebrity sign mate who shares your special traits.

Let the following chapters help you move in harmony with your natural Scorpio gifts. As the ancient oracle of Delphi advised, "Know thyself." To know yourself, as astrology helps you to do, is to gain confidence and strength.

You may wonder how astrologers determine what a Scorpio personality is like. To begin with, we use a type of recipe, blending several ingredients. First there's your Scorpio element: water. Water signs are emotional, creative, psychic. The way Scorpio operates: fixed—intense, focused, a controller. Then there's your sign's polarity, which adds a reactive, feminine, yin dimension. Let's not forget your planetary ruler: Pluto, the planet of transformation. Add your sign's place in the zodiac: eighth, the place of sex and power. Finally, stir in your symbol, the stinging Scorpion (or the soaring Eagle).

This recipe influences everything we say about Scorpio. Will a fixed, focused water sign be a good detective who gets to the bottom of the situation? Very likely. Scorpio tends to be intense, deeply emotional, single-minded.

But all Scorpios are not alike! Your individual astrological personality contains a blend of many other planets, colored by the signs they occupy, plus factors such as the sign coming over the horizon at the exact moment of your birth. However, the more Scorpio planets in your horoscope, the more likely you'll recognize yourself in the descriptions that follow. On the other hand, if many planets are grouped together in a different sign, they will color your horoscope accordingly, sometimes making a low-key, mellow sun sign come on much stronger. So if the Scorpio traits mentioned here don't describe you, there might be other factors flavoring your cosmic stew. (Look up your other planets in the tables in this book to find out what they might be!)

The Scorpio Man: Power Player

Yours is known as the sex sign of the zodiac. But if the truth be known, you're much more interested in issues of power and control. You're challenged by unsolved problems and mysteries of any kind. You're a natural detective who won't stop until you know what makes things and people tick. In spite of your aloof manner, you're always aware of what is going on (especially of who is running the show), and you're remarkably perceptive about people's true motives.

Beneath your deliberately cool surface, you may be far less secure. One of the most sensitive signs of the zodiac, you keep your vulnerability a dark secret to seal yourself off from rejection. When you do fall for someone, nothing less than total possession will do. Scorpio feels he should own the woman he loves (though he's also able to enjoy pure sex for its own sake elsewhere). Yours is the most possessive sign, with no toleration for disloyalty.

You are single-minded in pursuit of what you want, be it a job, a prize, or a person. It was with good reason that Scorpio fashion designer Calvin Klein named his first fragrance "Obsession." Your great concentration, intensity, and stamina make you a formidable competitor. But your love of power can degenerate into manipulation, bullying, and even violence if you are frustrated. You harbor a grudge and seek revenge when injured. As Teddy Roosevelt said, "Speak softly, but carry a big stick."

In a Relationship

When Scorpio falls in love, you are so single-minded about the object of your affection that, if you lose that love for any reason, you are devastated. Often this is the one experience that can teach Scorpio about healthy detachment and the wisdom of getting to know someone slowly and gradually for longevity's sake.

After issues of power and control are settled within the relationship, you become a loyal and devoted mate. But first you may go through a period of testing in which you are not above using emotional manipulation to gain the upper hand. You need a partner who will provide rational balance and perspective when you go to extremes and who will help you look on the lighter, brighter side of life.

The Scorpio Woman: Ms. Mystery

Like your male counterpart, the mysterious, mesmerizing Scorpio woman hides intense emotions under a cool, controlled facade. But inside, you are passionate, determined, and totally committed to everything you do. This makes you seem very stable and somewhat predictable. You're not one for surprises or spontaneous moves; there is usually a strategy behind every step you take. All your formidable energy is zeroed in on your goal. The Scorpio woman is rarely plagued by self-doubt. You know exactly where you are going and rarely waver from your path. Once committed, you remain loyal and dedicated, and you will patiently see your projects through to completion. Hillary Clinton and Condoleezza Rice embody these typical Scorpio traits.

Scorpio is the "heaviest" sign of the zodiac, so let those who skim the surface of life be forewarned. You delve deep and demand total commitment—anything less is not worthwhile. Since you are extremely vulnerable beneath your cool controlled surface, you are deeply hurt by betrayal. When disappointed, you can strike back with lethal accuracy.

The good girl/bad girl extremes of Scorpio are reflected in the sex-charged and power-charged roles Scorpio actresses have played in recent years, starting with Vivien Leigh as Scarlett O'Hara in *Gone With the Wind*. Jodie Foster and Julia Roberts both gained fame playing sexually charged roles in *Taxi Driver, The Accused,* and *Pretty Woman*. Scorpios Jodie Foster and Goldie Hawn have braved the Hollywood establishment by producing and directing their own projects.

Unfortunately, Scorpio intensity frightens away many who are not ready to commit to a bond that reaches to the soul level. The Scorpio woman considers this kind of fright a weakness, and so she blocks out many potentially interesting relationships. It is only after a period of tempering that you learn tolerance for a more balanced and rational relationship—and learn to give your partner space to be his own person.

A Scorpio woman is not one to play around with or take lightly. Though you may seem very sweet and naïve, you can quickly see through deception. An excellent detective, you sense immediately when something is hidden, yet you yourself are never completely open about your own motives. This secretiveness can cause suspicion and mistrust. Others wonder what is lurking beneath that unruffled surface.

Anger brings out your venomous side. Scorpio has a suspicious streak and often overreacts to imaginary slights. You tend to see things in black and white, and you go to extremes when you're upset. Then it is very difficult to coax you out of a black mood. You are more likely to get revenge than to forgive and forget.

In a Relationship

Much maligned as a femme fatale, the typical Scorpio is a one-man (at a time) woman, intensely loyal and devoted to your mate. Though you may experiment before settling down, as a

Scorpio you are looking for total commitment. After marriage, you're so completely involved with your husband that you can be devastated if the marriage fails. However, once committed, your intense involvement could backfire if you become overly demanding, possessive, and jealous. Then you will smother a more freedom-loving partner. You must learn not to give in to those negative suspicions, which can escalate into destructive paranoia.

You reach your full potential as a mate once you have learned to share yourself with your partner rather than try to control the relationship. On the plus side, as a Scorpio you will stay with your true mate after he earns your trust, even through the most difficult times, as Hillary Clinton demonstrated. You are someone he can count on to support him, no matter what the sacrifice. And, in the long run, you can transform his life for the better.

Scorpio in the Family

The Scorpio Parent

Scorpios are committed to everything they do, especially to being a good parent. Though you may not express your feelings openly, you are able to convey to your children a feeling of being deeply loved. It is this strong foundation of emotional security that gives your children confidence. Trust and loyalty are unspoken givens. You'll defend your children to the maximum, and you'll provide them with the ways and means to live up to your high hopes. But you are a strict parent who insists on control and discipline, which could create problems with an equally strong-willed child. You may have to learn lessons of flexibility and tolerance from your children. And you will also have to learn when to let go, to allow your children to follow their own interests in the outside world. However, your children always know you will be there for them, ready to provide a life raft in the roughest waters.

The Scorpio Stepparent

In marriage, Scorpios can be intensely possessive of a mate. It is especially important that you and your stepchildren get along before the marriage, and that you are sincerely willing to reach out to them. Otherwise, power struggles can develop. It would also help to discuss problems openly as they occur rather than let anger, hurt feelings, or misunderstandings build up. Be flexible enough to allow your mate time with the children, apart from you. Have some outside activities to help diffuse your energy, so it is not overly concentrated on the family.

The Scorpio Grandparent

Grandchildren can provide some of the most liberating, joyful experiences of your life. At last you can show your playful childlike side, with a fun-loving little playmate who demands nothing of you. You're free from the disciplining responsibilities of parenthood and the intense emotional commitment. You're no longer involved in power struggles or overworked, so you're free to spend happy times with the children. Grandchildren can also bring out the generosity in Scorpio, particularly when providing for their future security. You'll make a lasting impression on the youngest generation, and they'll make you feel born again!

CHAPTER 17

Scorpio Fashion and Decor Tips: Elevate You Mood with Scorpio Style!

In this year of serious concerns, why not put joy and imagination into your life by creating a harmonious environment and expressing your sun sign's natural flair in everything you do and wear? There are colors, sounds, fashion, and decor tips that fit Scorpio like the proverbial glove and that could brighten every day. Even small changes in decor could make you feel "home at last." A simple change of color in your walls or curtains, your special music in the air, and a wardrobe makeover inspired by a Scorpio designer or celebrity are natural mood elevators that boost your confidence and energy level. Even your vacations might be more fun if you tailor them to your natural Scorpio inclinations. Try these tips to enhance your lifestyle and express the Scorpio stylist in you.

Scorpio Fashion Secrets

Scorpios make an unforgettable fashion statement, whatever their style. Like other fixed signs, they usually stick to a trademark look, be it the sporty classic style of Jodie Foster, the avant-garde trendiness of Chloë Sevigny and Björk, or the ultrafeminine gamine look of Calista Flockhart. Many Scorpio women, like Lauren Hutton, prefer man-tailored styles with ambiguous sex appeal. Scorpios love to wear black, particularly black velvet or black leather and, like Demi Moore, will use intense makeup or none at all to dramatize their strong bone structure and mesmerizing eyes. Or they'll use dark glasses, like *Vogue* editor Anna Wintour, to enhance their air of mystery.

Because of your strong personality, Scorpio can pull off extreme styles that would be shocking on another sign. Designer Roberto Cavalli, a favorite of many stars who love to steal the show, is a master at the sexy entrance-maker look. Black dresses, black leather jackets, stiletto heels and sexy lingerie are Scorpio staples. Capes and trench coats play up your air of mystery and intrigue. Most Scorpios, however, should avoid contrived, complicated clothing. Stick to pure, simple, classic lines, especially if you're in a power position, like Hillary Clinton. For pure glamour, revisit vintage Scorpio beauties such as Grace Kelly (the cool kind of Scorpio beauty), Vivien Leigh (the fiery type), or sultry sexpot Hedy Lamarr in *Algiers*.

Scorpio Colors

Black and deep, rich burgundy are traditional Scorpio colors. But some Scorpios, particularly if they are pale blondes, prefer off-white tones or neutrals. The deep blues of the sea also resonate with Scorpio.

Your Scorpio Fashion Role Models

Calvin Klein's fashion style is pure Scorpio, with its streamlined, uncluttered sex appeal from head to toe. (Leave it to a Scorpio to put a woman in man-styled underwear and name a fragrance Obsession.) Scorpio-friendly designers Helmut Lang and Jil Sander do severely simple clothes that let your strong personality stand out. At the other extreme, there's Roberto Cavalli, the self-proclaimed King of Italian excess. Cavalli shows us how to show off in a riot of color, outrageous print combinations, and revealing silhouettes. Those who love the spotlight—from star athletes to Hollywood A-listers—are Cavalli fans. Zac Posen is a young Scorpio designer whose sexy feminine dresses appeal to celebrities and socialites.

Scorpio Home Makeover Tips

If you're a typical Scorpio, you care about your home decor very much or not at all. There's nothing wishy-washy about the ideal Scorpio atmosphere. Either it's a supersensual atmosphere, with dark woods, rich tapestry colors, sink-in upholstery, brocade walls, luxurious leather or suede coverings, and Oriental rugs. Or it's pared down to the essentials. In the latter case, rooms can be stark and minimal in one or two colors, often black and white.

Some Scorpios ignore their surroundings entirely, being focused on another agenda. This kind of Scorpio might live in a virtually unfurnished apartment or delegate the decor to someone else, simply because he or she is not involved or interested enough to decorate. For those who do care, marine motifs, voluptuous nudes, and dramatic ancient artifacts might appeal. Or you may go for the Victorian look, with carved wood furniture. You'll pay special attention to the bedroom, perhaps pulling out all the stops with satin sheets, mirrored walls, and seductive lighting effects.

Scorpio enjoys transforming the environment. You are often the one to buy a crumbling house or gut a forlorn apartment. Renovating from the ground up, tearing down and rebuilding, restoring a vintage building, or bringing a dull room to life would fully engage your energy. Rather than just a surface redo, you'll get right down to the plumbing and structure, stripping the walls and floors bare. Give yourself a beautiful bathroom with top-of-the-line fixtures. Or go all out with an indoor sauna or Jacuzzi to create your personal spa. Be sure there's a secret sanctuary somewhere to restore your spirit.

Scorpio Sounds

Scorpio loves intense music—thundering symphonies and dramatic operas with life-and-death themes. You also love sexy tangos, sensual cello sounds, Paul Simon, Bonnie Raitt, Joni Mitchell. Mysterious New Age music has Scorpio appeal. More avant-garde Scorpios go for powerful heavy-metal sounds with a driving beat and an undercurrent of danger. The black leather and biker paraphernalia side of the rock scene is pure Scorpio. Gospel music can also stir your soul. CD burners and iPods were made for Scorpio, as you love to control what you hear. Now you can make your own kind of music in whatever combination of sounds turns you on.

Scorpio Getaways

Scorpios relax to the sound of the pounding surf, your best tranquilizer, and thrill to the crashing waves. Find a beach that's away from the crowd, one that feels like yours alone, such as the deserted beaches of Martha's Vineyard, the Baja Peninsula, the surfing beaches of California, or the Caribbean in off-season.

You will never go to a place because it's "in," at least not for a vacation. You prefer a place where there is a challenge or a mystical experience such as a difficult mountain to scale, great fishing or skiing, unexplored terrain, the ruins of an ancient civilization. Australia, Brazil, Morocco, Norway, and China are exotic Scorpio destinations that fill the bill. You'll enjoy exploring the classic treasures of Greece, Mexico, and Peru, as well as the erotically decorated temples of India. In the U.S., visit the Scorpio states of Nevada, North Dakota, North Carolina, Oklahoma, and Washington.

Scorpios can travel with minimum luggage and are usually expert packers. Invest in some leather carry-on bags so you can skip the baggage claim and avoid lost luggage. Combination locks should keep your possessions secure, though you might want to look into a hidden money belt or a waist packet to store your vital items. Take wearable waterproof containers to the beach to hold credit cards and cash. Scorpios who are truly concerned with security can find clothes hangers with secret compartments to store valuables. Hidden pockets or compartments of any kind are very much a Scorpio thing.

Credit cards are ruled by Scorpio. Before you go, be sure to check which cards are accepted and how much cash you'll need. Investigate travel insurance and any special travel deal provided by your credit card company.

CHAPTER 18

The Scorpio Way to Stay Healthy and Age Well

This year we'll be focused on staying healthy to avoid the high costs of health care and to cope with stressful events. Some signs have an easier time than others committing to a health and diet regimen. With a lucky boost from Jupiter this year, Scorpio should have no trouble focusing on self-improvement in all areas. Astrology can clue you in to the specific Scorpio tendencies that contribute to good or ill health. So follow these sun-sign tips to help yourself become the healthiest Scorpio possible.

Diet for Self-Transformation

Scorpios never do anything halfway and need to be fully committed to their diet. Some Scorpios will go to great lengths to transform themselves, even resorting to extreme means like stomach stapling or gastric bypass. You are gifted with amazing focus and discipline and can stick with any diet, once you have made up your mind. The trick is to eliminate self-destructive food habits. Find a diet plan you can live with for a long time. This will help you avoid the yo-yo diet syndrome.

Take Control of Your Health

Though Scorpio usually has a strong constitution that can literally rise from the ashes of extreme illness or misfortune, resist the temptation to take this for granted or sabotage your health with self-destructive habits. Try to curb excessive tendencies in any area of your life. Know when to quit and when to seek help—and don't hesitate to ask for help when you need it.

Your sign is associated with the regenerative and eliminative organs. Therefore, it follows that sexual activity can be a source of good or ill health for Scorpio. It is important to examine your attitudes about sex, to follow safe sexual practices, and to seek balance in sex—as in all other areas of your life.

Exercise for Health and Stress Relief

It's no accident that Scorpio's month coincides with football season, which reminds us that sports are a very healthy way to defuse emotions and enjoy the thrill of winning. Many Scorpios enjoy the adrenaline rush of extreme sports and seek out a bit of danger and a competitive challenge. If you enjoy winter sports, be sure to prepare ahead of time for the ski slopes or the ice rink and remember to warm up your muscles before you go all out.

Water sports are a terrific outlet for Scorpio, so sign up for pool aerobics or competitive swimming and be sure to treat yourself to a vacation at a spectacular tropical beach resort. Somehow, just being near a saltwater environment can restore your equilibrium. Sailing and surfing, where you harness the power of the wind and the waves, should be especially thrilling for Scorpio. Some Scorpios take their love of water sports to extremes, searching for the highest waves for surfing and the most exciting reefs for deep water scuba diving. Be sure to balance your love of thrills with an equal concern for thorough training and safety measures.

Stay Forever Young

You're the sexy senior! The sign of Scorpio is associated with the sex organs and known for having an active sex life in the senior years. Your partner may well need Viagra! Scorpio is often called the "phoenix rising from the ashes" for your ability to survive illnesses and regain your health. However, you should pay special attention to the elimination and sexual functions of the body with regular examinations and colonoscopies. Water sports and vacations near the sea are excellent therapy for stressed-out Scorpios. Getting involved in something you care passionately about keeps Scorpio young at heart.

CHAPTER 19

Add Scorpio's Star Power to Your Career: What It Takes to Succeed in 2010

In today's tight job market, you'll need to pull out all the stops to land a great job. Scorpio has a combination of talents and abilities that can make you a natural winner. Tops on the list is your ability to focus and to handle pressure well. You understand the uses of power better than any other sign. You have great energy and drive and never take your eyes off the prize. If you develop and nurture your Scorpio talents, you'll be more likely to find a career you truly enjoy, as well as one that rewards you financially. Here's to your success!

Where to Look for Your Perfect Job

Scorpios are born survivors in the competitive workplace. You usually know exactly what you want and will put in the necessary groundwork to prepare for a top position. You are capable of getting and keeping great responsibility, though others may underestimate your quiet demeanor, at first mistaking it for shyness.

Scorpio talents often work best within a structured organization rather than in a freelance situation. Large companies give you a wide scope and plenty of potential power. Higher-ups soon notice how you stay cool in a crisis and keep your job well under control. As the zodiac's super sleuth, you shine in detective, research, or troubleshooting spots. Concentration and focus help in life-or-death fields, such as medicine, and in high-pressure television spots where you'll be the steady anchor. (Pat Sajak, Jane Pauley, Morley Safer, Walter Cronkite, and Dick Cavett are good examples in broadcasting.) Handling other people's money can be trusted to Scorpio accountants, financial planners, investment bankers, and brokers. Your sharp perception works for you in psychology, psychotherapy, or the theater. Both the fashion world (Calvin Klein) and fine arts (Picasso) know your strong statements. Stay away from jobs that have a dead end, that are in risky, fly-by-night businesses, or that require on-the-spot improvisation rather than steady discipline.

Live Up to Your Leadership Potential

You hire your staff with a keen perception of everyone's strengths and weaknesses. You are totally in command of all that happens in your domain and will rarely hand over the reins, even temporarily. Since you do not trust easily, you may be hesitant to delegate and so you take on too much responsibility yourself. Your suspiciousness could even degenerate into paranoia. But you care intensely about your work and are generous with others who are equally dedicated. A winner of power games, you can be lethal with competition. However, you are extremely supportive of anyone who gives you the proper respect and loyalty.

If you have dreams of running a business that will bring financial and personal satisfaction, some advice from those who achieved phenomenal success could help you make those dreams a reality. You needn't go further than Microsoft's Bill Gates, GE's Jack Welch, or CNN's Ted Turner to find businessmen who have weathered great storms and emerged with megasuccess through shrewd career maneuvers and careful planning. You are capable of taking on great responsibility, but may do so from behind the scenes or with a quiet unassuming demeanor. Scorpios specialize in transforming the lives of others. Ted Turner through his charitable donations and transformation of television news through CNN; Bill Gates through his foundations combating disease in Africa and his contributions to education; Jack Welch through his management of GE.

How to Work with Others

Since you aim for total control of your job, you will always have a motive behind your moves. You like work where there is a challenge and a chance to wield power, whether it's a weapon, a big machine, or a company checkbook. Sometimes Scorpio will work overtime to make yourself indispensable, simply for the power of being so needed! You are always aware of what is happening in the office, of who's doing what to whom. You are particularly good at assessing the weak points of others (or of the organization), and using this to your advantage. When you're interested in your work, you have unbeatable stamina, tolerating working conditions and hours that would make others rebel! You are very steady and stable on the job, rarely getting sidetracked to another profession or seduced by another organization.

The Scorpio Way to Get Ahead

In doing your personal plan of action, use your special Scorpio talents and abilities to bring you the highest return on your investment of time and energy. Choose a job where there is a weakness you can correct or chaos you can order and then take over! Play up your best characteristics:

- Cool control
- Stamina
- Perception
- Concentration
- Ability to handle pressure
- Steadiness
- Drive

CHAPTER 20

Learn from Scorpio Celebrities

You know how much fun it is when you find a famous person who shares your sun sign—and even your birthday! Why not turn your brush with fame into an education in astrology? Celebrities who capture the media's attention reflect the currrent planetary influences, as well as the unique star quality of their sun sign. Who's in this year may be out next year. You can learn from the hottest stellar spotlight stealers what the public is responding to and what this says about our current values.

If one of your famous sign mates intrigues you, explore his personality further by looking up his other planets using the tables in this book. You may even find his horoscope posted on astrology-related Internet sites like www.astrodatabank.com or www.stariq.com, which have charts of world events and headline makers. Then apply the effects of Venus, Mars, Saturn, and Jupiter to his sun-sign traits. It's a way to get up close and personal with your famous friend, and maybe learn some secrets not revealed to the public.

You're sure to have lots in common with your famous sign mates. Consider the leadership qualities of Hillary Clinton, Condoleezza Rice, and Joe Biden. Do you appreciate the high style of fashion designer Calvin Klein or the sexy swagger of Roberto Cavalli? Do you follow the career path of Bill Gates or cook to the recipes of Gordon Ramsay?

Get to know these famous Scorpios better and learn what makes their stars shine brightly.

Scorpio Celebrities

Sarah Bernhardt (10/23/1844)
Michael Crichton (10/23/42)
Kevin Kline (10/24/47)
Pablo Picasso (10/25/1881)
Tracy Nelson (10/25/63)
Pat Sajak (10/26/46)
Hillary Clinton (10/26/47)
Jaclyn Smith (10/26/47)
Keith Urban (10/26/67)
John Cleese (10/27/39)
Simon LeBon (10/27/58)
Marla Maples (10/27/63)
Kelly Osborne (10/27/84)
Evelyn Waugh (10/28/1903)
Dennis Franz (10/28/44)
Annie Potts (10/28/52)
Bill Gates (10/28/55)
Lauren Holly (10/28/63)
Julia Roberts (10/28/67)
Joaquin Phoenix (10/28/74)
Richard Dreyfuss (10/29/47)
Kate Jackson (10/29/48)
Winona Ryder (10/29/48)
Louis Malle (10/30/32)
Grace Slick (10/30/39)
Gavin Rossdale (10/30/67)
Ivanka Trump (10/30/81)
Dale Evans (10/31/12)
Dan Rather (10/31/31)
Diedre Hall (10/31/49)
Jane Pauley (10/31/50)
Harry Hamlin (10/31/51)
Vanilla Ice (10/31/68)
Lyle Lovett (11/1/57)
Jenny McCarthy (11/1/72)
Daniel Boone (11/2/1754)
Pat Buchanan (11/2/38)

Stefanie Powers (11/2/42)
k.d. lang (11/2/61)
Charles Bronson (11/3/22)
Roseanne (11/3/52)
Kate Capshaw (11/3/53)
Pauline Trigere (11/4/12)
Laura Bush (11/4/46)
Sean "P. Diddy" Combs (11/4/69)
Matthew McConaughey (11/4/69)
Roy Rogers (11/5/12)
Vivien Leigh (11/5/13)
Ike Turner (11/5/31)
Sam Shepard (11/5/43)
Tilda Swinton (11/5/61)
Famke Janssen (11/5/65)
Mike Nichols (11/6/31)
Maria Shriver (11/6/55)
Ethan Hawke (11/6/70)
Thandie Newton (11/6/72)
Rebecca Romijn (11/6/72)
Billy Graham (11/7/18)
Morley Safer (11/8/31)
Bonnie Raitt (11/8/49)
Alfre Woodard (11/8/52)
Gordon Ramsay (11/8/66)
Parker Posey (11/8/68)
Courtney Thorne-Smith (11/8/68)
Gretchen Mol (11/8/73)
Tara Reid (11/8/75)
Hedy Lamarr (11/9/13)
Carl Sagan (11/9/34)
Nick Lachey (11/9/73)
Ellen Pompeo (11/10/69)
Brittany Murphy (11/10/77)
Richard Burton (11/10/25)
Roy Scheider (11/10/32)
Demi Moore (11/11/62)
Calista Flockhart (11/11/64)
Leonardo DiCaprio (11/11/74)
Grace Kelly (11/12/29)

Anne Hathaway (11/12/82)
Richard Mulligan (11/13/32)
Chris Noth (11/13/54)
Whoopi Goldberg (11/13/55)
Aaron Copeland (11/14/1900)
Prince Charles (11/14/48)
Condoleezza Rice (11/14/54)
Yanni (11/14/54)
Josh Duhamel (11/14/72)
Ed Asner (11/15/29)
Roberto Cavalli (11/15/40)
Sam Waterston (11/15/40)
Diana Krall (11/16/64)
Dean McDermott (11/16/66)
Lisa Bonet (11/16/67)
Martin Scorsese (11/17/42)
Lauren Hutton (11/17/43)
Danny DeVito (11/17/44)
Dylan Walsh (11/l7/63)
Linda Evans (11/18/42)
Owen Wilson (11/18/68)
Chloë Sevigny (11/18/74)
Ted Turner (11/19/38)
Calvin Klein (11/19/42)
Ahmad Rashad (11/19/49)
Meg Ryan (11/19/61)
Jodie Foster (11/19/62)
Daria Werbowy (11/19/83)
Bo Derek (11/20/56)
Sean Young (11/20/59)
Marlo Thomas (11/21/38)
Goldie Hawn (11/21/45)
Mariel Hemingway (11/21/61)
Nicollette Sheridan (11/21/63)
Björk (11/21/65)

CHAPTER 21

Your Scorpio Relationships with Every Other Sign: The Green Lights and Red Flags

Are you looking for insight into a relationship? Perhaps it's someone you've met online, a new business partner, a roommate, or the proverbial stranger across a crowded room. After an initial attraction, you may be wondering if you'll still get along down the line. Or why supposedly incompatible signs sometimes have a magical attraction to each other. If things aren't working out, astrology could give you some clues as to why he or she is "not that into you."

Astrology has no magic formula for success in love, but it does offer a better understanding of the qualities each person brings to the relationship and how your partner is likely to react to your sun-sign characteristics. Knowing your potential partner's sign and how it relates to yours could give you some clues about what to expect down the line.

There is also the issue of the timing of a new relationship. From an astrological perspective, the people you meet at any given time provide the dynamic that you require at that moment. If you're an intense Scorpio, you might benefit from a more lighthearted Libra or a sports-loving Sagittarius companion at a certain time in your life.

The celebrity couples in this chapter can help you visualize each sun-sign combination. You'll note that some legendary lovers have stood the test of time, while others blazed, then broke up, and still others existed only in the fantasy world of film or television (but still captured our imagination). Traditional astrological wisdom holds that signs of the same element are naturally compatible. For Scorpio, that would be fellow water signs Cancer and Pisces. Also favored are signs of complementary elements, such as water signs with earth signs (Taurus, Virgo, Capricorn). In these relationships communication supposedly flows easily, and you'll feel comfortable together.

As you read the following matches, remember that there are no hard-and-fast rules; each combination has perks as well as peeves. So, when sparks fly and an irresistible magnetic pull draws you together, when disagreements and challenges fuel intrigue, mystery, passion, and sexy sparring matches, don't rule the relationship out. That person may provide the diversity, excitement, and challenge you need for an unforgettable romance, a stimulating friendship, or a successful business partnership!

Scorpio/Aries

THE GREEN LIGHTS:

One of the zodiac's challenging pairs, your Mars-ruled chemistry could ignite with frequent battles of the sexes. You both love a dare! Neither of you gives in, but you'll never bore each other (though you might wear each other out). Aries' direct, uncomplicated forcefulness especially intrigues Scorpio, and you are caught off-guard, for once.

THE RED FLAGS:

You both could play so hard to get that you never really connect! Aries never quite trusts secretive Scorpio, while Scorpio intrigues and power plays can fizzle under direct Aries fire. You are both jealous and controlling, but this dynamic duo can work if you focus on high ideas and mutual respect.

SIGN MATES:

Scorpio Danny DeVito and Aries Rhea Perlman
Scorpio Josh Duhamel and Aries Fergie

Scorpio/Taurus

THE GREEN LIGHTS:

Many marriages happen when these opposites attract. Taurus has a calming effect on Scorpio innate paranoia. And Taurus responds to Scorpio intensity and fascinating air of mystery. Together, these signs have the perfect complement of sensuality and sexuality.

THE RED FLAGS:

Problems of control are inevitable when you both want to run the show. Avoid long and bitter battles or silent stand-offs by drawing territorial lines from the start.

SIGN MATES:

Scorpio Sam Shepard and Taurus Jessica Lange
Scorpio Dean McDermott and Taurus Tori Spelling

Scorpio/Gemini

THE GREEN LIGHTS:

You're a fascinating mystery to each other. Gemini is immune to Scorpio paranoia, laughs away dark moods, and matches wits in power games. Scorpio intensity, focus, and sexual magnetism draw scattered Gemini like a moth to a flame.

THE RED FLAGS:

Scorpio can get heavy, possessive, and jealous—intense feelings that Gemini doesn't take seriously. To make this one last, Gemini needs to treat Scorpio like the one and only, while Scorpio must use a light touch, and learn not to take Gemini flirtations to heart.

SIGN MATES:

Scorpio Grace Kelly and Gemini Prince Rainier

Scorpio/Cancer

THE GREEN LIGHTS:

Cancer actually enjoys Scorpio intensity and possessiveness—it shows how much they care! And like Scorpio Prince Charles and Cancer Camilla Parker Bowles (also Princess Diana, another Cancer), this pair cares deeply about those they love. Strong emotions are a great bond that can survive heavy storms.

THE RED FLAGS:

Your Scorpio mysterious and melancholy moods can leave Cancer feeling isolated and insecure. And the more Cancer clings, the more Scorpio withdraws. Outside interests can lighten the mood or provide a means of escape.

SIGN MATES:

Scorpio Calista Flockhart and Cancer Harrison Ford
Scorpio Prince Charles and Cancer Camilla, Duchess of Cornwall

Scorpio/Leo

THE GREEN LIGHTS:

Scorpio innate power with Leo confidence and authority can make a fascinating high-profile combination like Scorpio Hillary and Leo Bill Clinton. There is great mutual respect and loyalty here, as well as sexual dynamite. You two magnetic, unconquerable heroes offer each other challenges to keep the sparks flying.

THE RED FLAGS:

Scorpio natural secretiveness and Leo openness could conflict, especially if Scorpio reveals a powerful will and need for control from under a deceptively quiet facade. And Leo is often surprised by the sheer intensity of your Scorpio drive and willpower. Though as a Scorpio you won't fight for the spotlight, you will often exercise control from behind the scenes. When these two intense, stubborn, demanding signs collide, it's a no-win situation.

SIGN MATES:

Scorpio Maria Shriver and Leo Arnold Schwarzenegger
Scorpio Hillary Clinton and Leo Bill Clinton

Scorpio/Virgo

THE GREEN LIGHTS:

With Scorpio, Virgo encounters intense feelings too powerful to intellectualize or analyze. This could be a grand passion, especially when Scorpio is challenged to uncover the Virgo earthy, sensual side. Your penetrating minds are simpatico, and so is your dedication to meaningful work (here is a fellow healer). Virgo provides the stability and structure that keep Scorpio on the right track.

THE RED FLAGS:

Virgo may cool off if Scorpio goes to extremes or plays manipulative games. Scorpio could find Virgo perfectionism irritating and the Virgo approach to sex too limited.

SIGN MATES:

Scorpio Diana Krall and Virgo Elvis Costello

Scorpio/Libra

THE GREEN LIGHTS:

The interplay of Scorpio intensity and Libra objectivity makes an exciting cat-and-mouse game. Libra intellect and flair blance your powerful Scorpio charisma. Scorpio adds warmth and substance to the cool Libra demeanor.

THE RED FLAGS:

Libra must learn to handle your sensitive Scorpio feelings with velvet gloves. When not taken seriously, Scorpio retaliates with a force that could send the Libra scales swinging way off balance. On the other hand, Scorpio must give Libra room to exercise his or her mental and social skills.

SIGN MATES:

Scorpio Gavin Rossdale and Libra Gwen Stefani

Scorpio/Scorpio

THE GREEN LIGHTS:

The list of legendary Scorpio-Scorpio couples reads like a historical who's who: Abigail and John Adams, Marie and Pierre Curie, Dale Evans and Roy Rogers. You'll match each other's intensity and commitment, knowing instinctively where to tread with caution.

THE RED FLAGS:

Since you both like to be in control, power struggles are always on the menu. Share some of your secrets. Air your grievances immediately rather than letting them fester.

SIGN MATES:

Scorpios Nick Lachey and Vanessa Minnillo

Scorpio/Sagittarius

THE GREEN LIGHTS:

Sagittarius sees an erotic adventure in Scorpio and doesn't mind playing with fire. Scorpio is impressed with Sagittarius high ideals, energy, and competitive spirit. Sagittarius humor defuses Scorpio intensity, while Scorpio provides the focus for Sagittarius to reach those goals.

THE RED FLAGS:

Scorpio sees through schemes and won't fall for a sales pitch unless it has substance. Sagittarius may object to your Scorpio drive for power rather than for higher goals. Sagittarius will flee from Scorpio possessiveness or heavy-handed controlling tactics.

SIGN MATES:

Scorpio Ted Turner and Sagittarius Jane Fonda

Scorpio/Capricorn

THE GREEN LIGHTS:

Sexy Scorpio takes the Capricorn mind off business. Though you could get wrapped up in each other, you are also turned on by power and position. You'll join forces to scale the heights.

THE RED FLAGS:

Capricorn has no patience for intrigue or hidden agendas. Scorpio will find this sign supremely focused on his or her own goals. Capricorn won't be easily diverted, even if this means leaving your Scorpio emotional needs—and ego—in the backseat.

SIGN MATES:

Scorpio Mike Nichols and Capricorn Diane Sawyer

Scorpio/Aquarius

THE GREEN LIGHTS:

Both of you respect each other's uncompromising position and mental focus. You will probably have an unconventional relationship spiced up by sexual experimentation and the element of the unexpected.

THE RED FLAGS:

Scorpio could feel that Aquarius is a loose cannon who is likely to sink the ship. Yours is not a sign that likes surprises, while Aquarius thrives on spontaneity. Or both of these fixed signs could come to a stubborn standoff. Aquarius runs hot and cold and can tune out Scorpio possessiveness. Scorpio may look elsewhere for intimacy and intensity.

SIGN MATES:

Scorpio Demi Moore and Aquarius Ashton Kutcher
Scorpio Rebecca Romijn and Aquarius Jerry O'Connell

Scorpio/Pisces

THE GREEN LIGHTS:

When these two signs click, nothing gets in their way. The Pisces desire to merge completely with a beloved is just the all-or-nothing message Scorpio has been waiting for. These two will play it to the hilt, often shedding previous spouses or bucking public opinion.

THE RED FLAGS:

Both signs are possessive, yet neither likes to be possessed. Scorpio could easily mistake Pisces vulnerability for weakness—a big mistake. Both signs fuel each other's escapist tendencies when dark moods hit. Learning to merge without submerging one's identity is an important lesson for this couple.

SIGN MATES:

Scorpio Goldie Hawn and Pisces Kurt Russell
Scorpio Richard Burton and Pisces Elizabeth Taylor

CHAPTER 22

The Big Picture for Scorpio in 2010

Welcome to 2010! This year is about leadership, getting a fresh start, and embracing new beginnings. Your originality and creativity are emphasized.

Your ruler, Pluto, starts the year in Capricorn, which it entered in 2008, then again in 2009, so you probably have a pretty good idea how this transit is impacting your life. Pluto will be in this sign until 2024, profoundly and permanently altering your conscious mind, the way you communicate, and your relationships with relatives and neighbors. Your professional goals will change as well. Pluto turns retrograde on April 6 and doesn't turn direct again until September 13. During this retrograde period, pay close attention to everything that happens concerning your daily life. Follow synchronicities; listen to your intuition.

Your coruler, Mars, begins the year retrograde in Leo, in the career sector of your chart, and turns direct again on March 10. During the retrograde period, you may be revisiting professional issues you thought were resolved, and things may not move forward as smoothly as you would like. It's best to use this period to plan rather than to pitch new ideas.

Mercury begins the year retrograde in Capricorn, which may mess up your daily movements and communication for the first two weeks of the year. But on January 15, it turns direct in Capricorn, where Venus is at that time, and suddenly you're filled with new ideas. If you're self-employed, there could be new contacts and contracts coming your way.

Late last year, Saturn entered Libra, where it will be until the fall of 2012. During this transit, you'll be delving deeply into your own unconscious, perhaps through formal therapy or some other means—meditation, for instance, or dream-recall work. You'll become more aware of the restrictions in your own life, and you may chafe against them. Saturn is about structures, and it rules our physical existence, so it's quite possible that new structures will begin to form for you in any number of areas—relationships, job, family, or your personal life.

On January 13, Saturn turns retrograde and remains that way until May 30. On July 21, it enters Libra again. During its brief visit to Virgo, the last for another thirty years, you have an opportunity to strengthen friendships and your network of acquaintances.

Neptune—the planet that symbolizes our illusions, idealism, all forms of escapism, and our higher selves—continues its journey through Aquarius, your fourth house. Neptune has been in this position since 1998, so by now you're well aware of how it impacts your home life. There can be psychic experiences with Neptune, so be prepared to explore your gut feelings, impulses, and dreams. When Neptune turns retrograde between May 31 and November 6, it enters a period of dormancy. Your home and family life may not function as smoothly as you would like.

Uranus—the planet that symbolizes your individualism and sudden and unexpected change—enters Aries on May 27, for a period of about seven years. Check your birth chart to find out exactly what area of your life will be affected by this transit. That area will experience sudden, unexpected change and new and exciting experiences and insights. Uranus's job is to shake up the status quo and get us out of the comfortable ruts into which we often fall. The best way to navigate this seven-year transit is to embrace change. Try new things, go back to school, find a new career path, change jobs or do whatever you feel will expand your universe and help you to evolve and achieve your potential. This transit will form a challenging angle to your sun that requires adjustments in attitude.

Uranus turns retrograde on July 5 and doesn't turn direct again until December 5. During this period, it retrogrades back into Pisces, your fifth house of pleasure and love.

Jupiter, the planet of expansion and luck, enters Pisces and your fifth house on January 17, speeds through it without any retrogrades, and enters Aries on June 6. On July 23, it turns retrograde, slips back into Pisces in early September, and remains there throughout the rest of the year. It enters Aries again in late January 2011, where it remains until early June 2011. While it's in Pisces, look for expansion and good luck generally with your love life, creativity, and everything you do for fun and pleasure. If you've wanted to start a family, Jupiter in Pisces could make things happen!

While Jupiter is in Aries, your daily work routine will undergo expansion. Think explosive growth. This can be positive or challenging depending on your circumstances. It may also make you into an entrepreneur!

If you have a copy of your natal chart, by all means check to see where both Pisces and Aries fall in your chart. This will tell you a great deal about the specific area of your life where expansion is what you're doing.

Romance and Creativity

There are two notable time periods this year that favor romance and creative endeavors. Between September 8 and the end of the year, Venus will be in your sign. This transit increases your sex appeal, charisma, and general self-confidence. If you're not involved when the transit begins, you probably won't be when the transit ends. Venus in your sign accentuates all your normal traits and characteristics. If you get involved under this transit, your passions will be running the show! But your intuition and emotions will be your guidance system.

Venus will be retrograde, though, between October 8 and November 18, so your love life could be a bit bumpy during this time. Don't buy any big-ticket items when Venus is retrograde.

The second great time period for romance and sex falls between February 11 and March 7, when Venus is transiting your fifth house of romance and creativity. This transit should bring smoothness and ease to your life in general. But it certainly adds all kinds of spice to your love life, and your muse is up close and very personal.

Career

The best career dates this year occur when Venus transits your tenth house and Cancer—from June 14 to July 10. This period should bring about a lot of communication with bosses and peers, increased networking, and perhaps some business travel. Other people will be receptive to your ideas. This is the time to make sales pitches. Venus brings ease and artistic sensibilities to your career. With Jupiter spending part of this year in Pisces, in the creativity and love section of your chart, just about everything you experience professionally can be used as creative fodder.

Another great time falls around the new moon in Scorpio on November 6. This moon happens just once a year and sets the tone for the next year. It should usher in new opportunities for your personal life and for many other areas of your life as well. You'll feel more appreciated, more recognized, more applauded!

Best Times For

Buying or selling a home: September 14 to October 28, while your coruler, Mars, transits your sign. This transit energizes everything that's important to you personally and gives you practically unlimited energy.

Family reunions: January 18 to February 11, while Venus transits Aquarius, in the home section of your chart.

Financial matters: October 28 to December 7, when Mars transits your second house of finances.

Signing contracts: When Mercury is moving direct! Especially good between October 20 and November 8.

Overseas travel, publishing, and higher-education endeavors: May 19 to June 14.

Mercury Retrogrades

Every year, Mercury—the planet of communication and travel—turns retrograde three times. During this period, it's wise not to sign contracts (unless you don't mind renegotiating when Mercury is moving direct), to check and recheck travel plans, and to communicate as succinctly as possible. Refrain from buying any big-ticket items or electronics during this time too. Often, computers and appliances go on the fritz, cars act up, data is lost—you get the idea. Be sure to back up all files before the dates below:

April 17–May 11: Mercury retrograde in Taurus, your seventh house of partnerships. Impacts both business and personal partnerships.

August 20–September 12: Mercury retrograde in Virgo, your eleventh house of friends, groups, wishes, and dreams.

December 10–December 30: Mercury retrograde in Capricorn, your third house—daily life, conscious thoughts, communications, relatives, and neighbors.

Eclipses

Solar eclipses tend to trigger external events that bring about change according to the sign and the house in which they fall. Lunar eclipses trigger inner, emotional events according to the sign and house in which they fall. Any eclipse marks both beginnings and endings. The solar and lunar eclipse in a pair fall in opposite signs.

If you were born under or around the time of an eclipse, it's to your advantage to take a look at your birth chart to find out exactly where the eclipses will impact you.

Most years feature four eclipses—two solar, two lunar, with the set separate by about two weeks. In 2009, there was a lunar eclipse in Cancer on December 31, so the first eclipse in 2010 is a solar eclipse in the opposite sign, Capricorn. This year, three of the eclipses occur either in Cancer or in Capricorn. Below are the dates for this year's eclipses:

January 15: solar, Capricorn, your third house. Events concerning your daily life are highlighted. New opportunities related to communication, relatives, neighbors, your neighborhood, and your community. Venus is also close to the eclipse degree, adding a protective quality and a nice touch of romance.

June 26: lunar, Capricorn. Your third house again. Emotions stirred concerning the areas mentioned above.

July 11: solar, Cancer, your ninth house of career. New opportunities related to higher education, publishing, overseas travel, your spiritual beliefs, and your worldview.

December 21: lunar, Gemini, your eighth house of shared resources.

Luckiest Day of the Year

There's at least one day a year when the sun and Jupiter link up in some way. This year, March 2 looks to be that day, with a nice backup on July 26.

Now let's find out what's in store for you, day by day.

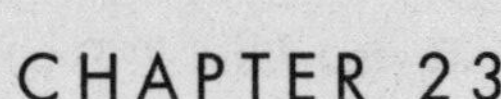

CHAPTER 23

Eighteen Months of Day-by-Day Predictions: July 2009 to December 2010

Moon sign times are calculated for Eastern Standard Time and Eastern Daylight Time. Please adjust for your local time zone.

JULY 2009

Wednesday, July 1 (Moon in Libra to Scorpio 1:20 a.m.) Sorry, but with Uranus going retrograde in your fifth house, it's not the greatest day for romance. You can expect erratic behavior along with some confusion and delays in your love life. The lesson is self-control. In spite of the adverse conditions, you can learn more about your motivations.

Thursday, July 2 (Moon in Scorpio) With the moon on your ascendant, the way you see yourself is the way others see you. You're recharged for the month ahead; you're more appealing to the public. Relations with the opposite sex go well. You're feeling physically vital with your thoughts and emotions aligned.

Friday, July 3 (Moon in Scorpio to Sagittarius 11:12 a.m.) Mercury moves into your ninth house. Your mind is extremely active as you discuss ideas, beliefs, and concepts. You express your opinions with authority on philosophy, religion, mythology, law, or publishing. It's a good day for teaching or writing.

Saturday, July 4 (Moon in Sagittarius) The moon is in your second house. You could gain a financial boost that feels like a jolt of energy. While that will make you feel more secure, you need to decide what your priorities are in handling your income. Curtail your spending, even if you've just received an increase in your finances.

Sunday, July 5 (Moon in Sagittarius to Capricorn 11:08 p.m.) Venus moves into your eighth house. You're in a position to gain financially through a partnership or an inheritance. A marriage could be motivated by a desire for financial security. Alternately, there could be a stronger sense of possessiveness and jealousy.

Monday, July 6 (Moon in Capricorn) Express yourself dynamically, but control your emotions. You can take what you know and share it with others, especially those with creative minds. A female relative or a neighbor could play a role.

Tuesday, July 7 (Moon in Capricorn) There's a lunar eclipse in your third house. You react emotionally to an event that relates to relatives or neighbors. It could relate to an event from long ago. Alternately, you might react with strong emotions to the results of anything that challenges your mental prowess.

Wednesday, July 8 (Moon in Capricorn to Aquarius 12:04 p.m.) You could be launching a journey into the unknown. Secrets and intrigue play a role as you dig deep for information. Avoid confusion and conflict; maintain your emotional balance. Hold off on making any major decisions.

Thursday, July 9 (Moon in Aquarius) Stay home, if that's possible, and tend to domestic duties. That could involve working on a home-repair project or tending to loved ones. Spend some time by yourself in quiet meditation.

Friday, July 10 (Moon in Aquarius) Complete a project, and get ready to move on. Clear up those odds and ends. Make room for something new. Accept what comes your way, but don't start anything. Use the day for reflection and expansion.

Saturday, July 11 (Moon in Aquarius to Pisces 12:44 a.m.) With Mars moving into your eighth house, you're using your native skills to investigate a matter of some importance. You tend to act aggressively regarding any joint ventures or shared resources. Thanks to Mars, your sexual drive is enhanced.

Sunday, July 12 (Moon in Pisces) Your sense of well-being relates to the state of affairs in a romantic relationship in which you're investing lots of emotion. You might enjoy taking a gamble, but be sure to weigh the odds carefully before you invest your assets. Follow your hunches.

Monday, July 13 (Moon in Pisces to Aries 11:40 a.m.) It's a number 3 day. You are relaxed but attentive. Your imagination is keen. You're curious and inventive. Enjoy the harmony, beauty, and pleasures of life. Beautify your home. Remain flexible. Your attitude determines everything.

Tuesday, July 14 (Moon in Aries) Others rely on you for help. You're the one they call upon in time of need. Be of service, but don't deny your own needs. Take care of any health-related issues. Exercise and diet are key.

Wednesday, July 15 (Moon in Aries to Taurus 6:30 p.m.) You tend to be versatile and changeable. Approach the day with an unconventional mind-set. Take a risk, but be careful not to spread out and diversify too much.

Thursday, July 16 (Moon in Taurus) You fit in just about anywhere. You direct your strong emotional energy toward getting along. You seek domestic tranquillity and security. Cooperation and partnership are key, which just might be a pleasant surprise for your partner.

Friday, July 17 (Moon in Taurus to Gemini 11:42 p.m.) Mercury moves into your tenth house. You communicate well with the public. You easily sense the public mood and can respond as required, much to the amazement of colleagues. Gain recognition for what you do. Go for it!

Saturday, July 18 (Moon in Gemini) You're back to your old self with intense emotional experiences that can affect your feelings about shared belongings. Security remains an important issue. If you are planning on making a major purchase, make sure that you and your partner are in agreement. Otherwise, you can expect a heated exchange.

Sunday, July 19 (Moon in Gemini) Complete a project that you've been putting off, especially something related to the home. Look beyond the immediate. Strive for universal appeal. Spiritual values surface.

Monday, July 20 (Moon in Gemini to Cancer 12:52 a.m.) You're at the top of your cycle. You get a fresh start as you nurture a new project that could relate to domestic matters. Be independent and creative. Take the lead; don't be afraid to turn in a new direction. Refuse to deal with people with negative attitudes. Stress originality.

Tuesday, July 21 (Moon in Cancer) There's a solar eclipse in your ninth house. Things taking place elsewhere affect your thinking. It could be the beginning or end of a trip or an educational experience. Whatever has eluded you, especially related to travel or education, is within your reach.

Wednesday, July 22 (Moon in Cancer to Leo 12:28 a.m.) With the moon in your tenth house, professional concerns take priority. Business is highlighted. Your prestige is elevated. You're warm toward fellow workers, but make sure you don't let your professional life mix with your personal life.

Thursday, July 23 (Moon in Leo) Tear down the old in order to rebuild. Be methodical and thorough. Revise; rewrite.

Emphasize quality and persevere to get things done. You're building a solid creative base.

Friday, July 24 (Moon in Leo to Virgo 12:24 a.m.) Friends play an important role. You find strength in numbers. You find meaning through friends and groups. Focus on your wishes and dreams. Examine your overall goals.

Saturday, July 25 (Moon in Virgo) Stick close to home, focus on tidying up the house, attend to the detail and loose ends. You may exhibit some perfectionist tendencies. Relax. Write in a journal. You write from a deep place with lots of details and colorful descriptions. Dig deep for information, especially about any health issues.

Sunday, July 26 (Moon in Virgo to Libra 2:26 a.m.) You investigate, analyze, or simply observe what's going on. You quickly come to a conclusion and wonder why others don't see it the way you do. Let others know what you want, but avoid self-deception. Maintain your emotional balance.

Monday, July 27 (Moon in Libra) Take time to reflect and meditate. Avoid confrontations. Unconscious attitudes can be difficult. So can relations with women. Work behind the scenes; keep your feelings to yourself. Unexpected money arrives.

Tuesday, July 28 (Moon in Libra to Scorpio 7:57 a.m.) Make room for something new. Clear your desk for tomorrow's new cycle. Accept what comes your way now. Set your goals and get to work. Strive for universal appeal.

Wednesday, July 29 (Moon in Scorpio) You get a fresh start with the moon in your sign on a number 1 day. Your feelings and thoughts are aligned. It's all about your health and your emotional self.

Thursday, July 30 (Moon in Scorpio to Sagittarius 5:10 p.m.) It's a number 2 day. Cooperation and partnership are highlighted. Your intuition comes into play as you focus on relationships. Don't make waves. Don't rush about or show resentment.

Friday, July 31 (Moon in Sagittarius) Venus moves into your ninth house. You're feeling intuitive and fond of the finer things in life. You would love a long romantic journey. An attachment with a person of foreign birth or a foreign country plays a role.

AUGUST 2009

Saturday, August 1 (Moon in Sagittarius) Expand your horizons. Focus on your finances and all money matters. Consider your priorities in spending your income. Plan for the future, but put off any big purchases for another few days. Your values play an important role.

Sunday, August 2 (Moon in Sagittarius to Capricorn 5:09 a.m.) Mercury moves into your eleventh house, so you can expect a lot of interesting exchanges with friends and members of a group who are helping you achieve your goals. Your social contacts pay off in a big way. You work well with others, especially those with artistic talents.

Monday, August 3 (Moon in Capricorn) Yesterday's energy related to communication flows on. Take what you know and share it with others. You make your point, but try not to get overemotional, especially with relatives. You take a few short trips handling your everyday chores. You accept an invitation to a social event.

Tuesday, August 4 (Moon in Capricorn to Aquarius 6:08 p.m.) It's a number 4 day. Focus on practical matters. Avoid confrontations. Control your impulses. Use your native energy to persevere and get things done. Stick with it, and you'll gain success and recognition for your hard work.

Wednesday, August 5 (Moon in Aquarius) There's a lunar eclipse in your fourth house. You react strongly to something going on in your home. A parent could play a role. Take time to retreat to a private place to relax and meditate.

Thursday, August 6 (Moon in Aquarius) Groups and social events are highlighted. Play your hunches. Look beyond the immediate. Help others, but dance to your own tune. You have a greater sense of freedom. You're dealing with new options. You get a new perspective.

Friday, August 7 (Moon in Aquarius to Pisces 6:35 a.m.) You'll find it beneficial to work on your own, especially if you're investigating a mystery. You dig deep for information, but don't make any absolute decisions until tomorrow. Go with the flow. Maintain your emotional balance.

Saturday, August 8 (Moon in Pisces) A spark of creative energy motors you ahead on a project. You take a risk, but you can pull it off. It's a good day for speculation, love, and sex for pleasure. Be aware that you tend to be more possessive of loved ones.

Sunday, August 9 (Moon in Pisces to Aries 5:24 p.m.) Finish whatever you started. Clear your desk; make room for something new. Alternately, clean a closet, your garage, or the attic. Take an inventory on where things are going in your life. Use the day for reflection and expansion.

Monday, August 10 (Moon in Aries) You're assertive and ready to take the lead. With the moon in Aries on a number 1 day, initiate new projects, launch new ideas, or brainstorm. However, be aware that emotions can be volatile. You're passionate, but impatient.

Tuesday, August 11 (Moon in Aries) Yesterday's aggressive energy flows on. You're extremely persuasive, especially if you're passionate about what you're doing, selling, or trying to convey. Wear bright colors. Imprint your style. Have an adventure.

Wednesday, August 12 (Moon in Aries to Taurus 1:51 a.m.) You started the week with a bang. Take a step back. You're feeling vital and optimistic. Your attitude determines everything. Relax and enjoy yourself. Spread your good news, but take time to listen to others. You get your batteries recharged.

Thursday, August 13 (Moon in Taurus) Cooperation is highlighted. You could get a contract for a joint project. Loved ones and partners are more important than usual, but it's difficult to remain detached and objective. Be careful that others don't manipulate your feelings.

Friday, August 14 (Moon in Taurus to Gemini 7:27 a.m.) Experiment, promote new ideas, and take chances. Speculation is highlighted. Make way for change. Find a new point of view. Approach the day in an unconventional way.

Saturday, August 15 (Moon in Gemini) Matters tend to get emotionally intense, especially if you're dealing with shared resources or belongings. You could attract the attention of people in power. Look into any issues related to taxes, inheritance, investments, or insurance.

Sunday, August 16 (Moon in Gemini to Cancer 10:14 a.m.) It's a number 7 day. There's an unmistakable sense of mystery surrounding the day. You investigate a secret or confidential matter. Look beneath the surface for answers or explanations. See things as they are, not how you would like them to be. You might discover deception, but find that others still can't see what's so obvious to you.

Monday, August 17 (Moon in Cancer) You feel a strong urge to break out of your usual routines and experience something new. Ideas, philosophies, and worldviews are more important. Sign up for a workshop or plan a long journey.

Tuesday, August 18 (Moon in Cancer to Leo 10:57 a.m.) Clear your desk for tomorrow's new cycle. Accept what comes your way now. Visualize the future, set your goals, and get to work. Strive for universal appeal. Spiritual values arise.

Wednesday, August 19 (Moon in Leo) You gain an elevation in prestige related to your profession and career. You make a strong emotional commitment to your profession; you get along well with coworkers. Material success and financial security play a role.

Thursday, August 20 (Moon in Leo to Virgo 11:01 a.m.) There's a new moon in your tenth house. New opportunities related to your profession arise. You get a boost in prestige. Business is highlighted. You get along well with fellow workers, who appreciate your efforts. You make a strong emotional commitment to your profession or to a role in public life.

Friday, August 21 (Moon in Virgo) The moon is in your eleventh house. Friends play a key role in helping you fulfill your wishes and dreams. You get along well with groups, especially when everyone is of like mind. You help the group's goals and you benefit in return. Friends play a key role in helping you fulfill your wishes and dreams.

Saturday, August 22 (Moon in Virgo to Libra 12:12 p.m.) Persevere to get things done. You're building a creative base for your future. Fulfill your obligations; stay focused. Revise; rewrite. Be methodical and thorough. There's no time for romance.

Sunday, August 23 (Moon in Libra) You might feel a need to withdraw. Things affecting the past play a role. It's a great day for a mystical or spiritual discipline. Relations with women can be difficult.

Monday, August 24 (Moon in Libra to Scorpio 4:17 p.m.) It's a number 6 day. Offer your advice and support. Do a good deed for someone. Be generous and tolerant. Diplomacy wins the way. An adjustment in your domestic life works out for the best. Be helpful, but dance to your own tune.

Tuesday, August 25 (Moon in Scorpio) With Mars in your ninth house, you're courageous in promoting your ideas. You have the ability to persuade others to follow your lead. Any long-distance travel will focus on adventure. Decisions are based on feelings rather than logic. There's a lot of internal chatter about your emotional self going on.

Wednesday, August 26 (Moon in Scorpio) Venus moves into your tenth house. You could be involved in an affair at work. A relationship at work could result in an elevation of status and recognition. You gain public recognition.

Thursday, August 27 (Moon in Scorpio to Sagittarius 12:16 a.m.) You see the big picture, not just the details. Don't limit yourself. Spiritual values arise. Worldviews are emphasized. You're restless, impulsive, and inquisitive. In romance, there's strong passion, but can you make a commitment?

Friday, August 28 (Moon in Sagittarius) The moon is in your second house. Expect emotional experiences related to money and your values. You have the opportunity to turn in a new direction. Creative people play a role. Stress originality. In romance, if you're looking, something new is developing.

Saturday, August 29 (Moon in Sagittarius to Capricorn 11:45 a.m.) The spotlight is on cooperation. You're emotional and sensitive. There could be some soul-searching related to relationships. A new one could be forming. Help comes through friends.

Sunday, August 30 (Moon in Capricorn) Get your ideas across as you go about your everyday activities. You may be in the car a lot. Stay in conscious control of your emotions. Be aware that your thinking may be unduly influenced by the past. Female relatives play a role.

Monday, August 31 (Moon in Capricorn) As the month ends, tear down the old in order to rebuild. Be methodical and thorough. You're developing a new creative base for the future. Take care of your obligations. Stay on task.

Tuesday, September 1 (Moon in Capricorn to Aquarius 12:43 a.m.) Your individuality is stressed as the month begins. Your visionary abilities are heightened. You have a greater sense of freedom. You're dealing with new ideas. You get a new perspective.

Wednesday, September 2 (Moon in Aquarius) Stick close to home, if possible. Work on a home-repair project. Beautify your home. Change a bad habit. A parent could play a role. You feel a close tie to your roots.

Thursday, September 3 (Moon in Aquarius to Pisces 12:59 p.m.) You're at the right place at the right time. Missing papers or objects are found. You can overcome bureaucratic red tape. Be practical with your money. Be methodical and thorough. Revise and rewrite. In romance, you might feel somewhat inhibited.

Friday, September 4 (Moon in Pisces) There's a full moon in your fifth house. Find time to explore the creative aspects of your life. You reap what you have sown. Take a chance; experiment. Be aware that your emotions tend to overpower your intellect.

Saturday, September 5 (Moon in Pisces to Aries 11:15 p.m.) Focus on making people happy. Diplomacy wins the way. Do a good deed for someone. Visit someone who is ill or in need of help. Be understanding and avoid confrontations. Dance to your own tune.

Sunday, September 6 (Moon in Aries) Mercury goes retrograde in your twelfth house. You could be feeling confused about the direction of your life. You might want to withdraw today and work on your own. Think carefully before you act over the next three weeks. There's a tendency to undo all the positive actions you've taken. Avoid any self-destructive tendencies. Be aware of hidden enemies.

Monday, September 7 (Moon in Aries) It's a service day. Others rely on you. You improve, edit, and refine the work of others. Keep your resolutions about exercise; watch your diet. Attend to details related to your health. Make a doctor or a dentist appointment.

Tuesday, September 8 (Moon in Aries to Taurus 7:19 a.m.) You're completing a cycle. Finish what you started. Visualize the future, set your goals, and get to work. Look beyond the immediate. Strive for universal appeal. But don't start anything new until tomorrow.

Wednesday, September 9 (Moon in Taurus) You get a fresh start related to a partnership, either business or personal. A legal matter comes to your attention. Women play a prominent role. You tend to get along well with others, but it's difficult to go with the flow.

Thursday, September 10 (Moon in Taurus to Gemini 1:18 p.m.) Yesterday's energy related to partnerships flows on. Cooperation is highlighted. Use your intuition to get a sense of your day. Be kind and understanding. Don't make waves. Don't rush or show resentment. Let things develop.

Friday, September 11 (Moon in Gemini) Pluto goes direct in your third house. You tend to comprehend what baffles others. You're a deep thinker, but you also tend to read too much into what people say. You might also believe that you know what's going on behind closed doors.

Saturday, September 12 (Moon in Gemini to Cancer 5:20 p.m.) Tear down the old in order to rebuild. Be methodical and thorough. Revise; rewrite. Emphasize quality. Persevere to get things done. You're building a solid creative base.

Sunday, September 13 (Moon in Cancer) With the moon in your ninth house, you feel a need to get away. Foreigners or a foreign country play a role. Plan a long journey or discuss worldviews, ideas, or philosophy.

Monday, September 14 (Moon in Cancer to Leo 7:40 p.m.) It's another service day. Do a good deed. Be understanding and avoid confrontations. Diplomacy wins the way, especially when dealing with someone who's nagging or making unfair demands on your time.

Tuesday, September 15 (Moon in Leo) The moon is in your tenth house. Business dealings are highlighted. You gain responsibilities and prestige. You tend to put a lot of energy into your professional life, and that could mean that you're ignoring domestic obligations. Also, it's best not to bring your career concerns home.

Wednesday, September 16 (Moon in Leo to Virgo 8:56 p.m.) It's your power day. Expect a financial coup. Unexpected money comes your way, especially if you try a different approach. You're playing with power, so be careful not to hurt others.

Thursday, September 17 (Moon in Virgo) The moon is in your eleventh house. Friends play an important role, especially a Pisces and a Cancer. You get along better with your coworkers. Focus on your wishes and dreams. Examine your overall goals.

Friday, September 18 (Moon in Virgo to Libra 10:26 p.m.) There's a new moon in your eleventh house. Begin a new project, especially if your talented friends are involved. You work well with a group. Your wishes and dreams are coming true.

Saturday, September 19 (Moon in Libra) After all your interactions with friends and associates yesterday, you feel like turning inward. Unconscious attitudes can be difficult. Keep your feelings secret. It's a great day for a mystical or spiritual discipline. Your intuition is heightened.

Sunday, September 20 (Moon in Libra) Venus moves into your eleventh house. You gain through your association with friends, especially those who are creative. You also may find some answers related to a health and diet issue.

Monday, September 21 (Moon in Libra to Scorpio 1:52 a.m.) Your organizational skills are highlighted. Tear down the old in order to rebuild. Be methodical and thorough. Persevere to get things done, but don't get sloppy. You're building a creative base for your future.

Tuesday, September 22 (Moon in Scorpio) The moon is on your ascendant. The way you see yourself is the way others see you. You're physically vital; relations with the opposite sex go well. Your thoughts and feelings are aligned.

Wednesday, September 23 (Moon in Scorpio to Sagittarius 8:44 a.m.) An adjustment in your domestic life might be necessary. Be understanding and diplomatic. Don't force anything on those around you. It's best to be sympathetic, kind, and compassionate, even if others are nagging. However, know when to say enough is enough.

Thursday, September 24 (Moon in Sagittarius) Money and material goods are important to you and give you a sense of security. It's not the objects themselves that are important, but the feelings and memories you associate with them. Watch your spending. Look at your priorities in handling your income.

Friday, September 25 (Moon in Sagittarius to Capricorn 7:19 p.m.) It's another money day. Expect a windfall. Business dealings go well. You can go far with your plans and achieve financial success. You have a chance to gain recognition, fame, and power.

Saturday, September 26 (Moon in Capricorn) You're probably shopping and taking care of your everyday needs. Get in touch with others, especially relatives or neighbors. You'll have a message to pass on. Be careful while driving. Be aware that your thinking could be unduly influenced by the past.

Sunday, September 27 (Moon in Capricorn) Take care of your domestic needs. Spend time with family and getting your house in order. You could be feeling stressed from all the extra work that has piled up. Maintain your emotional balance. Don't ignore your exercise routine.

Monday, September 28 (Moon in Capricorn to Aquarius 8:07 a.m.) Partnerships and cooperation are highlighted as the week begins. You're more sensitive to the needs of others. Don't rush or show resentment. Be kind and understanding. Your intuition focuses on relationships.

Tuesday, September 29 (Moon in Aquarius) Mercury goes direct in your fourth house. That means any confusion, miscommunication, and delays that you've been experiencing, especially in your home, recede into the past. You get your ideas across. Everything works better now, including computers and other electronic equipment.

Wednesday, September 30 (Moon in Aquarius to Pisces 8:27 p.m.) Get organized. Tear down the old in order to rebuild. Revise; rewrite. Be methodical and thorough. Clean out your desk. Missing papers are found. You're building a creative base. Look beyond the immediate. In romance, you could feel somewhat repressed.

OCTOBER 2009

Thursday, October 1 (Moon in Pisces) You start out the month in a creative mood. Take a chance; experiment. Be aware that your emotions tend to overpower your intellect. You're possessive of loved ones and protective of children.

Friday, October 2 (Moon in Pisces) Yesterday's energy flows on. You're compassionate, sensitive, and inspired. Keep track of your dreams. Ideas are ripe. Your imagination is highlighted. Pursue universal knowledge, eternal truths, spirituality, and deep healing.

Saturday, October 3 (Moon in Pisces to Aries 6:21 a.m.) Get ready for change. Think freedom, no restrictions. Promote new ideas; follow your curiosity. Approach the day with an unconventional mind-set.

Sunday, October 4 (Moon in Aries) There's a full moon in your sixth house. It's a time of completion related to your work serving others. You reap what you've sown. Others rely on you for help, but dance to your own tune. Don't let your fears hold you back.

Monday, October 5 (Moon in Aries to Taurus 1:34 p.m.) You work best on your own. Knowledge is essential to success. You detect deception and recognize insincerity with ease. Gather information and dig deep, but don't make any absolute decisions until tomorrow.

Tuesday, October 6 (Moon in Taurus) Loved ones and partners are more important than usual. A legal matter comes to your attention. You comprehend the nuances of a situation, but it's difficult to go with the flow. Be careful that others don't manipulate your feelings.

Wednesday, October 7 (Moon in Taurus to Gemini 6:47 p.m.) Finish what you started. Visualize the future, set your goals, and get to work. Look beyond the immediate. Make room for something new, but don't start anything.

Thursday, October 8 (Moon in Gemini) Security is an important issue with you. Managing shared resources takes on new importance. Be aware that your experiences could be more intense than usual. An interest in metaphysics plays a role as you get a fresh start.

Friday, October 9 (Moon in Gemini to Cancer 10:48 p.m.) Cooperation is highlighted. Let your intuition focus on relationships. Don't make waves. Don't rush or show resentment. Let things develop. Show your appreciation for others.

Saturday, October 10 (Moon in Cancer) You're feeling moody. Water plays a prominent role. You're intuitive and sensitive to other people's moods. Do something with your children or loved ones.

Sunday, October 11 (Moon in Cancer) You're thinking about your philosophy of life. You analyze and scrutinize. While you lay it all out for friends or a group, you don't feel much emotional commitment to correcting the situation.

Monday, October 12 (Moon in Cancer to Leo 2:03 a.m.) Jupiter goes direct in your fourth house. Things will be expanding for you over the next year, especially related to your home and family. Your parents play a greater role now.

Tuesday, October 13 (Moon in Leo) You gain a promotion or an elevation in prestige. You get along well with fellow workers, who are appreciative. You're in the public eye, so avoid any emotional displays.

Wednesday, October 14 (Moon in Leo to Virgo 4:46 a.m.) Venus moves into your twelfth house. You feel a love of secrecy and solitude. You're compassionate, but you may want to withdraw from the action. Your emotions are tightly controlled by your subconscious.

Thursday, October 15 (Moon in Virgo) Friends play a significant role, especially a Cancer and a Pisces. Take a look at your goals and make sure that they're still an expression of who you are. You work well in a group of like-minded people, especially if you're pursuing a project for the common good.

Friday, October 16 (Moon in Virgo to Libra 7:30 a.m.) You're focused on your professional life. You feel ambitious; you seek a boost in your status. Be aware that you're playing with power, so try not to hurt anyone.

Saturday, October 17 (Moon in Libra) Romance is highlighted. A relationship figures prominently. You communicate your deepest feelings with that special person. You might want to stay home and work things out, if there's conflict. Attend the opening of a gallery show.

Sunday, October 18 (Moon in Libra to Scorpio 11:23 a.m.) There's a new moon in your twelfth house. Opportunities to work behind the scenes or explore your own unconscious arise. Start meditating.

Monday, October 19 (Moon in Scorpio) The focus today is on your self-awareness and general health. You're particularly sensitive to other people's feelings. It's all about the emotional self. Your feelings and thoughts are aligned, but you can also change your mind about a matter on a moment's notice.

Tuesday, October 20 (Moon in Scorpio to Sagittarius 5:50 p.m.) Get everything in order. You can overcome any bureaucratic red tape. You're in the right place at the right time. Emphasize quality. Revise and rewrite. You're building a creative base.

Wednesday, October 21 (Moon in Sagittarius) Expect emotional experiences related to money and values. You feel most comfortable surrounded by familiar objects, but put off any big purchases for a few days. Look at your priorities in spending your income. It's a good time for investments.

Thursday, October 22 (Moon in Sagittarius) You're restless, impulsive, and inquisitive. There's passion in relationships. Spiritual values arise. Worldviews are emphasized. Look for ways to expand.

Friday, October 23 (Moon in Sagittarius to Capricorn 3:40 a.m.) You could be launching a journey into the unknown. Secrets and intrigue play a role. You work hard, digging deep for information. Avoid confusion and conflict; maintain your emotional balance. Hold off on making any major decisions.

Saturday, October 24 (Moon in Capricorn) You have an emotional need to pursue your studies of subjects that interest you. Your intellectual curiosity requires continued nurturing and growth. Research a foreign destination; plan or dream about a long journey.

Sunday, October 25 (Moon in Capricorn to Aquarius 3:08 p.m.) Complete a project. Clear up odds and ends. Make room for something new, especially if you can work with others. Spend the day applying the finishing touches, reflecting on what you've accomplished, and examining your wishes and dreams.

Monday, October 26 (Moon in Aquarius) Your individuality is stressed as you launch a new project. Your visionary abilities are heightened. You have a greater sense of freedom. You're dealing with new ideas. You get a new perspective.

Tuesday, October 27 (Moon in Aquarius) Stay close to home, if possible, and spend time with family. Do something to beautify your home. Take time for quiet reflection on everything that has been happening in your life. Focus on recalling your dreams.

Wednesday, October 28 (Moon in Aquarius to Pisces 3:46 a.m.) Mercury moves into your first house. Over the next couple of weeks, you show a more intellectual outlook. Others might think you've undergone a transformation in your personality. You communicate very well on a variety of subjects, and others are impressed.

Thursday, October 29 (Moon in Pisces) Saturn moves into your twelfth house. You're beginning a two-and-a-half-year transit in which you'll have to confront everything that's hidden in your life. In particular, you'll be required to meet your obligations in relationships.

Friday, October 30 (Moon in Pisces to Aries 1:57 p.m.) It's a number 5 day. That means you're open to change and want to loosen any restrictions. You're willing to take a risk and experiment.

Saturday, October 31 (Moon in Aries) You end the month on a service day. Help others, but don't deny your own needs. Keep your resolutions about exercise; watch your diet. Attend to details related to your health. Make a doctor or a dentist appointment.

Sunday, November 1 (Moon in Aries to Taurus 7:45 p.m.) If you want to move ahead on a creative venture, you need to work hard. Control your impulses. Persevere. You're building a creative base for the future. Emphasize quality.

Monday, November 2 (Moon in Taurus) Your hard work pays off. You reap what you have sown. But don't stop. Persevere; remain determined and committed. A partner plays an important role. A legal matter comes to your attention.

Tuesday, November 3 (Moon in Taurus to Gemini 11:53 p.m.) Be diplomatic, resourceful, and helpful, but avoid scattering your energies. A domestic change works out for the best. Be generous and tolerant. Don't be confrontational. You feel a need to be accepted. You're looking for security, but you have a hard time going with the flow.

Wednesday, November 4 (Moon in Gemini) Neptune moves into your fourth house and will remain there for years. It signifies strong emotional ties with your home; your mother might be playing a significant role. Alcohol or drugs may bring some uncertainty into your home life.

Thursday, November 5 (Moon in Gemini) You could be attracting powerful people. Your experiences could be intense, especially related to shared belongings. An interest in metaphysics plays a role.

Friday, November 6 (Moon in Gemini to Cancer 2:43 a.m.) It's a number 9 day. Finish what you started. Look beyond the immediate. Visualize the future, set your goals, and get to work. Clear up odds and ends. Take an inventory on where things are going in your life. Make a donation to a worthy cause.

Saturday, November 7 (Moon in Cancer) Venus moves into your first house. Others notice your grace and friendly outlook. Your presence is quite pleasing to others. You're outgoing and making new friends. Guard against vanity.

Sunday, November 8 (Moon in Cancer to Leo 5:23 a.m.) You're on! Strut your stuff. Drama, perhaps involving children, is highlighted. You're creative and passionate. Romance feels majestic. Dress boldly. Showmanship is emphasized. A partner plays a major role.

Monday, November 9 (Moon in Leo) With the moon in your tenth house, you start the week fully focused on your professional life. You're responsive to the needs of the public. You make a strong emotional commitment, but avoid excessive emotional displays in public. Be careful about mixing your personal life with your professional world.

Tuesday, November 10 (Moon in Leo to Virgo 8:31 a.m.) After all the glamour and attention in recent days, focus on your work. Be methodical and thorough. Control your impulses. Emphasize quality.

Wednesday, November 11 (Moon in Virgo) Friends play a key role. You get along well with members of a group. A strong sense of companionship is key and helps you pursue your wishes and dreams. Your interests are so diverse that you might need to focus on your goals and make sure that they are an expression of who you really are.

Thursday, November 12 (Moon in Virgo to Libra 12:23 p.m.) It's a service-oriented day. Focus on making people happy, but avoid scattering your energies. Be diplomatic in dealing with others. Domestic purchases are highlighted. Some change or adjustment at home works out for the best.

Friday, November 13 (Moon in Libra) Secret sorrows or hidden fears surface. They could involve issues from your childhood. Retreat and pursue your interests behind the scenes. Reflect and meditate.

Saturday, November 14 (Moon in Libra to Scorpio 5:25 p.m.) It's your power day. Unexpected money arrives. Open your mind to a new approach that could bring in big bucks. You pull off a financial coup.

Sunday, November 15 (Moon in Scorpio) Moneymaking ideas come to mind with no apparent effort. You're in the flow, and you get your ideas across. Your values are more oriented toward gaining material wealth than ethical, moral, or philosophical matters.

Monday, November 16 (Moon in Scorpio) There's a new moon in your first house. New opportunities related to your personal life arise. Maybe you want to move or embark on a new romance. Whatever your personal desires are, you have the chance to fulfill those dreams.

Tuesday, November 17 (Moon in Scorpio to Sagittarius 12:23 a.m.) It's a number two day; the focus is on cooperation. Use your intuition to get a sense of the day. A new relationship could be developing, but there could be much soul-searching related to it. Don't rush or show resentment. Let things develop.

Wednesday, November 18 (Moon in Sagittarius) You see the big picture, not just the details. There's passion in a relationship, but it can be a problem making a commitment. You're restless, impulsive, and inquisitive. Make use of your sense of humor.

Thursday, November 19 (Moon in Sagittarius to Capricorn 10:01 a.m.) It's a number 4 day. Fulfill your obligations. Get everything organized. Revise; rewrite. Don't get sloppy. You're building foundations for an outlet for your creativity. You're at the right place at the right time.

Friday, November 20 (Moon in Capricorn) The moon is in your third house. Trust your hunches. Express yourself dynamically, but control your emotions, especially in discussions with relatives and neighbors. Take what you know and share it with others, especially those with creative minds.

Saturday, November 21 (Moon in Capricorn to Aquarius 10:11 p.m.) Focus on making people happy. Be generous and tolerant, but dance to your own tune. Domestic purchases are highlighted. Some change or adjustment at home works out for the best.

Sunday, November 22 (Moon in Aquarius) The moon is in your fourth house. Spend time at home with family and loved ones. Work on a project to beautify your home. Retreat to a private place and spend some time in meditation.

Monday, November 23 (Moon in Aquarius) Groups and social events are highlighted. You have a greater sense of freedom. You're dealing with new options. You get a new perspective. You're seeking alternatives.

Tuesday, November 24 (Moon in Aquarius to Pisces 11:08 a.m.) Finish what you've started. Clear your desk and get ready for something new. Look beyond the immediate. Strive for universal appeal. Follow your intuition.

Wednesday, November 25 (Moon in Pisces) Follow your heart on a creative project. You can tap deeply into the collective unconscious for inspiration. In love, there's greater emotional depth. You might be feeling somewhat possessive of a loved one or child. Pets play a role.

Thursday, November 26 (Moon in Pisces to Aries 10:11 p.m.) It's a number 2 day. Your spouse or partner is at your side. Don't make waves or show resentment, but take time to consider the direction you're headed and your motivation for continuing on this path. Your intuition focuses on relationships.

Friday, November 27 (Moon in Aries) Initiate projects, launch new ideas, and brainstorm. You're extremely persuasive, especially if you're passionate about what you're doing. Wear bright colors. Imprint your style. A Taurus and a Leo play an important role.

Saturday, November 28 (Moon in Aries) Attend to daily details and be of service. Help others where you can, but don't overlook your own needs. Pay attention to your health and diet. Friends play an important role, especially a Leo and an Aquarius.

Sunday, November 29 (Moon in Aries to Taurus 5:35 a.m.) Get ready for change. Let go of old ways of doing things; find a new point of view. Experiment, promote new ideas, and take chances. Think outside the box.

Monday, November 30 (Moon in Taurus) Partnerships and legal matters are on the table. A relationship takes on new meaning. Be aware that any conflicts could be more emotional than usual. You feel a need to be accepted. You're looking for security, but you have a hard time going with the flow.

DECEMBER 2009

Tuesday, December 1 (Moon in Taurus to Gemini 9:24 a.m.) Venus moves into your second house of money. You could make a lovely sum of money, and it could relate to an artistic endeavor. Meanwhile, with Uranus going direct in your ninth house, you can expect sudden and unexpected changes in your education or your philosophy of life. You could also abruptly decide to take a long journey. Some chaos and erratic behavior could result.

Wednesday, December 2 (Moon in Gemini) There's a full moon in your eighth house. You reap what you've sown regarding your sense of security. You could receive an inheritance or deal with shared money or possessions. Alternately, you could be gaining recognition for your work with a social movement.

Thursday, December 3 (Moon in Gemini to Cancer 11:01 a.m.) You could be exploring a mystery. Secrets, intrigue, and confidential information play a role. You investigate, analyze, or simply observe what's going on. You come to a conclusion and wonder why others don't see it your way. You can detect deception and recognize insincerity with ease.

Friday, December 4 (Moon in Cancer) Your mind is active; you yearn for new experiences. You're a dreamer and a thinker. You may feel a need to get away. Plan a long trip or sign up for a workshop or seminar.

Saturday, December 5 (Moon in Cancer to Leo 12:08 p.m.) Mercury moves into your third house. Yesterday's energy flows on with new intensity. Ideas abound. You're witty and clever; you express yourself smoothly.

Sunday, December 6 (Moon in Leo) You're creative and passionate. Romance and love are highlighted. You're impulsive and honest. Publicize yourself or whatever you're doing.

Monday, December 7 (Moon in Leo to Virgo, 2:07 p.m.) It's a number 2 day. The spotlight is on relationships; cooperation is highlighted. Use your intuition to get a sense of your day. Be kind and understanding. Don't make waves. Help comes through friends or a partner.

Tuesday, December 8 (Moon in Virgo) You get along well with others, exchanging thoughts and ideas. You feel grounded when working with a group. You're a problem solver with a knack for focusing on the details, especially if you're dedicated to helping others. You're opening your heart and simultaneously pursuing your wishes and dreams.

Wednesday, December 9 (Moon in Virgo to Libra 5:48 p.m.) Persevere to get things done. Stay focused. Don't get sloppy. Be methodical and thorough. Write and rewrite. Tear down the old in order to rebuild. You're establishing a creative base for your future. In romance, you might be feeling somewhat inhibited in showing affection.

Thursday, December 10 (Moon in Libra) Retreat to a private place and work behind the scenes. Unconscious attitudes can be difficult. So can relations with women. Keep your feelings secret. Follow your intuition. Pursue a mystical or spiritual discipline.

Friday, December 11 (Moon in Libra to Scorpio 11:32 p.m.) It's another service day. Diplomacy wins the way. Be generous, tolerant, and understanding. Do a good deed for someone. Focus on making people around you happy. A domestic adjustment works out for the best.

Saturday, December 12 (Moon in Scorpio) With the moon in your first house, your self-awareness and appearance are important. You're dealing with the person you are becoming. You may feel moody. Your feelings and thoughts are aligned.

Sunday, December 13 (Moon in Scorpio) You're passionate; your sexuality is heightened. You're sensitive to other people's feelings. You could have some intense emotional experiences. Control issues might arise. It's best to forgive and forget.

Monday, December 14 (Moon in Scorpio to Sagittarius 7:25 a.m.) It's a number 9 day. Complete projects and get ready for something new. Clear up odds and ends. Take an inventory on where things are going in your life. Make a donation to a worthy cause. Look beyond the present.

Tuesday, December 15 (Moon in Sagittarius) You see the big picture, not just the details. You're restless, impulsive, and inquisitive. Travel is indicated. Alternately, you could be dealing with a matter related to the law or publishing. Expect emotional experiences related to money.

Wednesday, December 16 (Moon in Sagittarius to Capricorn 5:32 p.m.) There's a new moon in your money house, the second house. That means new opportunities that can bring in substantial income arise. You tend to equate your financial assets with emotional security. Look at your priorities in handling any new income.

Thursday, December 17 (Moon in Capricorn) The moon is in your third house. You communicate well with others, and you make your opinions known. Be careful to maintain conscious control of your emotions when getting your ideas across. Your thinking can be unduly influenced by the past. Expect a lot of short trips as you finish up your holiday shopping.

Friday, December 18 (Moon in Capricorn) Your ambition and drive to succeed are highlighted. Your responsibilities increase. You may feel stressed. Don't speculate or take any unnecessary risks. Maintain emotional balance. Your domestic scene needs attention.

Saturday, December 19 (Moon in Capricorn to Aquarius 5:39 a.m.) It's a number 5 day. You're open to change and variety; you desire to loosen any restrictions. You're willing to take a risk and experiment. Variety is the spice of life and change is good. Think outside the box.

Sunday, December 20 (Moon in Aquarius) Mars goes retrograde in your tenth house. You have a strong need for a boost in your status or a raise. However, in the next few weeks you'll feel that you're being blocked from achieving that career goal. Turn inward and use your energies to focus on a project to improve your bargaining power. Avoid showing anger or resentment.

Monday, December 21 (Moon in Aquarius to Pisces 6:42 p.m.) You investigate, analyze, or simply observe what's going on. You detect deception and recognize insincerity with ease. Gather information, but don't make any absolute decisions until tomorrow. Maintain your emotional balance.

Tuesday, December 22 (Moon in Pisces) The moon moves into your fifth house. Your emotions tend to overpower your intellect, but you're in touch with your creative side. You also might be more possessive of loved ones and protective of children. Animals play a role.

Wednesday, December 23 (Moon in Pisces) Imagination is highlighted. Watch for psychic events. Keep track of your dreams. Ideas are ripe. It's a day for deep healing.

Thursday, December 24 (Moon in Pisces to Aries 6:40 a.m.) It's a number 1 day. Be independent; refuse to deal with people with closed minds. Don't be afraid to turn in a new direction. Trust your hunches. Your intuition is highlighted. In romance, there could be something new developing.

Friday, December 25 (Moon in Aries) As Venus moves into your third house, your artistic talents flourish, especially in a social setting. You're warm and friendly. Merry Christmas!

Saturday, December 26 (Moon in Aries to Taurus 3:27 a.m.) Mercury goes retrograde in your third house. During the next three weeks, you could be feeling somewhat uncertain or insecure about your ability to communicate effectively. Expect some confusion in your communication with others, especially relatives. You could also butt heads with a neighbor over a misunderstanding.

Sunday, December 27 (Moon in Taurus) The focus turns to personal relationships. Loved ones and partners are more important than usual. You feel a need to be accepted. You're looking for security, but you have a hard time going with the flow. Be careful that others don't manipulate your feelings.

Monday, December 28 (Moon in Taurus to Gemini 8:15 p.m.) A change of scenery would do you good. Let go of old structures. Promote new ideas; follow your curiosity. Approach the day with an unconventional mind-set. Freedom of thought and action is key.

Tuesday, December 29 (Moon in Gemini) Mysteries of life and death and higher realms draw your attention. You explore a past life through hypnotic regression or ponder life after death. Alternately, you communicate with others about jointly held possessions, an inheritance, taxes, or insurance.

Wednesday, December 30 (Moon in Gemini to Cancer 9:46 p.m.) It's a number 7 day; the mystical energy from yesterday flows on. Get ready for a journey into the unknown as you explore a mystery. Work on your own and dig deep for information. Don't make any absolute decisions until tomorrow.

Thursday, December 31 (Moon in Cancer) There's a lunar eclipse in your ninth house. As the year ends, you can expect to experience an emotional reaction to a personal realization related to your education or long-distance travel. It could involve your thoughts about a foreign-born person. Whatever internal emotional experience you undergo, it could affect your ideas or philosophy.

HAPPY NEW YEAR!

JANUARY 2010

Friday, January 1 (Moon in Cancer to Leo 10:42 p.m.) Mercury turned retrograde last month and is still that way today, which may throw a wrench into your New Year's Day plans. But not to worry. With your intuitive ability, you probably have planned for the unexpected and readjusted your schedule. Tonight, the moon enters Leo and the career sector of your chart, so even though it's the weekend, you're primed and ready for work.

Saturday, January 2 (Moon in Leo) Whether you dive into work today or stay at home, you're in the mood for beautifying your personal environment (and perhaps yourself as well!) in some way. This could entail painting in bolder colors, adding fresh flowers, or even practicing some sort of feng shui to emphasize certain energies. Just don't buy any big-ticket items until after Mercury turns direct on January 15.

Sunday, January 3 (Moon in Leo to Virgo 10:53 p.m.) Over the next two days, your social calendar suddenly heats up. Pick and choose wisely, because right now you've got a lot of obligations to meet. However, with Venus in compatible earth sign Capricorn, the possibilities in your love life certainly look very nice right now. So if a friend wants to introduce you to someone, by all means get out there and be seen.

Monday, January 4 (Moon in Virgo) It's a good day to make appointments with doctors and dentists and to play catch up on the maintenance of your health. You also may want to consider joining a gym or signing up for yoga. If you don't think you can commit to daily exercise of this kind, then consider daily walks.

Tuesday, January 5 (Moon in Virgo) You're very precise today about everything. From your work to your home life, your personal relationships and even your inner, emotional life, you're after details. How does it all connect? How can you create the conditions in which all these working parts come together in your favor?

Wednesday, January 6 (Moon in Virgo to Libra 12:59 a.m.) With the moon in Libra today, you're in a social mood, but may not feel like physically being around people. So a good compromise is to update your blog, connect with people through e-mail, and work on a Web site.

Thursday, January 7 (Moon in Libra) You're clearing the decks today for when the moon enters your sign tomorrow morning. That means you should tie up loose ends, complete projects, and meet obligations. Then put together your agenda for the next two and a half days so you can maximize the energy.

Friday, January 8 (Moon in Libra to Scorpio 6:01 a.m.) The next two and a half days are your power days, when your head and your heart are in complete agreement. Today, focus on research and investigation. Your intuitive abilities are especially strong, and it would be wise to listen to that inner voice.

Saturday, January 9 (Moon in Scorpio) Venus in Capricorn and the moon in Scorpio complement each other and create what could be a very romantic and creative day. In fact, love may be closer than you think—right in your backyard or just up the street. If romance isn't what you're looking for, then the energy of this combination could manifest itself in your creative drive.

Sunday, January 10 (Moon in Scorpio to Sagittarius 2:10 p.m.) Personal security issues could be your focus. What makes you feel the most secure: a certain amount in your bank account or family and friends on whom you can depend? Define these parameters for yourself if you haven't done so already.

Monday, January 11 (Moon in Sagittarius) With Mercury still retrograde and the moon in the financial sector of your chart, you'd better check and recheck your bank statements. If you do online banking, be sure the site is secure.

Tuesday, January 12 (Moon in Sagittarius) In another three days, Mercury turns direct. So if you've been thinking about vacation or travel, do some virtual traveling today. But don't commit until after January 15. Also, don't sign any contracts until after that date.

Wednesday, January 13 (Moon in Sagittarius to Capricorn 12:54 a.m.) Saturn turns retrograde today in Libra and remains like that until May 30. This period should be one of reflection for you, where issues you thought were resolved could crop up. Deal with them. Then move on.

Thursday, January 14 (Moon in Capricorn) The day's focus is on your neighborhood or community, your relationships with siblings, and your career goals. The Capricorn moon helps you to clarify your career ambitions, and makes it easier to organize and prioritize.

Friday, January 15 (Moon in Capricorn to Aquarius 1:17 p.m.) Mercury turns direct in Capricorn, and there's a solar eclipse in Capricorn. Read the section under eclipses in the big-picture section. Count on major activity and movement today. New opportunities surface, so be on your toes!

Saturday, January 16 (Moon in Aquarius) You're on the cutting edge of thought and trends today. You'll be plenty stubborn too, but that's what is called for in the situations that surface. Try to go with the flow. A situation at home or within your family may require your attention.

Sunday, January 17 (Moon in Aquarius) Read about Jupiter's activities in the big-picture section. Today, Jupiter enters Pisces and your fifth house. This transit lasts until early June and expands your romantic and creative possibilities. If you've considered starting a family, this transit could make it happen!

Monday, January 18 (Moon in Aquarius to Pisces 2:18 a.m.) Venus enters Aquarius, where it will be until February 11. During this transit, your love life and your creative life should go well. If you don't have a home office, you may be setting one up during this period. It's also possible that you'll be involved in a home-beautification or -renovation project of some kind.

Tuesday, January 19 (Moon in Pisces) The moon joins Jupiter in Pisces. This combination should make for an enormously creative day. Your intuition is in high gear too, and if you can use it to plug in to what you're doing creatively, your output may astonish you.

Wednesday, January 20 (Moon in Pisces to Aries 2:37 p.m.) Unless you have a lot of natal planets in fire signs, you may find this lunar transit irritating. It could cause you to be impatient, restless, perhaps even reckless. Strive to listen to other people's sides. Engage employees and coworkers in discussions.

Thursday, January 21 (Moon in Aries) If you find work boring today, do something daring. Take a risk. Pitch an idea you've been keeping to yourself. Propose an agenda. Back it up with facts and passion. And then step aside and watch people flock to this movement you've created.

Friday, January 22 (Moon in Aries) There's plenty of passion in your love today. In fact, some of that passion could surface as jealousy. Try not to smother the one you love. You wouldn't like it if you were being smothered with love.

Saturday, January 23 (Moon in Aries to Taurus 12:41 a.m.) The moon enters your opposite sign, bringing your attention to your romantic and business partnerships. You may be looking for ways to improve these relationships. Thing is, the answers are already at your fingertips. Go within.

Sunday, January 24 (Moon in Taurus) With Mercury now direct in Capricorn, the moon in Capricorn's earth sign brother, Jupiter, and Uranus in fellow water sign Pisces, the stars are stacked in your favor. The only question is what you're going to do with all this energy. For starters, plan and strategize. Set goals.

Monday, January 25 (Moon in Taurus to Gemini 7:12 a.m.) The moon in Gemini may prompt you to be more chatty than you usually are, to let secrets out of the bag. Be careful that you don't reveal so much that you feel uncomfortable later on. The best use of this transit may be to stick to online conversations today, so you can think before you express yourself.

Tuesday, January 26 (Moon in Gemini) Networking is a great way to meet people and make contacts that might benefit you down the road. If you're on a search for information, use your usual sources first, and then turn to the Internet, chat rooms, and blogs.

Wednesday, January 27 (Moon in Gemini to Cancer 10:02 a.m.) This water-sign moon is probably much more comfortable for you. It increases your intuition, may cause you to be more nurturing and compassionate, and places some of your focus on matters connected to education, publishing, and overseas travel.

Thursday, January 28 (Moon in Cancer) This could be the day you book that flight to some far-flung corner of the world that you've been wanting to visit. The exotic certainly beckons. Be sure to plan ahead. You dislike getting caught unprepared.

Friday, January 29 (Moon in Cancer to Leo 10:10 a.m.) The moon enters the career sector of your chart.

You've got your finger on the pulse of what your bosses and peers are looking for. The big challenge is whether you're looking for the same thing. In some way, you're out in front of the public more today.

Saturday, January 30 (Moon in Leo) The full moon in Leo features news about career matters. There may be a lot going on in general today, and you'll need to slow down and catch your breath. Mars is just a degree from this full moon, so you could be somewhat temperamental.

Sunday, January 31 (Moon in Leo to Virgo 9:23 a.m.) The Virgo moon can sometimes create an atmosphere of criticism or pickiness. Just keep your opinions to yourself. And if someone in your immediate environment is really bugging you, write it all down.

FEBRUARY 2010

Monday, February 1 (Moon in Virgo) Friends and group associations take center stage today. It's possible that you're working on a group project of some kind that requires cooperation and teamwork. These concepts certainly aren't foreign to you, but you generally prefer working on your own.

Tuesday, February 2 (Moon in Virgo to Libra 9:42 a.m.) When the moon enters Libra this morning, you may feel a sudden need to get off by yourself and do your own thing. If possible, work out of your house and stay in touch through e-mail. You may have to emerge from your shell for a social function, but basically you're clearing the decks for when the moon enters your sign on Thursday.

Wednesday, February 3 (Moon in Libra) You may be struggling to achieve balance in your life right now. You work hard in one area, and another area suffers. The best you can do is divide your time as equally as possible. By tomorrow, it will all be a nonissue anyway.

Thursday, February 4 (Moon in Libra to Scorpio 12:56 p.m.) Breathe. The moon enters your sign early this afternoon. Feels good, doesn't it? Now your head and your heart are in sync, and it's easier to do all the things that you enjoy and that you feel obligated to do.

Friday, February 5 (Moon in Scorpio) Another power day. Keep your concentration focused on whatever it is you're trying to accomplish today. And once you've achieved your goal, kick back and chill. You've earned it.

Saturday, February 6 (Moon in Scorpio to Sagittarius 8:04 p.m.) This evening, the moon enters Sagittarius and you're on fire with ideas. Mars forms a harmonious angle to this moon, so you've got a double whammy of energy to see you through almost anything. In fact, the next two days may be quite good for career matters.

Sunday, February 7 (Moon in Sagittarius) With Mars still moving retrograde through the career sector of your chart, you have an opportunity to review and revisit projects and agendas and ideas that you thought you'd put to rest last year. You'll find value in many of these items, so be sure to keep them in a file that you can open after March 10, when Mars turns direct again.

Monday, February 8 (Moon in Sagittarius) Money, money, money—that's your focus today, and not in a greedy sense. You should define your relationship with and attitudes about money.

Tuesday, February 9 (Moon in Sagittarius to Capricorn 6:45 a.m.) This earth-sign moon is very much to your liking. It sharpens your communication skills and allows you to be more diligent in planning and strategizing career. You may get tapped for some sort of community project today. Be sure you have the time before you commit to it.

Wednesday, February 10 (Moon in Capricorn) Mercury enters Aquarius, your fourth house—his transit lasts until

March 1 and should bring increased communication at home. Your mind is especially active during this transit, so be sure to keep a notebook handy, even at night. You never know when a dream may spark a creative idea!

Thursday, February 11 (Moon in Capricorn to Aquarius 7:25 p.m.) Until March 7, you're in one of the most romantic and creative times for you all year. Thank Venus in Pisces for that. Any relationships that begin under this transit will have a deeply intuitive component. You and your partner will communicate so well that you may finish each other's sentences!

Friday, February 12 (Moon in Aquarius) Today's new moon in Aquarius ushers in opportunities related to your home and family. If your house is on the market, for instance, then it could sell in the next few weeks. Someone may move in or out. You may decide to expand your existing home or to refurbish it in some way.

Saturday, February 13 (Moon in Aquarius) With both Mercury and the moon in Aquarius, your emotions and intellect are on the same track. One feeds the other. If you've ever doubted the connection between mind, body, and emotions, today is the day to experiment. Prove it to yourself.

Sunday, February 14 (Moon in Aquarius to Pisces 8:24 a.m.) Happy Valentine's Day! Whether you're involved or not, be sure to show your appreciation for all the people in your life you love. If you are involved, then plan something special with your partner. It doesn't have to be fancy or expensive as long as it's something you both enjoy.

Monday, February 15 (Moon in Pisces) Your emotions concerning a romantic relationship may seem completely exaggerated today. It doesn't mean that what you feel is incorrect, only that your feelings are overblown. Wait until the moon is in Aries and then check back in with your emotional self!

Tuesday, February 16 (Moon in Pisces to Aries 8:31 p.m.) Your daily work routine may be filled with challenges today.

You leap right in with your usual resolve and have things cleaned up by the end of the day. You may have to think outside the box to get to where you want to be, so rely on your intuition to show you the way.

Wednesday, February 17 (Moon in Aries) With Mercury and Mars in signs that are compatible with the Aries moon, you've got plenty of energy today. Your physical energy carries you through some long work hours, and by this evening, you're ready to let off steam. Venus and Jupiter, by the way, are still transiting Pisces and your fifth house of romance. So perhaps the way to unwind this evening is with the one you love.

Thursday, February 18 (Moon in Aries) You take a risk today, and it could pay off in a major way. The risk may be something as simple as changing details in your daily work routine or as complex and big as changing jobs. If you follow your inner guidance, then you come out on top.

Friday, February 19 (Moon in Aries to Taurus 6:56 a.m.) The moon enters your opposite sign today, so partnerships are your focus. It's possible that a business or romantic partner needs additional support, which you gladly provide. Discussions with this person could involve financial matters.

Saturday, February 20 (Moon in Taurus) You're especially stubborn right now. A partner may actually turn this quality around so that it appears to be a flaw in your character. Don't buy into that. There are reasons you were born as a fixed water sign, and part of that reason may be to develop a skin thick enough so that criticism rolls off of you.

Sunday, February 21 (Moon in Taurus to Gemini 2:47 p.m.) You may be looking into such mundane matters as taxes, insurance, and wills. It's a good day to delve into any or all of these areas. You and someone with whom you share financial resources may be discussing money.

Monday, February 22 (Moon in Gemini) You're networking like mad today, perhaps to gather support for a project or idea that you're trying to promote. Be sure that you back up this idea or project with solid facts and marketing analysis. That will impress potential supporters.

Tuesday, February 23 (Moon in Gemini to Cancer 7:29 p.m.) When the moon enters Cancer this evening, it will form beneficial angles with Jupiter, Venus, and Uranus. This brings an excitement factor into whatever unfolds for you today. Any opportunities that surface will expand your world in some way. Romance and creative endeavors could be the beneficiaries.

Wednesday, February 24 (Moon in Cancer) You're more aware of your family and your home today and how both factor in to what makes you feel emotionally secure in life. You could be planning a trip and researching foreign destinations. Make your travel plans on either side of the dates for the next Mercury retrograde—April 17 to May 11.

Thursday, February 25 (Moon in Cancer to Leo 9:09 p.m.) Tonight, the moon reaches the highest point in your chart—the career sector. So lay out your professional agenda for the next two days, and don't hesitate to strut your stuff if the opportunity arises. Now is the time to get out and be seen and heard.

Friday, February 26 (Moon in Leo) In two days, the moon will be full, so it's possible that you're feeling the effects already. Full moons usually generate a lot of frenetic activity, so be careful that you don't speed.

Saturday, February 27 (Moon in Leo to Virgo 8:53 p.m.) The moon enters earth sign Virgo, which is compatible with your sun. This transit places emphasis on friends and involvement with groups. It also makes you more attentive to details. You're connecting the dots.

Sunday, February 28 (Moon in Virgo) Here's that full moon in Virgo. It actually should be quite pleasant for you, very social. Pluto forms a harmonious angle to this moon, indicating that you're in a position of power. Don't abuse your holds over others. You could regret it tomorrow!

MARCH 2010

Monday, March 1 (Moon in Virgo to Libra 8:32 p.m.) Mercury enters Pisces, and your fifth house, where it will be for the next seventeen days. This transit practically guarantees a lot of discussions with a romantic partner or about a creative project. Until March 7, Mercury and Venus are traveling together in Pisces, and all your creative projects have a distinctly intuitive texture to them.

Tuesday, March 2 (Moon in Libra) You're expected to be a team player today, and that may not suit your mood. Grin and bear it. You'll have plenty of time later in the day to chill out and be alone.

Wednesday, March 3 (Moon in Libra to Scorpio 10:12 p.m.) The moon enters your sign late this evening. Set your agenda now for the next couple of days so you can maximize the energy of this transit. Rather than tying up loose ends, which should have been done with the moon in Libra, launch new ideas and projects.

Thursday, March 4 (Moon in Scorpio) You're feeling quite good today, with your mind and heart in agreement on all the important stuff. It's a good day to investigate and research, to look for the bottom line in whatever you're doing. Whether it's a project or a relationship, you're in the groove.

Friday, March 5 (Moon in Scorpio) With the moon in your sign and Venus, Jupiter, and Uranus in fellow water sign Pisces, the day shapes up to be quite romantic and creative. Your imagination and intuition are especially strong. If you have a hunch about something, definitely follow it. It won't steer you wrong.

Saturday, March 6 (Moon in Scorpio to Sagittarius 3:37 a.m.) Money is your focus today. What you earn, what you spend, how you can earn and save more. In fact, you may want to save money for a child's college education, a trip, or even a big-ticket item like an appliance. Your attitude toward money is also central to your thinking today.

Sunday, March 7 (Moon in Sagittarius) Venus enters Aries and your sixth house, where it will be until March 31. This transit may have you charging ahead of the pack to implement something truly different in your daily work life. For part of this transit, Mars will be moving direct in Leo, another fire sign, so the energy will propel you to forge your own path.

Monday, March 8 (Moon in Sagittarius to Capricorn 1:15 p.m.) This earth-sign moon is very comfortable for you. Today, you're able to ground your ideas and dreams and to lay out a plan or strategy for implementing and achieving them. Relatives play into the day's activities. In fact, one of these people or even a neighbor may prove helpful in figuring things out.

Tuesday, March 9 (Moon in Capricorn) Your communication skills are remarkable today. You're able to talk or write about complex ideas in a way that other people can easily understand. Others are receptive too. So whether you're teaching a workshop, explaining rules to your kids, or pitching an idea, don't freeze up. You've got the facts on your side.

Wednesday, March 10 (Moon in Capricorn) Mars, which corules your sign, turns direct in Leo, in your tenth house, a bonus for career matters. Anything that has been stalled the last few months or that has seemed to languish in limbo can now move ahead. Between now and March 31, when Venus changes signs, these two planets complement each other and add passion and fire to whatever you're doing.

Thursday, March 11 (Moon in Capricorn to Aquarius 1:44 a.m.) Your home and family take precedence today. It could be that a parent or some other member of your family needs additional support or guidance on an important matter.

You may feel a conflict between obligations at home and in your professional life.

Friday, March 12 (Moon in Aquarius) You're the visionary. You can spot a cutting-edge trend before it arrives and use it to your own advantage. Test the vision against your intuition first and see if it resonates internally. If it does, take the appropriate steps to make things happen.

Saturday, March 13 (Moon in Aquarius to Pisces 2:44 p.m.) Here's another day when the moon links up with both Jupiter and Uranus. Your muse is up close and personal today, providing insights that expand your creative venues. Emotionally, you're in a very nice place, which usually means that the rest of your life is unfolding well.

Sunday, March 14—Daylight Saving Time Begins (Moon in Pisces) Some terrific surprise in your love life surfaces today. You and your partner may decide it's time to take the relationship to a deeper level of commitment. You could decide to move in together, get engaged, or even set a date for marriage.

Monday, March 15 (Moon in Pisces) Today's new moon in Pisces should usher in new romantic and creative opportunities. Uranus and Mercury form close conjunctions to this moon, so there's plenty of excitement, and events are moving quickly. Expect the unexpected. Lots of talk and discussion.

Tuesday, March 16 (Moon in Pisces to Aries 3:32 a.m.) The moon enters Aries and your sixth house. This should give you quite a head start. You're not afraid to forge your own path or take risks. Follow your instincts, and don't bother listening to the naysayers.

Wednesday, March 17 (Moon in Aries) Mercury enters Aries, joining the moon and Venus in your sixth house. The combination creates an emotional atmosphere that prompts you to speak your mind with coworkers and employees. It's as if you simply can't hold back. So let it rip, if you must. But try not to hurt anyone else.

Thursday, March 18 (Moon in Aries to Taurus 1:30 p.m.) The moon enters your opposite sign, bringing your concentration to a partnership. Regardless of the issues that surface, it's important to discuss them in a calm, rational way. Even if you feel enormously impatient to just get things wrapped up, give the situation the time and consideration it deserves.

Friday, March 19 (Moon in Taurus) The Taurus moon grounds your emotions and, yes, may make you more stubborn than usual. That's fine. It probably fits exactly what the situation calls for today. Uranus in Pisces forms a beneficial angle to this moon, so there's an element of excitability.

Saturday, March 20 (Moon in Taurus to Gemini 9:29 p.m.) The moon enters Gemini, a chatty sign that excels at networking and the collection and dissemination of information. Mars in Leo, a compatible fire sign, lends itself to bolstering the energy of this moon and your career potential. Sounds like you should be networking with peers and bosses.

Sunday, March 21 (Moon in Gemini) If you feel divided emotionally, blame the Gemini moon. The sign for Gemini is the twins, so Geminis are capable of seeing two sides of an issue, of playing both ends against the middle. Now apply this duality to your emotions, and you'll understand why you feel divided.

Monday, March 22 (Moon in Gemini) You may get together with friends today. Whether it's a brainstorming session or a social function, the bottom line is the same: great ideas, excellent communication, and good company.

Tuesday, March 23 (Moon in Gemini to Cancer 3:16 a.m.) The Cancer moon is more familiar and comfortable for you because it's a fellow water sign. Today, you nurture yourself and others. Your mother or another nurturing female in your life plays an important part in events today. Areas of focus may include: higher education, publishing, overseas travel, your spiritual beliefs, and your worldview.

Wednesday, March 24 (Moon in Cancer) Intuition and imagination, emotions and your inner world—these are your focal points today. Use them wisely and get prepared for the moon entering your career sector tomorrow. Saturn forms a beneficial angle to this moon, which helps to bring solid results.

Thursday, March 25 (Moon in Cancer to Leo 6:40 a.m.) Here it is, the moon in Leo and your career sector. It's time to show what you're really made of. Don't hesitate to step up to the plate and hit those home runs. There may be people around you who think you're boasting. Ignore them.

Friday, March 26 (Moon in Leo) The moon and Mars travel together today, igniting passion that spills over into all professional matters. Emotionally, this is a combination that can smash obstacles and move mountains. When any desire is backed by this kind of powerful emotion, miracles happen.

Saturday, March 27 (Moon in Leo to Virgo 7:58 a.m.) Time to be social and network. Join groups that support your passions and interests. Take care of things like doctor and dentist appointments, signing up for yoga classes, or joining a gym. The Virgo moon can be health conscious, so it's a good time to try new nutritional programs, new vitamins, or new alternative therapies.

Sunday, March 28 (Moon in Virgo) With both Mercury and Venus still traveling together in Aries for another few days and Mars still in fire sign Leo, you've got plenty of enthusiasm for whatever you tackle. In romance, you may be deeply attracted to someone.

Monday, March 29 (Moon in Virgo to Libra 8:22 a.m.) Today's full moon in Libra occurs in your twelfth house, illuminating an issue that has been hidden. Saturn forms a wide conjunction to this moon, indicating that the information you uncover or the news you hear is serious.

Tuesday, March 30 (Moon in Libra) Hunker down for today. You need some solitude to achieve whatever you're working on. You get the job done, of course—you usually do—but you may have to put in some longer hours. Just do the work and move on.

Wednesday, March 31 (Moon in Libra to Scorpio 9:42 a.m.) Venus enters Taurus, your opposite sign, and puts your romantic focus on your spouse or partner. You and a partner could decide to get married or to move in together. Or you may discover issues that need to be ironed out before you deepen your commitment.

APRIL 2010

Thursday, April 1 (Moon in Scorpio) The moon is in your sign, and you hit the ground running, ready to tackle whatever gets in your way. The beauty of it all is that you won't encounter many obstacles today. So pick your passion, and dive in.

Friday, April 2 (Moon in Scorpio to Sagittarius 11:54 p.m.) Mercury joins Venus in Taurus, your opposite sign. This combination, which lasts until April 25, makes it much easier for you and a business or romantic partner to discuss the finer details of your relationship. You may be more stubborn about certain things today and should try to see things from the other person's perspective.

Saturday, April 3 (Moon in Sagittarius) Now the moon and Mars are both traveling in fire signs, stimulating the financial and career sectors of your chart. Today could be the day that you land a salary increase or receive a royalty check or a check for some other service you have performed. In fact, you and your partner could come up with some joint creative project that would be both marketable and profitable. Start brainstorming!

Sunday, April 4 (Moon in Sagittarius to Capricorn 10:08 p.m.) Once the moon enters Capricorn this evening, you're in a very good place emotionally to start planning your long-range goals. You're able to list your needs and desires in such a clear-cut way that even people who don't know you would get it! In the short term, set up your agenda tonight for the next few days.

Monday, April 5 (Moon in Capricorn) Any method can be improved. But unless you have the time and the energy to figure out how to improve what you're doing, stick with what works. Today, the tried and true will be the way to go.

Tuesday, April 6 (Moon in Capricorn) Pluto turns retrograde today in Capricorn. The impact will be subtle because Pluto moves so slowly. Between now and September 13, when it turns direct again, you'll become more conscious of your own thought process. You may be revamping how you communicate too. Read more about Pluto in the big-picture section.

Wednesday, April 7 (Moon in Capricorn to Aquarius 9:51 a.m.) Your focus shifts to the future. You may be looking for the next trend, the next cutting-edge idea, or the next wave in books, movies, or fashion. Your home could become your base of operations.

Thursday, April 8 (Moon in Aquarius) With Venus still in your opposite sign, you and your partner may be sticking close to home this weekend. So rent some movies, stock up on popcorn, and settle in to chill with the one you love.

Friday, April 9 (Moon in Aquarius to Pisces 10:48 p.m.) The moon joins Jupiter and Uranus in Pisces, in your fifth house. This combination, with Venus in Taurus tossed into the soup, really increases the possibility of excitement in romance and in your creative ventures. Things may be unfolding quickly, so be on your toes.

Saturday, April 10 (Moon in Pisces) Intuition and imagination serve you very well today. Whether you're dealing with your kids, a creative project, a romantic relationship, or simply whatever you do for enjoyment, it's wise to heed your intuition. Yours often manifests itself as a hunch or as a sudden impulse to do something different.

Sunday, April 11 (Moon in Pisces) Keep a notepad and pencil on the nightstand. Your dreams may be especially vivid, and they could convey information that you need. The bottom line always interests you, and a dream tonight may reveal exactly what that bottom line is.

Monday, April 12 (Moon in Pisces to Aries 10:31 a.m.) Appropriately for a Monday, your focus shifts to your daily work routine. You'll take real risks today, perhaps in an attempt to shake out ideas from your coworkers or employees, and at the end of the day, it pays off. Just be careful not to be so blunt that you create hostility or bad feelings.

Tuesday, April 13 (Moon in Aries) How far can you take a single idea? That's your challenge for today. And the idea can be connected to virtually any area of your life. All you have to do is run with it. You get help from a Sagittarius or a Leo.

Wednesday, April 14 (Moon in Aries to Taurus 7:55 p.m.) Today's new moon in Aries should usher in opportunities in your daily work routine. If you've been thinking about setting up a home-based business, this new moon could bring about the conditions that enable you to do. Other possibilities? You change jobs, change your schedule so that it suits your lifestyle, or take leave to do something that really fires your passions.

Thursday, April 15 (Moon in Taurus) Tax day. Instead of griping about taxes—as most of us tend to do—be grateful that you have the money to pay them. In fact, whatever you spend today, be sure to express gratitude for your job, home, family, and everything else that you value.

Friday, April 16 (Moon in Taurus) You and your partner may be in deep talks about your relationship. After all, Venus is also in Taurus right now, and the combination brings a nice flow of communication and good feelings. You both want things to work. All you need is a little time to iron out small differences. If you're not involved now, this combination could bring a very nice creative project with someone whose passions match your own.

Saturday, April 17 (Moon in Taurus to Gemini 3:09 a.m.) Mercury turns retrograde in Taurus today and doesn't turn direct again until May 11. Think of this as a temporary glitch in another pretty good month. The retrograde means miscommunication, travel snafus, and possible trouble with computers, but it can also bring old friends back into your life. Time to review, rewrite, and revise.

Sunday, April 18 (Moon in Gemini) Network and communicate. And even though Mercury is retrograde, you can do this by keeping your communications clear and simple. Check and recheck whatever you write. You may be gathering information of some sort and then disseminating it to others.

Monday, April 19 (Moon in Gemini to Cancer 8:40 a.m.) As the moon enters Cancer, your focus shifts to goals connected to education, publishing, overseas travel, and perhaps the expansion of a business or product to overseas markets. Cancer is also about nurturing—how you nurture others as well as yourself. Your mom or another nurturing female could play a role in events today.

Tuesday, April 20 (Moon in Cancer) If you're planning a trip—domestically or internationally—be sure you make your plans after May 11, when Mercury turns direct. But in the event that you can't do that, be as flexible as possible while traveling, and try to take your bag onboard rather than checking it. Be sure to have a backup plan!

Wednesday, April 21 (Moon in Cancer to Leo 12:43 p.m.) Your focus shifts to career matters. And with the moon joining Mars in the career sector of your chart, you've got plenty of energy to achieve your goals. Emotionally, you could be somewhat volatile. Be sure to take a few deep breaths throughout the day and detach from results. Focus on the process.

Thursday, April 22 (Moon in Leo) Show what you can do. Not to prove it to others, but to prove it to yourself. Deep down, you know you have what it takes. You simply have to decode your intuition and then act on the information.

Friday, April 23 (Moon in Leo to Virgo 3:25 p.m.) The Virgo moon asks that you pay close attention to the details, especially important while Mercury is retrograde. Regardless of which area of your life is dominant today, you'll find that you're better off by connecting the dots rather than looking for the larger, grander scheme of things. Conquer the small stuff. And when the moon enters your sign on April 27, dive into the big picture.

Saturday, April 24 (Moon in Virgo) Your social life picks up this weekend. Your biggest challenge, in fact, may be in deciding exactly how you want to spend your free time. Which invitation should you accept? Or should the party be at your house? If it's at your place, you may spend hours planning.

Sunday, April 25 (Moon in Virgo to Libra 5:18 p.m.) Venus enters Gemini and your eighth house, and will be there until May 19. This transit usually makes it easier to obtain a mortgage and other loans. But with Mercury retrograde, you'll have to act between May 12 and May 19.You may hear of leads on good deals through friends. Hold off until after May 11 regardless.

Monday, April 26 (Moon in Libra) You may be in a social mood, but another part of you is content to close your door and do your own thing. So you can go either way today. One thing is certain. You'll be able to see the other person's point of view in any discussion.

Tuesday, April 27 (Moon in Libra to Scorpio 7:30 p.m.) The moon is in your sign, and your roll begins. Even though Mercury is still retrograde, you're able to make enormous strides with something that has captured your interest or even your passion. It could be a relationship, a creative endeavor, or virtually anything.

Wednesday, April 28 (Moon in Scorpio) Today's full moon in your sign should be quite pleasant, although a bit faster-paced than usual. Pluto forms a harmonious angle to this moon, suggesting that power issues or dealing with authority is part of the larger picture. Mercury is exactly opposite this moon, suggesting some communication tensions or misunderstandings.

Thursday, April 29 (Moon in Scorpio to Sagittarius 11:36 p.m.) A day to mull over financial matters. This means checking and rechecking bank statements, making sure your online banking site is secure, and updating your virus software. You get the idea. With Mercury still retrograde, errors are possible.

Friday, April 30 (Moon in Sagittarius) If you're a computer gamer, you may be hitting the stores today in search of some new game that you heard about or which has been released recently. If you're in search of the special gift for someone, check the online stores.

MAY 2010

Saturday, May 1 (Moon in Sagittarius) You're looking for the big picture about what your priorities are. And these are life priorities, not just your agenda for the day. So you may be asking the kinds of questions that are difficult to answer. What, for instance, do you want to do with the time you have on the planet? What kind of impact do you want to have? How can you achieve that?

Sunday, May 2 (Moon in Sagittarius to Capricorn 7:00 a.m.) The moon hooks up with Pluto in your third house. The combination leads to some very powerful emotions—the kinds that can move mountains or crush the opposition. Best to use the energy in a balanced way. You may be dealing with relatives today.

Monday, May 3 (Moon in Capricorn) Turn some of the power of the moon-Pluto combination toward your career goals. Think about where you would like to be professionally six months from now. A year down the road. Five years. What do you have to start doing now to achieve these goals? How can you connect the dots?

Tuesday, May 4 (Moon in Capricorn to Aquarius 5:52 p.m.) As the moon enters Aquarius and your fourth house, your focus shifts to home. You may be researching your family history. What you uncover may surprise you.

Wednesday, May 5 (Moon in Aquarius) People may think of you as a visionary. You probably don't think of yourself that way, but it's what you are, especially when you turn up the volume on your considerable intuitive talents. So don't hesitate to call it as you see it today. You'll easily convince others to fall into line with your vision.

Thursday, May 6 (Moon in Aquarius) Hang on for another five days. Mercury turns direct on May 11 and even though you're champing at the bit for things to move forward again, it's best to bide your time. After May 11, you'll be able to make your travel plans and negotiate your deals.

Friday, May 7 (Moon in Aquarius to Pisces 6:34 a.m.) The moon joins Uranus and Jupiter in your fifth house. This combination occurs two and a half days every month, and it should heighten not only your love life and creativity but your general mood as well. There's often an abruptness to events that happen when these three planets travel together. Sudden insights into romantic relationships and your own creative process are possible.

Saturday, May 8 (Moon in Pisces) At the end of the month, Uranus moves into Aries and out of your fifth house. So enjoy this triple water energy while it lasts! Today's focus is on children. You may be looking at a creative project with innocence and enthusiasm.

Sunday, May 9 (Moon in Pisces to Aries 6:30 p.m.) You may be preparing a project or working on an idea that you'll be presenting at work tomorrow. This could be something on which you hope to work alone, but the reality may be that you have to be part of a team. Grin and bear it.

Monday, May 10 (Moon in Aries) With both the moon and Mars in fire signs, you've got plenty of passion and impatience built up inside of you. Pour it into a creative project or, better yet, into an exercise routine. In fact, if you don't have a regular exercise routine yet, today is the day to design one. Make sure it's something you know you can commit to on a daily basis.

Tuesday, May 11 (Moon in Aries) Mercury finally turns direct in Taurus! With both Jupiter and Uranus in compatible water sign Pisces and Pluto in compatible earth sign Capricorn, your partnerships are the day's focus. In business, you're able to reach common ground with a partner and agree on the basics. In a committed relationship, it's easier to work out any differences now that surfaced when Mercury was retrograde. Overall, life improves.

Wednesday, May 12 (Moon in Aries to Taurus 3:49 a.m.) If you feel a bit blue today, it could be because this is the down period of the month, the day before the new moon. It would help to spend quiet moments with yourself, in a place where you feel peaceful. This spot could be one you create within your own home or perhaps some place outside. And while you're quiet like this, give some thought for what you would like to attract into your life with tomorrow's new moon.

Thursday, May 13 (Moon in Taurus) Today's new moon in Taurus should be especially nice to you. It occurs in your seventh house of partnerships and should attract new opportunities to meet people to whom you're attracted. If you're involved already, then this new moon could bring you and your partner much closer. You may decide to take the relationship to the next level.

Friday, May 14 (Moon in Taurus to Gemini 10:19 a.m.) Other people are willing to share their time, energy, and expertise with you. It's also a good day to apply for a mortgage or loan, to scrutinize your insurance and tax situation, and to set things in motion in terms of a will. In other words, tend to the mundane.

Saturday, May 15 (Moon in Gemini) The moon links up with Venus in Gemini, in your eighth house. The combination could bring about some curious and intriguing psychic experiences. You may decide to sign up for a workshop or seminar on intuitive development, schedule a past-life regression, or visit a community of psychics. It's an excellent day to file paperwork for a loan or mortgage.

Sunday, May 16 (Moon in Gemini to Cancer 2:47 p.m.) When the moon enters fellow water sign Cancer this afternoon, you'll feel more in the flow. If you're self-employed, you may be considering how to expand your product or services to an overseas market. You may have to call on the expertise of a friend or family member to put together your plan. It's time to expand your venues.

Monday, May 17 (Moon in Cancer) Nurturing is a vital component of Cancer. Today you're both the person who is nurtured and the nurturer. Your mother or a motherlike figure may play into the day's events. You also may be nurturing a creative project or specific goal. If so, how can you best make this project or goal work? What additional steps do you need to take to make things happen?

Tuesday, May 18 (Moon in Cancer to Leo 6:07 p.m.) Over the next few days, people will be looking to you as the person with the answers. They'll think you can do anything. And even if you feel you're trying to dance on the head of a pin, you'll pull it all together with panache. In other words, you're going to show them exactly how competent you are!

Wednesday, May 19 (Moon in Leo) Venus enters Cancer and your ninth house, where it will be until June 14. This beautiful transit could attract a romantic relationship with a foreign-born individual. If you're traveling overseas, you can count on the next three weeks or so to unfold smoothly. If you're a writer, then definitely submit your manuscript during this transit. If you've submitted it already, then this could be the time period in which you hear good news!

Thursday, May 20 (Moon in Leo to Virgo 8:59 p.m.) Once the moon enters Virgo tonight, you may want to line up your social activities for the weekend, and take time to schedule dentist or doctor appointments.

Friday, May 21 (Moon in Virgo) As your social calendar heats up, you may decide to join a group of like-minded individual. It could be anything from a political group to a theater group, a bridge or chess club, or a writers' group. It depends on where your interests lie. The point is to spend time with people who support your passions and interests.

Saturday, May 22 (Moon in Virgo to Libra 11:50 p.m.) Whenever the moon enters your twelfth house, a part of you relishes the chance for solitude, and another part of you wants to reach out to friends. The reaching part of the equation is due to Libra, a sign for which relationships are important. Keep this in mind over the course of the next two days.

Sunday, May 23 (Moon in Libra) You're clearing the decks and tying up loose ends so that when the moon enters your sign on Tuesday, you'll be ready to take on new projects, relationships, events, and situations. You may want to make some sort of symbolic gesture that shows you're serious about creating space in your life for the new. Clean out your garage, attic, or closets.

Monday, May 24 (Moon in Libra) Do some research into feng shui, and find the area of your home that relates to the part of your life you would like to bolster. Then get to work on clearing and enhancing the energy through color and object placements. And just watch what begins to happen in your life!

Tuesday, May 25 (Moon in Libra to Scorpio 3:18 a.m.) The moon enters your sign very early this morning. So right from the get-go, the texture of everything is much different. You *feel* the change in the air. You've got your agenda set up for the next few days, and you dive into one thing after another with the kind of intensity and passion by which you are known.

Wednesday, May 26 (Moon in Scorpio) The last few days of this month are guaranteed to be hectic, what with some major transits coming up. So if work is your greatest pleasure, then keep your nose to the grindstone today, and finish whatever you have started. If you're in the mood for pleasure and fun, then take the day off and indulge yourself!

Thursday, May 27 (Moon in Scorpio to Sagittarius 8:16 a.m.) Today's full moon in Sagittarius coincides with Uranus's entrance into Aries. For a review of the latter, read the big-picture section of what Uranus's transit into Aries means for you. Uranus forms a wide but beneficial angle to this moon, indicating the possibility of excitement and unpredictability to whatever happens today.

Friday, May 28 (Moon in Sagittarius) If you didn't hear news about money yesterday, it's possible that you will today. Or you have a great insight into your relationship with money or into whatever it is that you value in life. What makes you feel emotionally secure: a solid family base, a certain amount of money in the bank, friends, or your work? These questions are some you'll be asking yourself today.

Saturday, May 29 (Moon in Sagittarius to Capricorn 3:44 p.m.) The moon joins Pluto in your third house. This combination can work in many different ways, but usually on a subtle level. You may experience especially powerful emotions or have powerfully intuitive feelings or even become involved in a confrontation with a powerful person. It all depends on your particular emotional makeup.

Sunday, May 30 (Moon in Capricorn) Saturn turns direct today in Virgo. It will enter Libra again on July 21, but until then, it forms a beneficial angle to your sun and solidifies the structures in your life. You'll be able to make great professional strides while Saturn is forming such a strong angle to your sun. So get busy!

Monday, May 31 (Moon in Capricorn) Plan ahead. Strategize. Be clear and concise about your goals, whether personal or professional. Remember that you attract what you focus on. So place your focus on what is upbeat and positive!

JUNE 2010

Tuesday, June 1 (Moon in Capricorn to Aquarius 2:08 a.m.) You may be sticking close to home today, tinkering with a home-improvement project or working out of your home office. You could be touching base with clients, family members, or neighbors through e-mail, perhaps in anticipation of a reunion.

Wednesday, June 2 (Moon in Aquarius) Your family and the people closest to you may not be aware of just how rich your inner life is. This richness often comes to you through dreams and when you're in creative periods. Today, that richness seeps into your conscious mind, and you wow the competition!

Thursday, June 3 (Moon in Aquarius to Pisces 2:34 p.m.) The moon enters your fifth house—and shares that space only with Jupiter now because Uranus has entered Aries. So there should be a calm flow to the day and feelings of optimism. Things seem to connect seamlessly

Friday, June 4 (Moon in Pisces) Your imagination and intuition are heightened. You may have excellent dream recall today and tomorrow, so be sure to keep a notebook and pen near your bed. As you drift off to sleep tonight, ask for insights into a concern you have and give yourself a suggestion to wake up right after the dream so you'll remember it.

Saturday, June 5 (Moon in Pisces) Now that summer is almost here, your internal climate is shifting as well. You may be in the mood for a slower pace, a looser schedule, and more time for yourself and your loved ones. So today, take steps to make these desires a reality.

Sunday, June 6 (Moon in Pisces to Aries 2:51 a.m.) Jupiter enters Aries and your sixth house today. Between now and

July 23, when it begins its retrograde back into Pisces, your daily work routine will expand in unimagined ways. You may have greater responsibilities, be expanding your office, move your office to your home—the possibilities are practically infinite.

Monday, June 7 (Moon in Aries) Your coruler, Mars, enters Virgo and your eleventh house today until July 29. During this transit, you'll be working hard to achieve a particular wish or dream that you have. The means to do this may come to you through friends, a network of acquaintances, or even a group to which you belong.

Tuesday, June 8 (Moon in Aries to Taurus 12:42 p.m.) Partnerships are highlighted again, specifically how your values and those of your partner mesh. Any disparity in your values doesn't have to become an issue, but it's always smart to understand where the other person is coming from.

Wednesday, June 9 (Moon in Taurus) If you're accused of being stubborn today, don't bother arguing the point. You tend to be stubborn about things that matter to you, and then you really dig in your heels and refuse to budge. You apply this quality in other ways too. When you start something, you keep at it until it's done exactly the way you want it.

Thursday, June 10 (Moon in Taurus to Gemini 7:12 p.m.) Mercury enters Gemini, where it will be until June 25. During this period, your conscious mind actively seeks answers to difficult and challenging questions. What happens when we die? Is it possible for the living and the dead to communicate? Is reincarnation true?

Friday, June 11 (Moon in Gemini) You may join an online community that explores the nature of reality and tackles the kinds of questions you were asking yourself yesterday. With both the moon and Mercury in the sign of the twins, you're in the mood to discuss and debate the issues that interest you right now.

Saturday, June 12 (Moon in Gemini to Cancer 10:51 p.m.) Today's new moon in Gemini ushers in new opportunities to explore the big issues mentioned on June 11. A teacher who helps you find the answers you seek may surface. Or you may act as a teacher for someone else. Saturn forms a wide and challenging angle to this moon, so there could be some tension in the events that unfold. On the other hand, Neptune forms a wide and beneficial angle to the moon, suggesting elements of inspiration and spirituality.

Sunday, June 13 (Moon in Cancer) Make your travel plans today. The more exotic the location, the better. Just be sure to travel on either side of the next Mercury retrograde, which falls between August 20 and September 12. This moon also favors educational and publishing ventures. So if you've got a manuscript stuck away in a drawer somewhere, it may be time to dust it off and find out what it will take to finish it.

Monday, June 14 (Moon in Cancer to Leo 11:55 p.m.) Venus enters Leo and your tenth house, where it will be until July 10. This period is one of the best all year for career matters. Some possibilities? A raise, a promotion, or, if you've been looking, a brand-new career path. Women are helpful during this period, and if you work in the arts, you'll have a chance to showcase your work.

Tuesday, June 15 (Moon in Leo) Today and tomorrow, focus as closely as you can on your career. Pay attention to the various relationships, situations, and events that unfold. Don't hesitate to talk about and promote your own ideas, agenda, and products. The public should be very receptive to what you've got to say.

Wednesday, June 16 (Moon in Leo) You should get out and about today. Meet with people, network, and attend a social function. The contacts you make could prove invaluable to your career and to you personally. Dress for success today. You'll be in the public eye more than usual.

Thursday, June 17 (Moon in Leo to Virgo 2:41 a.m.) The moon joins Mars in Virgo. The combination heightens the likelihood of an active social life this weekend, even though the moon will have moved on by then. Just the same, you should have your choice of things to do this weekend. In the end, you may opt for time with a friend or a partner.

Friday, June 18 (Moon in Virgo) You're a stickler for detail today. Sometimes, this can take the form of harsh self-criticism or criticism of others. If that's how your day seems to start off, make an effort to turn your focus on work or a creative project. In other words, scrutinize details in things rather than in people.

Saturday, June 19 (Moon in Virgo to Libra, 4:13 a.m.) Balance takes center stage today in your life. It's not that you have to balance one thing with another, but that you have to discover how to balance your inner energy with external demands. Not an easy task, but today and tomorrow you have the solitude and the free time necessary to do it.

Sunday, June 20 (Moon in Libra) Art, music, dance, writing, photography—any sort of creative endeavor is therapy to your soul today. Yoga would qualify too. Through artistic play, you find the balance you need, and you are able to clear yourself mentally so that you're in a very good place when the moon enters your sign tomorrow.

Monday, June 21 (Moon in Libra to Scorpio 8:14 a.m.) With the moon entering your sign today and your ruler, Pluto, in compatible earth sign Capricorn, you're primed for success. You're able to take the smallest task and make it important to the overall functioning of whatever you're doing. Pluto puts you in the communication power seat. You speak, and people listen.

Tuesday, June 22 (Moon in Scorpio) On June 26, there's a lunar eclipse in Capricorn, in your third house, and Pluto falls in exactly the same degree. You may be feeling the impact of this already, a kind of surge of power that comes over you at odd times, as if all your circuits are overloading. Take a few deep breaths.

Wednesday, June 23 (Moon in Scorpio to Sagittarius 2:11 p.m.) Uranus and Jupiter in Aries form harmonious angles to this Sagittarius moon. So, financially, expect sudden developments that somehow expand your money base. It could be an unexpected raise, a payment for a service rendered, or even a royalty check. Don't spend it all in one place.

Thursday, June 24 (Moon in Sagittarius) You can see the forest, and for today, that's all you need to see. Don't worry about the details, about the stuff going on behind the scenes, about the whispered conversations you imagine are happening in the hallways. Keep your eyes on the forest.

Friday, June 25 (Moon in Sagittarius to Capricorn 11:22 p.m.) Mercury enters fellow water sign Cancer, where it will be until July 9. This should be a very nice period for you, particularly because it falls over the July Fourth weekend, when many of us will be visiting family and friends and generally nurturing our relationships with these people.

Saturday, June 26 (Moon in Capricorn) This powerful lunar eclipse in Capricorn triggers strong emotions related to relatives, writing and other forms of communication, and with anything connected to your community or neighborhood. It forms a harmonious angle to your sun, suggesting that your power base could be boosted somehow. If you're a writer, hold off submitting a manuscript until you reach the new moon next month.

Sunday, June 27 (Moon in Capricorn) The Capricorn moon could easily turn you into a control freak. You know the type: the person who insists on directing the day's activities even though direction isn't needed; the parent who turns a fun day into a misery of rules and regulations; the friend who insists on doing things his or her way even though another way would be better. So don't plan anything today. Go with the flow.

Monday, June 28 (Moon in Capricorn to Aquarius 9:53 a.m.) Get together today with one of your groups—coworkers, a book group, or a theater or writers' group. Whatever it is, immerse yourself in the collective. And if you don't belong to any groups, then go to a spot where there are a lot of people and listen to how people speak and what they talk about. Observe. Learn.

Tuesday, June 29 (Moon in Aquarius) You may feel emotionally detached today, which is probably a good thing. Your mind will be clearer, your heart calmer. But because Aquarius is a fixed sign, just like Scorpio, pity the fool who tries to change your mind about something near and dear to you. You won't budge.

Wednesday, June 30 (Moon in Aquarius to Pisces 10:11 p.m.) Breathe. The moon is in a fellow water sign again, in your fifth house of romance, creativity, and children. This moon is one you probably enjoy because it deepens your intuitive connection to the environment around you. So kick back, shut your eyes, and relax. That's sure to get your creative adrenaline pumping.

JULY 2010

Thursday, July 1 (Moon in Pisces) This lunar transit really should be one of your favorites. For a couple of days each month, the universe rewards you by providing space in which you can do anything you enjoy. So what's your greatest pleasure: travel, a creative ambition, kids, romance, hiking, or swimming? Whatever it, indulge yourself.

Friday, July 2 (Moon in Pisces) With Venus still in Leo and your tenth house, your greatest pleasure today may be a romance going on between you and a coworker or just doing your thing at work! Regardless, the day is yours to enjoy.

Saturday, July 3 (Moon in Pisces to Aries 10:45 a.m.) The moon joins Uranus and Jupiter, which are both in Aries and your sixth house now. Just in time for the long July Fourth holiday! You may, in fact, find that you need to work part of this long weekend. It's not that anyone is breathing down your neck; this compulsion comes from within.

Sunday, July 4 (Moon in Aries) Happy Independence Day! Whether you stay in town or leave to spend the weekend elsewhere, you're certain to take your work along—even if it's only in your head! Engage yourself in some creative way. Perhaps there's a manuscript gathering dust in your drawer or a portfolio that could be updated. You may want to give some thought to the idea of freedom and what it means to you.

Monday, July 5 (Moon in Aries to Taurus 9:30 p.m.) Uranus turns retrograde in Aries and begins its journey back into Pisces, which begins again on August 13. Read more about Uranus's movement in the big-picture section. For today, hold on to your hat. It's possible that you have to revisit an issue at work that you thought was resolved.

Wednesday, July 7 (Moon in Taurus) The moon enters your opposite sign and your focus shifts to a partner—business or romantic—or, if you're in your teens, to friends. This moon also prompts questions about emotional security. What makes you feel most secure within your world: a certain amount of money in your bank account, your family, or your business or job?

Thursday, July 8 (Moon in Taurus to Gemini 4:51 a.m.) On July 11, there's a solar eclipse in Cancer. Give some thought today to what kinds of new experiences and opportunities you would like this solar eclipse to bring into your life. Make a list. Imagine these things happening. Back your imagining with emotion and intense desire. Then step aside, and let the universe do its work.

Friday, July 9 (Moon in Gemini) Mercury enters Leo and the career sector of your chart. Between now and July 27, you may be traveling for work. You should be pitching your ideas and generally pushing your agenda and goals forward. Discuss your ideas with coworkers and bosses. You'll be surprised at how much support you have.

Saturday, July 10 (Moon in Gemini to Cancer 8:38 a.m.) Venus enters Virgo today, where it will be until August 6. During this transit, it's possible that a romance begins with someone you meet through friends or through a group to which you belong. This person could be a friend already, and you both realize you have more in common than you thought.

Sunday, July 11 (Moon in Cancer) Today's solar eclipse in Cancer occurs in your ninth house and should usher in new opportunities in foreign travel, publishing, education, and the development and expansion of your worldview. Heady stuff, right? And since Cancer is about nurturing, there will be new opportunities for you to nurture someone else. You may also have the opportunity to nurture a creative project.

Monday, July 12 (Moon in Cancer to Leo 9:54 a.m.) The moon is in Leo, and this combination should boost your popularity quotient at work! Everyone loves you today and believes you have the answers. So if there's a particular idea or project you want to push, you can easily gather the support you need.

Tuesday, July 13 (Moon in Leo) If you feel overwhelmed by responsibility today, then leave work early and do something for yourself. Go to a spa. Get a massage. Take in a movie. Buy a book you've coveted. Spend time with your kids or a pet. You get the idea here. Today is about *you.*

Wednesday, July 14 (Moon in Leo to Virgo 10:15 a.m.) The moon joins Venus in Virgo, a very nice combination that heightens your social life, friendships, and wishes and dreams. Everything in these areas should proceed smoothly until August 6, when Venus enters Libra and your twelfth house. So get together with friends, join a group, and get involved.

Thursday, July 15 (Moon in Virgo) There's a service component to the Virgo moon, where you do something for someone else without any thought of compensation. It could be a friend, neighbor, or relative. Whoever it is, you're happy to help.

Friday, July 16 (Moon in Virgo to Libra 11:25 a.m.) The moon enters Libra and your twelfth house—a sure sign that it's time to clear the decks and tie up loose ends again. You're getting prepared for Sunday, when the moon enters your sign, always a high point in every monthly cycle. So do something to unclutter your life today. Clean closets; bundle up clothes you no longer wear and donate them to a homeless shelter. Clean out the garage, the attic, and your desk.

Saturday, July 17 (Moon in Libra) You and a friend or several friends may take in an art exhibit, attend an opera, or do something else that boosts your creative soul. Change is in the air. You can taste it. The question is, how can you initiate change in your own life?

Sunday, July 18 (Moon in Libra to Scorpio 2:43 p.m.) The moon enters your sign this afternoon, and you feel the change in your mood almost immediately. Suddenly, it all makes sense. The inner you and the outer you are in agreement on the basics and then some! So tackle something you've had on the back burner. You'll burn through it in no time.

Monday, July 19 (Moon in Scorpio) With Venus in Virgo and the moon in your own sign, your love life should be picking up right now. You and your partner are defining your relationship and may be ready to take it to the next level of commitment. If you're living together or already married, then your home life may be changing in some way. A birth? Someone moves in?

Tuesday, July 20 (Moon in Scorpio to Sagittarius 8:49 p.m.) The moon enters your second house. This transit often brings your finances up front and center. How much are you earning and spending? Do they balance out? Are you able to save some of what you earn? These are questions you'll be trying to answer today.

Wednesday, July 21 (Moon in Sagittarius) With the big picture firmly in your mind, you set out to plot a course toward the ultimate goal. Think of it as a quest. How are you going to get from point A to point Z? What detours will you have to take? What's the shortest distance between these two points?

Thursday, July 22 (Moon in Sagittarius) If you're feeling nomadic, blame the Sagittarius moon. You may want to indulge your restlessness by driving to a town or city you've never visited before. Be adventurous. Walk around, talk to people, and see what you discover about yourself in the process.

Friday, July 23 (Moon in Sagittarius to Capricorn 5:40 a.m.) The moon joins Pluto in your third house. This will be happening several days a month for the next thirteen or fourteen years. So pay attention to the feelings you have today and to the events and situations that unfold. They're part of a larger pattern.

Saturday, July 24 (Moon in Capricorn) Your career ambitions are at the heart of your activities. Even though it's Saturday, you may find yourself planning and strategizing with a friend or sibling about something coming up next week at work. Or a friend or sibling could be helping you put together a professional résumé.

Sunday, July 25 (Moon in Capricorn to Aquarius 4:39 p.m.) Today's full moon in Aquarius occurs in your fourth house. Expect news related to family and home and a lot of activity generally centered in and around your home. The intuitive qualities that you have are heightened in some way around the time of this full moon.

Monday, July 26 (Moon in Aquarius) Read a totally different kind of book from what you normally read. Not only will your intellect expand with possibilities, but an entire new universe of ideas will open for you. Aquarius loves an intellectual challenge. One of your parents or someone else within your family group may require additional help.

Tuesday, July 27 (Moon in Aquarius) Mercury enters Virgo, joining Venus in your eleventh house. This duo is sure to bring increased communication with a romantic partner or with an artistic friend. There's plenty of energy to go around in any kind of group gathering. If a romance begins under these transits, it may be with someone who is first and foremost a friend.

Wednesday, July 28 (Moon in Aquarius to Pisces 5:00 a.m.) A creative project that you may have put on hold some months ago now seizes your passion again. You dive into it with a new perspective. You may get help from an unexpected source. Be gracious in your appreciation for this helper.

Thursday, July 29 (Moon in Pisces) Mars enters Libra, joining Saturn in your twelfth house. Between now and September 14, when Mars enters your sign, you'll be working hard behind the scenes. Whether the work is related to your work, your personal life, or your creativity, your focus will be intense. This is a good time to take up meditation or even therapy, if you're so inclined.

Friday, July 30 (Moon in Pisces to Aries 5:42 p.m.) The moons joins Jupiter and Uranus in your sixth house. This trio of planets really has you zipping through your workday like a crazy person, probably trying to do too much at once. Pause, take a deep breath, and delegate. By the end of the day, you'll be glad that you did.

Saturday, July 31 (Moon in Aries) You can turn your physical energy toward your personal life today. It's Saturday, right? So whether you're tackling home-improvement projects or traveling, throwing a party or pursuing something that interests you, you're on fire.

AUGUST 2010

Sunday, August 1 (Moon in Aries) You enter August at a breakneck speed, trying to cover all the bases. But you're just one person, and until you're cloned, it's best to keep your tasks to a manageable number so you don't wear yourself out before September gets here. Jupiter is trying to expand your daily work routine, but may be doing it in a way that makes you feel scattered.

Monday, August 2 (Moon in Aries to Taurus 5:13 a.m.) What is it that you want and value in a personal relationship? In a business partnership? You wrestle with these questions today even though, at some level, you already know the answers. Look to your friendships. Which ones have the qualities that make you feel most comfortable? List the qualities. That's the place to start.

Tuesday, August 3 (Moon in Taurus) It's only Tuesday, and already the social invites are coming in for this weekend. But you may have your eye on someone who interests you romantically. If you're involved already, then the energy could unfold in a creative way, through a project you're involved in with other people.

Wednesday, August 4 (Moon in Taurus to Gemini 1:54 p.m.) This isn't your favorite moon, unless you have natal planets in Gemini. That said, it does prompt you to network and touch base with friends, clients, and acquaintances. It boots you out of yourself and into the larger world of people and information. In a mundane sense, this transit favors tax and insurance matters.

Thursday, August 5 (Moon in Gemini) You could feel restless today and not be able to figure out why. Sometimes, the why really is irrelevant. Just go with the flow of what you're feeling and understand that your emotions are the gauge by which you can measure whether you're in the right place within yourself.

Friday, August 6 (Moon in Gemini to Cancer 6:50 p.m.) Venus enters Libra, where it will be until September 8. If a romance begins under this transit, it could have a secretive quality to it. If the relationship itself is being kept a secret, that won't last after Venus enters your sign next month!

Saturday, August 7 (Moon in Cancer) Your mood is much gentler today, more nurturing, and probably more intuitive. If you're headed off to college or grad school soon, you may be making final preparations. If you're a writer in search of a publisher, then submit your manuscript while the moon is in Cancer.

Sunday, August 8 (Moon in Cancer to Leo 8:23 p.m.) The moon enters the career sector of your chart. The energy of this transit isn't anything new to you. But since being informed is to be empowered, set your agenda today for tomorrow. Since tomorrow is a new moon, you'll be glad that you did!

Monday, August 9 (Moon in Leo) Okay, this new moon in the career sector of your chart bodes very well for new professional opportunities headed your way. This moon happens only once a year and should bring exactly the right opportunities you've been looking for in terms of your career. You could gain new responsibilities, a promotion, recognition by peers and bosses, or even a new career opportunity altogether.

Tuesday, August 10 (Moon in Leo to Virgo 8:02 p.m.) In just ten days, Mercury will turn retrograde in Virgo, in your eleventh house. Before that happens, be sure to buy big-ticket items and make your travel plans. You may also want to consider buying an external hard drive for your computer to back up all your files.

Wednesday, August 11 (Moon in Virgo) You're into that perfectionist groove today. And that tendency may be focused on a romantic relationship or a creative project. How can you improve one or both? What do you need to do to make these improvements? Best to stick with yourself rather than expecting the other person to change.

Thursday, August 12 (Moon in Virgo to Libra 7:44 p.m.) The moon joins Venus in your twelfth house. This duo heightens emotions in a romantic relationship. You may feel caught up in the whirlwind of it all, barely able to catch your breath.

Or you could feel somewhat uneasy that things are moving too quickly. Just take it all in stride.

Friday, August 13 (Moon in Libra) You're seeking balance today. It's possible that you need more time to yourself. Not only do you go through periods where you crave solitude, but you need those periods to maintain your mental, emotional, and spiritual health. So don't hesitate to take off work early if you're feeling squeezed.

Saturday, August 14 (Moon in Libra to Scorpio 9:27 p.m.) The moon enters your sign this evening, and you feel as if a weight has fallen off of your shoulders. Now that you're in a lighter state of being, you may want to socialize a bit more over the weekend. You'll be the life of the party.

Sunday, August 15 (Moon in Scorpio) Another power day. One activity that is favored when the moon is in your sign is meditation. Your sign is especially designed for deep introspection, and meditation is one way to achieve this. There are numerous techniques available online, or hit your local bookstore and look in the self-help section.

Monday, August 16 (Moon in Scorpio) Mercury will be turning retrograde in Virgo and your eleventh house on August 20, and be lending itself to some mischief and miscommunication with friends. Be sure to treat your friends gently right now, and warn them about the retrograde so everyone is aware of it.

Tuesday, August 17 (Moon in Scorpio to Sagittarius 2:35 a.m.) Check and recheck bank accounts. When Mercury is about to turn retrograde, you can start experiencing some of snafus. With the moon in your financial sector today, you have an opportunity to stay on top of things. It's also wise to make sure your tax and insurance payments are up-to-date.

Wednesday, August 18 (Moon in Sagittarius) You could be virtual traveling today. Pick any spot on the globe that interests you and figure out how expensive this trip would be. If you can afford it, plan it after Mercury turns direct on September 12 and before or after the next retrograde period, which falls between December 10 and December 30.

Thursday, August 19 (Moon in Sagittarius to Capricorn 11:18 a.m.) As the moon enters your third house, you probably feel more grounded, and you're better able to plan and figure things out in a rational, reasoned way. Your relatives could play a role in the day's events. And if not them, a neighbor. Or all three. Back up computer files. Tomorrow Mercury turns retrograde.

Friday, August 20 (Moon in Capricorn) Mercury turns retrograde in Virgo. You should be prepared for it. On other fronts, Jupiter and Uranus in Aries and your sixth house continue to toss sudden changes your way, which force you to alter something in your work routine. The alteration could expand your opportunities in some way.

Saturday, August 21 (Moon in Capricorn to Aquarius 10:38 p.m.) The moon is in flux, which often leads you into a disoriented, confused period. It doesn't last long, but it does prompt you to question everything. Hang on. Once the moon is solidly in Aquarius, you'll feel a hundred percent better.

Sunday, August 22 (Moon in Aquarius) Things at home could be a bit strange. Blame Mercury's mischief. If an appliance goes on the fritz, it's best to wait until after September 12 to replace it. However, the upside of the retrograde is that old friends may begin to surface.

Monday, August 23 (Moon in Aquarius) Your actions today generate a buzz. You're thinking very far outside the box, and people like what they're hearing. It's likely that your ideas will catch the attention of someone who will prove to be one of your biggest supporters.

Tuesday, August 24 (Moon in Aquarius to Pisces 11:11 a.m.) Today's full moon in Pisces and your fifth house should be quite romantic and creative. The insights you gain and the news you hear should have you celebrating. Pluto forms a tight and beneficial angle to this moon—and to your sun—indicating that you're in the driver's seat.

Wednesday, August 25 (Moon in Pisces) You're moving at the speed of light on a creative project. It could involve your kids, if you have children. It's the sort of thing you're very good at: connecting the dots on an intuitive level and then explaining it to others who may lack your expertise.

Thursday, August 26 (Moon in Pisces to Aries 11:49 p.m.) Emotionally, you're on fire. And this spills over into other areas of your life and helps slam through any obstacles that you may face. Even though brute force isn't always the best way to vanquish an obstacle, it works this time. It's part of that Uranus transit. Then Jupiter comes along and vacuums up the pieces and rearranges them in a way that expands your venue and opportunities.

Friday, August 27 (Moon in Aries) Drama is on your plate today. It may revolve around home and family, but it would be to your advantage to see where it actually falls in your natal chart. That will tell you where the drama will be. Mars is opposite this moon, which creates tension.

Saturday, August 28 (Moon in Aries) It's time to take stock of where you're going and where you have been. What would you like to accomplish during the last four months of the year? How can you best do this? Make a list. Write it all out. That makes it more real.

Sunday, August 29 (Moon in Aries to Taurus 11:36 a.m.) When the moon is opposite your sun, you may feel that only you are right and correct. It's a good idea to attempt to be more flexible, to slip into the other person's shoes for a few moments and see things from that person's perspective.

Monday, August 30 (Moon in Taurus) Stubborn? Who, you? Not a chance, right? Well, today you are stubborn and then some. It's because the Taurus moon, like your Scorpio sun, is a fixed sign. This means that you are slow to change your opinions and beliefs. It takes more than just a debate. You must be convinced on an intuitive level.

Tuesday, August 31 (Moon in Taurus to Gemini 9:20 p.m.) Go celebrate. It's almost the end of summer. It really is time for you to carve out time for yourself and your own interests. It's not selfishness. For you, it's self-preservation.

SEPTEMBER 2010

Wednesday, September 1 (Moon in Gemini) People step up to the plate to share their time and expertise with you. It's as if you sent out a call for help, and everyone answered, even people you don't know. Well, maybe not total strangers, but certainly people you hadn't expected.

Thursday, September 2 (Moon in Gemini) Network and communicate—that's the name of the game today. How you do it is entirely up to you. Have a party, go to a party, or send out a telepathic hello! The new contacts you make now could be important down the road, so be organized with business cards, addresses, e-mail addresses, and the like.

Friday, September 3 (Moon in Gemini to Cancer 3:51 a.m.) This moon is more to your liking. It enhances your intuition and imagination, and deepens your emotions. Today, the areas that are highlighted include publishing, education, your spiritual beliefs, and overseas travel. If you're a writer, hold off submitting until after Mercury is direct.

Saturday, September 4 (Moon in Cancer) The long Labor Day weekend may have you hanging out at home. Traveling when everyone else does is something you rarely enjoy. Perhaps your trip out of town will happen after September 12! You may be beautifying your home in some way, adding fresh flowers or repainting rooms.

Sunday, September 5 (Moon in Cancer to Leo 6:46 a.m.) There's an element of the showman in you today. For some reason, you're out in front of the public more than usual. Whether you're involved in a charity event or throwing a party, the public's eyes are on you.

Monday, September 6 (Moon in Leo) Can you hang in there another six days? Once Mercury turns direct, it's like a stone flying out of a slingshot. Everything starts shooting forward again. So don't let the events today get you down or slow you down. Keep revising and reviewing your plans and projects.

Tuesday, September 7 (Moon in Leo to Virgo 6:54 a.m.) The moon joins retrograde Mercury. Ouch. This duo can feel pretty strange if only because the retrograde could bring some confusion to what you think and feel. And since these transits occur in the friendship area of your chart, be gentle with your friends, and ask the same of them in return!

Wednesday, September 8 (Moon in Virgo) Today's new moon in Virgo should usher in opportunities for you to work toward achieving your dreams. New people enter your life as well; they facilitate your means for doing this. Mercury forms a wide conjunction to this moon, suggesting a lot of debate and discussion. Today also marks the beginning of Venus's transit through your sign, which will be one of the most romantic and creative times for you all year. Read more about this transit in the big-picture section.

Thursday, September 9 (Moon in Virgo to Libra 6:02 a.m.) Think back to a happy childhood memory. Muster the emotions you felt then. And as you go through your day today, use those early emotions to enhance your mood now, as an adult. If this doesn't work for you, then find something—anything—in your environment to appreciate.

Friday, September 10 (Moon in Libra) Team up with a partner or a friend or even a family member, and explore your past lives together. Do this through meditation, dream recall, or with a regression therapist. As an intuitive Scorpio, you may have had glimpses of past lives already. A regression would snap it all into focus.

Saturday, September 11 (Moon in Libra to Scorpio 6:22 a.m.) It's that time of month again, when the moon enters your sign. It happens early—a major plus. It means that upon awakening, you're immediately in that groove called *Scorpio,* with your head and heart in complete agreement. You're ready to investigate, research, and get to the bottom line. But the bottom line of what? Well, it could be a relationship. Right now, Venus is in your sign also.

Sunday, September 12 (Moon in Scorpio) Mercury turns direct in Virgo, a very nice bonus that should enhance your love life, your creativity, your career—well, you get the picture. The planets are lined up in your favor now. Use this abundant energy with the care and wisdom it deserves!

Monday, September 13 (Moon in Scorpio to Sagittarius 9:52 a.m.) Pluto turns direct today in Capricorn. Let's take stock. Pluto and Mercury are both in earth signs compatible with your sign, Venus is in your sign, and tomorrow Mars joins Venus. Whew. Your love life, sexuality, and physical energy are about to go through the roof. Buckle up. It's going to be a wild ride.

Tuesday, September 14 (Moon in Sagittarius) Mars enters your sign, where it will be until October 28. While Venus and Mars travel together, you can be sure that the chemistry between you and a romantic partner is exquisite. You're not only on the same page, but may be feeling the same things too. Think of this connection as the telepathy of emotions.

Wednesday, September 15 (Moon in Sagittarius to Capricorn 5:30 p.m.) It could be one of those days when you brainstorm with coworkers or even with your family members or close friends. Whether you're getting ready to launch a product or pitch an idea, the people around you are supportive. Their ideas are good, so don't be too firmly wedded to the notion that your way is the only way!

Thursday, September 16 (Moon in Capricorn) The sign for Capricorn is the goat. Goats are among the most sure-footed creatures, so today, that's how you are emotionally. You feel certain that whatever you're doing is exactly the right way to go about things.

Friday, September 17 (Moon in Capricorn) Now that Mercury is moving direct, you're in a much better place in terms of just about everything. With Venus still in your sign, your love life is yielding some nice surprises, and your creative drive is exceptionally strong. You feel sexy and seductive, and your self-confidence should be at record levels.

Saturday, September 18 (Moon in Capricorn to Aquarius 4:35 a.m.) It's an idea day, and your inspiration comes from numerous sources. But the greatest source may be within your own family. Your partner or a parent or one of your kids says or does something, and suddenly you're off and running with an idea. Record it. Write it down. And when the moon enters Pisces, tackle it and flesh it out.

Sunday, September 19 (Moon in Aquarius) You may be playing around with divination systems today. It can be anything—tarot cards, the I Ching, astrology, or even unconventional systems like cloud reading. Or opening a dictionary at random and pointing at a word. As the intuitive of the zodiac, you really don't need an external system. But sometimes it's a good thing to have for confirmation about what you're feeling.

Monday, September 20 (Moon in Aquarius to Pisces 5:15 p.m.) Tackle those ideas you recorded on Saturday. Your imagination and intuition are heightened with the moon in Pisces, and it's much easier to access information now. You can turn all these ideas into creative fodder, and you probably will do so before the moon enters Aries on Thursday.

Tuesday, September 21 (Moon in Pisces) If you have kids, then today they are a source of joy and wonder for you. It's as if you suddenly see the world through their eyes and realize just how rooted in the moment they are. Try this every morning when you awaken and feel not quite as optimistic as you would like.

Wednesday, September 22 (Moon in Pisces) Venus and Mars are both in your sign. This combination is practically a guarantee for a lively love life, and your sexuality is heightened as well. Life in general should be proceeding much more smoothly now. Other people think you're the person with the answers, and they flock to you in droves.

Thursday, September 23 (Moon in Pisces to Aries 5:47 a.m.) Today's full moon in Aries highlights an issue at work, perhaps with a coworker or a boss or an employee, if you own your own business. Pluto forms a challenging angle to this moon, suggesting some underlying tensions that will require diplomacy and tact on your part.

Friday, September 24 (Moon in Aries) You're out in front of the pack today, doing what you do best with fearless abandon: leading others. Your ideas are cutting edge, your physical energy is ideal, and people are willing to support what you're doing. You could be short on patience. Try not to lose your cool.

Saturday, September 25 (Moon in Aries to Taurus 5:17 p.m.) The moon enters your opposite sign, and your focus shifts to a partnership. Whether it's romance or business, the insights you bring into this relationship are excellent. But your partner may have his or her own insights as well, and you should be willing to discuss and debate the fine points.

Sunday, September 26 (Moon in Taurus) Choose your battles wisely. Some things just aren't worth getting disturbed about. Use your energy to tackle the real dilemmas and challenges in your life, not the stuff that others make up out of thin air. Maintain your position. Don't surrender.

Monday, September 27 (Moon in Taurus) With both Venus and Mars opposite this moon, there could be tension between you and someone close to you. A Mars opposition, in particular, can lead to rash actions and words, so be careful what you say and how you say it. Also, don't speed under this transit, because if you get pulled over, the ticket is yours.

Tuesday, September 28 (Moon in Taurus to Gemini 3:12 a.m.) A workshop or seminar may be on your agenda today. It may not even be a formal setting, but someone's kitchen table, where an expert on a particular topic is waxing eloquently about the pros and cons. Whether it's tax advice or information on wills, listen closely, and then make up your own mind about how to proceed.

Wednesday, September 29 (Moon in Gemini) You know the drill. Time to gather and disseminate information, to network, and to touch base with clients, family, friends. If you've made friends through e-mail with people you've never met personally, now is the time to set up a meeting. It probably will feel like a gathering of friends from other lives.

Thursday, September 30 (Moon in Gemini to Cancer 10:47 a.m.) There are always people who tell you that something is impossible or not valid. You've proven naysayers wrong time and again, and you'll do so today.

OCTOBER 2010

Friday, October 1 (Moon in Cancer) On October 8, Venus will turn retrograde, which could affect your romantic relationships and your creative endeavors. Prepare for it now by making sure that your creative work is precisely where you want it to be. Try to keep things with your romantic partner on an even keel.

Saturday, October 2 (Moon in Cancer to Leo 3:22 p.m.) Showtime! By this afternoon, you're in a mood for friends, great discussions, and socializing. And since you like to be in control of situations, have the gathering at your place. Be creative. Celebrate the advent of fall. It's equally possible that you'll be involved in some sort of work-related stuff today. Maybe you can combine the two?

Sunday, October 3 (Moon in Leo) Mercury enters Libra and your twelfth house, where it will be until October 20. The next few weeks will feature a lot of talk and debate behind the scenes. It may be related to a younger person who is having trouble in his or her personal life or could concern contracts that are pending. Once Mercury enters Scorpio on October 20, the issue should be pretty much settled.

Monday, October 4 (Moon in Leo to Virgo 5:00 p.m.) The moon enters your eleventh house, usually a social placement for the moon. In fact, today would be a great day to get together a publicity campaign. Whether you're publicizing your company's product or your own work, the public is receptive.

Tuesday, October 5 (Moon in Virgo) Virgo can be a health-conscious sign, so it's possible that you're on a new kick—yoga classes, a new gym membership, or even a new nutritional program. Make sure you can commit to what you start.

Wednesday, October 6 (Moon in Virgo to Libra 4:52 p.m.) Prepare today for tomorrow's new moon in Libra. List the kinds of people and experiences you would like to manifest in your life under the influence of this new moon. Back the list with deep emotion and desire. Then get out of your own way so the universe can bring all these goodies your way!

Thursday, October 7 (Moon in Libra) Today's new moon in Libra ushers in opportunities to work with people, perhaps in some sort of artistic field, and there's a genuine thrust toward creative opportunities for you. Mercury and Saturn form wide conjunctions to the new moon, indicating that offers that come your way will be serious and that there will be a lot of talk and conversation before you decide.

Friday, October 8 (Moon in Libra to Scorpio 4:52 p.m.) Okay, Venus turns retrograde today in your sign and turns direct again on November 18. During this period, there may be bumps in a relationship or with a creative project. But just as likely are annoyances that somehow impact your physical comfort—faulty air-conditioning or heat, home renovations that drag on, and that sort of thing.

Saturday, October 9 (Moon in Scorpio) The moon now travels with retrograde Venus and Mars in your sign. It's not as problematic as it sounds, but because Venus isn't behaving, there could be some minor snafus with plans you and a partner have made. You've got plenty of energy, and it carries you through whatever challenges you meet today, which really should be minimal.

Sunday, October 10 (Moon in Scorpio to Sagittarius 7:09 p.m.) It's a day when your focus shifts to exotic places. Even if you're just virtual traveling, your imagination and your restlessness are accentuated. So perhaps it's time to take off for parts unknown. Plan your travel on either side of the next Mercury retrograde dates from December 10 to December 30.

Monday, October 11 (Moon in Sagittarius) You're in search of the big picture. You actually shouldn't have to search too far and wide; you can just look within and glean the answers psychically. But if you don't believe you can do it that way, then the door will shut, and you'll have to go the more traditional route and sift through facts and figures and talk to the experts.

Tuesday, October 12 (Moon in Sagittarius) If you can imagine it, you can attain it. Your values play an important role today, and you may, in fact, need to clarify your priorities before you can imagine what it is that you really desire. Once you do that, half the battle is won!

Wednesday, October 13 (Moon in Sagittarius to Capricorn 1:17 a.m.) Whenever the moon hooks up with Pluto in Capricorn—as it will be doing several times a month until 2024—you'll be wrestling with power issues. But since Capricorn is an earth sign compatible with your water-sign sun, the struggle is in *defining* your own power. Who are you in the depths of your own soul? Who do you want to be?

Thursday, October 14 (Moon in Capricorn) If you're still examining power issues today, it would be to your advantage to talk to a sibling or trusted friend and ask how that person perceives you. Sometimes, another person's input about who we are can be reassuring. Or shocking. Or it simply confirms what we already know. But it's always insightful.

Friday, October 15 (Moon in Capricorn to Aquarius 11:24 a.m.) Think of it this way. It's Friday and you've wrapped up most of your work (you're the type who is usually way ahead), so why not treat yourself and knock off early today? You may even decide to head out of town this weekend, perhaps to some favorite spot where you can kick back, relax, and do whatever it is that you enjoy most.

Saturday, October 16 (Moon in Aquarius) Whether you're out of town or sticking close to home today, you've got plenty on your plate. In the event that you feel overwhelmed or rushed, take time out to exercise, read, or engage some other activity that relaxes you and takes your mind off whatever is going on. Even some yoga stretching and postures could loosen up the tension.

Sunday, October 17 (Moon in Aquarius to Pisces 11:52 p.m.) With Venus retrograde and Mars still in your sign, today should be astonishingly delicious! It's all about you and your romantic partner or you and your muse or you and your kids. Or it could be all three. Take your pick. There's plenty of psychic energy crackling through the air, which is usually exciting for you.

Monday, October 18 (Moon in Pisces) Synchronicities abound today. You know the drill on this stuff. You mention someone's name, and that person calls or you get an e-mail from them. Or a certain number or sequence of numbers keeps popping up today. Or you're mulling over a puzzling issue and turn on the radio—and a song is playing that somehow offers insights or an answer about that issue. It means you're right on track.

Tuesday, October 19 (Moon in Pisces) Tomorrow, Mercury enters your sign, which will put three planets in Scorpio. Gear up today for this one. Things are about to get busy, complex, passionate, and emotional. You may want to spend much of today embroiled in your creative projects or in research.

Wednesday, October 20 (Moon in Pisces to Aries 12:24 p.m.) Mercury joins Venus and Mars in your sign. The combination of these three planets in Scorpio suggests that you and a partner will be involved in heavy-duty conversation. You may be defining your relationship or spelling out your expectations. This combination also points to an intense time for research, investigation, psychic development, and high drama!

Thursday, October 21 (Moon in Aries) Adding the fiery Aries moon to an already intense and complex picture could do one of several things. You may be urged to blaze your own path in a relationship, with a work project, or just in terms of something you're seeking. You are pretty fearless emotionally right now, so that can add or detract from everything else, depending on your focus.

Friday, October 22 (Moon in Aries to Taurus 11:31 p.m.) Today's full moon in Aries highlights your daily work routine. It's possible that you receive news about a job for which you've applied. If that's the case, the job may allow you to integrate more of your ideals and spiritual beliefs into your daily work. If there has been anything hidden from you at work, this full moon will illuminate it.

Saturday, October 23 (Moon in Taurus) Your partner—business or romantic—may need your attention and support today. It's possible you haven't been giving this relationship the attention it deserves recently, and things are starting to fray a bit at the seams. So take the time to sort things out.

Sunday, October 24 (Moon in Taurus) It may be beautification time at your place. It can be anything from new furniture and fresh paint on the walls to adding touches like fresh flowers or new potted plants. The Taurus moon enjoys being surrounded by beauty. Indulge yourself.

Monday, October 25 (Moon in Taurus to Gemini 8:48 a.m.) If it's true that timing is everything, then today is an excellent time to review your taxes. Are there any more tax benefits you can get this year? Do you need new office equipment? Make a note of everything, but don't buy big-ticket items until after Venus turns direct on November 18.

Tuesday, October 26 (Moon in Gemini) Your phone seems to ring constantly today, your in-box fills up by the moment, and you may have trouble allocating your time. And that means you should be delegating. Have someone else answer the mail and the e-mail. Get your family members involved if it's stuff at home that is piling up. Engage others. They'll be delighted to help. All you had to do was ask.

Wednesday, October 27 (Moon in Gemini to Cancer 4:15 p.m.) Here's that nice, familiar Cancer moon again. Time to chill. Meditate. Dive into something that really fires up your passions. This moon asks only that you nurture others, yourself, your pets, your plants—whatever and whoever is in need of attention.

Thursday, October 28 (Moon in Cancer) Mars enters Sagittarius, where it will be until December 7. During this transit, you'll be working harder and possibly longer hours to bring home your daily bread. You could take another job with better pay and benefits. It's important to remain upbeat, on top of things, and to enjoy every second of every day.

Friday, October 29 (Moon in Cancer to Leo 9:39 p.m.) While some of the day could focus on education, publishing, foreign interests, or even your worldview, this evening is reserved for your career. You may be brainstorming with a peer or boss about a new product, service, or idea. Don't hesitate to speak your mind.

Saturday, October 30 (Moon in Leo) There could be some minor tensions today between professional and personal obligations. You get it sorted out, you always do, but the sorting itself may drive you a bit nuts. If this is the night kids trick-or-treat, then be sure to be stocked up on all the appropriate goodies.

Sunday, October 31 (Moon in Leo) Happy Halloween! Regardless of your age, join in the festivities. One thing that appeals to a Scorpio is delving into the mysterious and the truly magical. And since the Hollow's Eve is the night when the portal opens between the living and the dead, have a séance!

NOVEMBER 2010

Monday, November 1 (Moon in Leo to Virgo 12:51 a.m.) Today's Virgo moon forms harmonious angles to Mercury and retrograde Venus in your sign. The combination means you're able to anchor your intuitive hunches on details. Now all you have to do is connect the dots and figure out what the big picture is. Wait until the new moon is in your sign to do that!

Tuesday, November 2 (Moon in Virgo) You're meticulous in the way you plot and plan the script of your life. It's not as if you're sitting around with a pencil and paper, but you've got it all in your head and your heart, where it counts. Today you may have to fine-tune a bit. But basically, you're right on track.

Wednesday, November 3 (Moon in Virgo to Libra 2:19 a.m.) Start tying up loose ends. Don't procrastinate on last-minute items. You want to clear the decks for Saturday's new moon in your sign. Make a list of the kinds of people, experiences, and opportunities you would like to manifest in your life under this new moon. It happens only once a year and sets the tone for the next twelve months.

Thursday, November 4 (Moon in Libra) You may be looking ahead already to the Thanksgiving holidays, if you celebrate that day where you live. It's one of the biggest travel holidays of the year, and if you're tired of long security lines and the hassle that is so often associated with air travel, maybe the festivities should be at your house this year.

Friday, November 5 (Moon in Libra to Scorpio 3:16 a.m.) The moon enters your sign today, and yes, you're ready for it. There are any number of projects at work you can tackle, but an equal number of things at home and in your personal life may require your attention. So pick and choose.

Saturday, November 6 (Moon in Scorpio) Today's new moon in your sign should usher in new opportunities in just about every area of your life. It's the most important new moon for you every year, and if you're ready for it, and know what you would like to manifest in your life, it can prove to be fantastic. There may be an abruptness to events that unfold around this time that prompts a lot of discussion.

Sunday, November 7—Daylight Saving Time Ends (Moon in Scorpio to Sagittarius 4:28 a.m.) Neptune turned direct yesterday in Aquarius. The impact on you and your home life will be subtle because Neptune moves so slowly. Nonetheless, certain things at home—with your partner, your parents, or even a child—should begin to straighten out. You have a clearer idea how to integrate your spirituality more firmly in your home life.

Monday, November 8 (Moon in Sagittarius) Mercury enters Sagittarius and your second house, where it remains until November 30. During this period, a lot of your conversations focus on money and your values. Are your values reflected in how you earn your living? How can you earn more money or spend less? A contract is possible during this time. Just be sure you sign before Mercury turns retrograde on December 10!

Tuesday, November 9 (Moon in Sagittarius to Capricorn 9:37 a.m.) The moon joins Pluto in your third house. Once again, you learn just how powerful emotions can be. Whatever you focus on, you get.

Wednesday, November 10 (Moon in Capricorn) Organization is what today is about. Whether you're organizing your family or your closet, employees or your own desk, your kids or your attic, the goal is the same: to organize what you own and to give away or toss out what you no longer use.

Thursday, November 11 (Moon in Capricorn to Aquarius 6:33 p.m.) The moon joins Neptune in your fourth house. Your emotional concentration shifts to your spirituality, idealism, and compassion. You may be asking yourself how you can incorporate these qualities more readily into your daily life. You could start by volunteering at a local homeless shelter or even at the animal shelter.

Friday, November 12 (Moon in Aquarius) With both Mars and Mercury in Sagittarius, your conscious mind now moves as quickly as your body. If you've been looking for a job, your pavement-pounding should pay off—maybe not today, but certainly before Mars leaves Sagittarius on December 7 and most likely around the new moon in Sagittarius on December 5. Don't get discouraged. Keep believing in yourself.

Saturday, November 13 (Moon in Aquarius) Heady ideas, a grand vision, the energy to carry it out—sounds like a politician, doesn't it? Well, today that's the role you play for others. They look to you as the person who will lead them into the future. Better be sure you're prepared for this one!

Sunday, November 14 (Moon in Aquarius to Pisces 6:25 a.m.) The moon joins Uranus and Jupiter in your fifth house. These three planets won't be meeting up next year. So enjoy this energy while it lasts. Expect the unexpected in romance and creative ventures, and trust that Jupiter will continue to expand your creative and romantic options through the end of the year. If you've thought about starting a family, now is the time when the stars support your desire.

Monday, November 15 (Moon in Pisces) Another glorious day when everything works seamlessly, with hardly any effort on your part. If entertaining is something you enjoy, then start planning your Thanksgiving festivities today. If you enjoy being with pets or photographing animals (or anything else), then do that today. In others words, today is about *your* pleasure.

Tuesday, November 16 (Moon in Pisces to Aries 7:00 p.m.) The moon today brings you headaches and aggravation. Or it can bring you to a place where you know you're on the right track despite what people around you may be saying. Who're you going to believe? The others or yourself? The answer to that one is easy. Yourself, of course.

Wednesday, November 17 (Moon in Aries) It's a good idea to start clearing your desk in anticipation of the Thanksgiving holidays. If you work in a profession that tends to slow down during the holidays, then don't launch anything new. Just keep a file on your ideas and thoughts. Then, early next year, get out that file and go to work!

Thursday, November 18 (Moon in Aries) Both Venus and Jupiter turn direct today, major good news for your love life, your creativity, and just about anything else you can think of. If you've put off buying a big-ticket item—a car, an appliance, or even a computer—go shopping tomorrow! Jupiter now rushes forward for its appointment with Aries early in 2011.

Friday, November 19 (Moon in Aries to Taurus 6:05 a.m.) So here you are, with the moon in your opposite sign once again. By now you should have a general idea how this transit manifests itself in your life. The details vary, of course, but the big picture is that your focus shifts from yourself to others. Pluto forms a harmonious angle to this moon, suggesting you're in the seat of power.

Saturday, November 20 (Moon in Taurus) It's important to ground yourself today. Think of it as a reality-check day. Consult with your business or romantic partner about the particulars. He or she will be a fount of information.

Sunday, November 21 (Moon in Taurus to Gemini 2:46 p.m.) Today's full moon in Taurus receives beneficial angles from both Jupiter and Uranus. Any news that comes your way today is likely to do so in an unexpected way, and it will expand your life in some way. Or be lucky for you in some way. Maybe this news is about your guest list for Thanksgiving dinner?

Monday, November 22 (Moon in Gemini) As the days close in on the Thanksgiving holidays, plans could be in flux, travel schedules shifting, and the guest list expanding or shrinking. You take it all in stride and make adjustments accordingly. You stay on top of the e-mail lists and the phone calls; you're in charge of networking.

Tuesday, November 23 (Moon in Gemini to Cancer 9:14 p.m.) You're starting to gear up for the long holiday weekend, and you turn to the nurturing environment that so many family members and friends may associate with you. It isn't that you're Mother Earth (unless you have a heavy Cancer influence in your natal chart), but that you intuitively grasp the hearts of others.

Wednesday, November 24 (Moon in Cancer) Tending to the home fires, to the details of arrivals and needs of your guests, and to your own well-being—that about sums it up today. However, if you're en route elsewhere for Thanksgiving or spending the weekend with friends, be sure you don't speed. Mars in Sagittarius could prompt you to ignore the speed limits!

Thursday, November 25 (Moon in Cancer) Happy Thanksgiving! With Venus in direct motion for the past week and both Mars and Mercury in Sagittarius, the conversation is lively and diverse. You're already looking toward tomorrow and the next day, wondering what's coming up. Don't. Try to stay rooted in the moment.

Friday, November 26 (Moon in Cancer to Leo 2:01 a.m.) You may be tempted to do some work today. Even if you stay at home to do it, you need to put things right in your own mind. So save a few hours for work today. It may be nothing more than touching base with people through e-mail and pinning down appointments and times.

Saturday, November 27 (Moon in Leo) It's never too early to start thinking about plans for New Year's Eve, particularly with a Mercury retrograde occurring between December 10 and December 30. If you wait until that period to make your plans (holiday travel falls in here too), you can count on everything changing. If flux and change is something you find exciting, wait until the last moment.

Sunday, November 28 (Moon in Leo to Virgo 5:34 a.m.) Friends are important to you—not just acquaintances, but real friends, the kind of friends you can depend on when things get rough. So celebrate your close friends today. Take everyone out to lunch. If some particular hobby is common to all of you, then get together to discuss it.

Monday, November 29 (Moon in Virgo) Start thinking about what you've accomplished this year. Are you pleased with how the year has gone? Are there people you wish you had gotten to know better? Things you regret? Are you proud of where you've gone? Take note and begin to think about your New Year's resolutions.

Tuesday, November 30 (Moon in Virgo to Libra 8:16 a.m.) Between now and December 10, while Mercury is moving direct in Capricorn, your conscious mind is very focused. Then, on December 10, Mercury turns retrograde, and you'll be revising and reviewing what you've been doing.

Wednesday, December 1 (Moon in Libra) It's a great day for meditation and contemplation. This doesn't mean you have to sit and stare at your navel for hours, with your legs crossed lotus style. It's easier to contemplate while you're doing something so familiar to you that you can do it on automatic. Make note of your observations.

Thursday, December 2 (Moon in Libra to Scorpio 10:44 a.m.) The moon enters your sign, so here's another power day. Thanks to your innate focus, you probably have your agenda all laid out. But if you're winging it, then rely heavily on your intuition and follow your inner guidance system, and you won't be disappointed.

Friday, December 3 (Moon in Scorpio) You seem to be making up for lost time. It may spring from some inner feeling of urgency, or you simply may be compelled to achieve the rest of the items on your wish list for the year. Just be sure to schedule downtime. You'll need it.

Saturday, December 4 (Moon in Scorpio to Sagittarius 2:00 p.m.) You're working up to the new moon in Sagittarius, which is tomorrow. Since this new moon concerns your finances, you may want to give some thought today about the kinds of financial experiences you would like to surface in your life. Sagittarius is also about education, travel, publishing, and foreign cultures. If your interests and goals lie in any of these areas, include them in your brainstorming.

Sunday, December 5 (Moon in Sagittarius) Today's new moon in Sagittarius could be quite spectacular for you. It should usher in new financial opportunities—a raise, for instance, or a better-paying job. With Mars also in Sagittarius now, in the later degrees, you've got plenty of physical energy to actively seek what you want. Uranus also turns direct, in Pisces, releasing feelings of constraint in your love life and with your creativity.

Monday, December 6 (Moon in Sagittarius to Capricorn 7:17 p.m.) You're planning again. It's as if you can't help doing that when the moon is in Capricorn. Your energy is very directed toward something that you want. So what is it you want? Define it.

Tuesday, December 7 (Moon in Capricorn) Mars joins the moon in Capricorn. You're revved up. Mars will be in your sign through the end of the year, urging you to remain focused and directed. It's almost as if you're wearing blinders. So be sure to take the blinders off once in a while so you can see what's in your peripheral vision.

Wednesday, December 8 (Moon in Capricorn) Building is what the Capricorn moon does very well. So whether you're building bridges in relationships or building a career, a family, or a route to the achievement of your goals, you're exceptionally focused, determined.

Thursday, December 9 (Moon in Capricorn to Aquarius 3:32 a.m.) Back up your computer files today. Make double backups—like on an external disk drive and on a flash drive. Mercury turns retrograde tomorrow. It's a good idea to finish up your holiday shopping today, especially if you're buying big-ticket items. If you do shop while Mercury is retrograde, be sure to save the receipts as you may be returning items. Solidify New Year's plans.

Friday, December 10 (Moon in Aquarius) Mercury turns retrograde in Capricorn and remains that way until December 30. Mars is also in Capricorn now, so you've got plenty of physical energy in your daily life to accomplish whatever needs to be done. Mars in Capricorn urges you to get regular physical exercise. If you don't have an exercise program yet, between now and the end of the year is a good time to start!

Saturday, December 11 (Moon in Aquarius to Pisces 2:41 p.m.) The moon joins Jupiter and Uranus in your fifth house, Mars, Mercury retrograde, and Pluto are in compatible earth sign Capricorn, and Venus is in your sign. With the stars stacked in your favor like this, you may want to do special stuff from now through Monday. Whether it's spending time with the people you love or diving into a creative project or simply doing what you enjoy, today and the next two days are made to order for you.

Sunday, December 12 (Moon in Pisces) Your imagination and intuition slam into overdrive. You're so psychic today that you're able to glean all kinds of information—maybe more than you want or need!—just by shifting your focus from one person or situation to another. It's likely that your dreams are especially vivid and may address issues about which you're concerned. They may address future events and situations. Keep a notepad and pen handy on your nightstand.

Monday, December 13 (Moon in Pisces) During this Mercury retrograde period, people you haven't seen for a while may be showing up in your life again. One of these individuals could be a former lover or spouse who dropped out of your life some time ago. Don't allow this individual to push your buttons. You've evolved well beyond that.

Tuesday, December 14 (Moon in Pisces to Aries 3:15 a.m.) A certain restlessness grips you today. It could be connected to a work issue—perhaps with an employee or a coworker—but could involve just about any close relationship in your life. You may have to strike out on your own, without the support you thought you had. It's fine. You'll win either way.

Wednesday, December 15 (Moon in Aries) You may be finishing up last-minute holiday shopping. Try to pay cash for everything so you don't end up despairing in January when the credit card bills come due. Be sure to stretch your dollars by buying gifts that fit the individuals—as opposed to buying just to buy!

Thursday, December 16 (Moon in Aries to Taurus 2:49 p.m.) You and your partner may want to get away for a few days by yourselves before the holiday crush of visitors arrive. It doesn't have to be an expensive getaway. If it's warm where you live, go camping. If it's winter, search the Internet for lodging deals.

Friday, December 17 (Moon in Taurus) Today's Taurus moon forms a harmonious angle with all the other planets that are in earth and water signs. So, once again, you're in a very powerful and positive place emotionally. Use the force of your emotions to bring about change in whatever area of your life you want it. It may not all happen today, but you can at least get the ball rolling!

Saturday, December 18 (Moon in Taurus to Gemini 11:38 p.m.) You've got plenty of help today. Others are willing and even eager to share their time and resources with you. In fact, you may want to network a bit via e-mail and blogs, touching base with clients, friends, family, and Internet buddies before you become embroiled in whatever task you've taken on today.

Sunday, December 19 (Moon in Gemini) This moon is somewhat impersonal at times. It enables you to detach from the emotional high drama and chaos around you and to find a bastion of reason and calmness. It's also a moon that needs information. So feed your heart and your head today.

Monday, December 20 (Moon in Gemini) It may seem like an odd time, so close to the holidays, to focus on insurance, taxes, wills, and that sort of thing. But it's also nearly the year's end, and you may want to consult with an accountant about purchases you can make or money you can save that will bring a lower tax bill.

Tuesday, December 21 (Moon in Gemini to Cancer 5:22 a.m.) Today's full moon in Gemini is also a lunar eclipse. There could be emotional issues surrounding the very stuff you were working on yesterday. Uranus forms a challenging angle to this moon, indicating that whatever triggers your upset is unexpected. Sounds like you may discover that you could owe more taxes than you thought.

Wednesday, December 22 (Moon in Cancer) If visitors are arriving at your place—or you're on your way to someone else's house for the holidays—you've got that warm, fuzzy feeling in the pit of your stomach. It's the Cancer moon that brings on that feeling, triggering memories of home and hearth, perhaps from your early childhood.

Thursday, December 23 (Moon in Cancer to Leo 8:51 a.m.) The last thing you'll want to worry about today is something at work. But with the Leo moon entering the professional sector of your chart, you may have to do exactly that. If it can be taken care of by phone or e-mail, great. If you're out of town, it may just have to wait.

Friday, December 24 (Moon in Leo) Remember that Mercury is still retrograde in your third house of relatives and neighbors. It's probably safest to stay away from touchy hot-button subjects like religion and politics. The environment for miscommunication is just too fertile.

Saturday, December 25 (Moon in Leo to Virgo 11:15 a.m.) Merry Christmas! However you celebrate today, be sure to show your appreciation for the special people in your life. That should go without saying, but sometimes these people are the ones we take for granted. According to the law of attraction, the more you find to appreciate in your life, the likelier it is that you attract more of the same.

Sunday, December 26 (Moon in Virgo) Avoid the post-Christmas rush at the mall. You're not particularly crazy about crowds, and if you have gifts to return, you can do it next week. It's a good day to sort, to tend to details, or to cement a relationship with someone in your circle of friends.

Monday, December 27 (Moon in Virgo to Libra 1:39 p.m.) A part of you wants to surround yourself with friends and family. But the other part of you craves solitude, and that side of you may win. If you still have guests at your house—or are a guest at someone else's house—sneak away for a few hours. You need the time by yourself to recharge.

Tuesday, December 28 (Moon in Libra) Your New Year's plans, despite your best intentions, may be in flux. That's par for a Mercury retrograde. Remain flexible and go with the flow where this is concerned. Work on your resolutions for 2011. Those may change before Mercury turns direct on December 30, but at least you're on your way.

Wednesday, December 29 (Moon in Libra to Scorpio 4:50 p.m.) How terrific is it that the last three days of the year feature a moon in your sign? In fact, you are so in the groove that nothing daunts you. So get out and do whatever your little old heart desires. The universe has gifted you with three days to do your own thing.

Thursday, December 30 (Moon in Scorpio) Mercury turns direct again. Finish up your list of resolutions; try to tailor them so that they're realistic enough to achieve. Save the return and exchange of gifts until tomorrow, when Mercury will be fully stabilized. Your passions are running high and furiously today, and you may have to pause to catch your breath.

Friday, December 31 (Moon in Scorpio) Looking back, what would you change about this year? What do you regret? What makes you proud? Were you distracted from your goals? Did you adhere to the plan you set up early in the year? No answers? Fine. Think about it tomorrow!

HAPPY NEW YEAR!

SYDNEY OMARR

Born on August 5, 1926, in Philadelphia, Pennsylvania, Sydney Omarr was the only person ever given full-time duty in the U.S. Army as an astrologer. He is regarded as the most erudite astrologer of our time and the best known, through his syndicated column and his radio and television programs (he was Merv Griffin's "resident astrologer"). Omarr has been called the most "knowledgeable astrologer since Evangeline Adams." His forecasts of Nixon's downfall, the end of World War II in mid-August of 1945, the assassination of John F. Kennedy, Roosevelt's election to a fourth term and his death in office . . . these and many others are on the record and quoted enough to be considered "legendary."

ABOUT THE SERIES

This is one of a series of twelve *Sydney Omarr® Day-by-Day Astrological Guides* for the signs of 2010. For questions and comments about the book, go to www.tjmacgregor.com.